Dedicated to the three grand ladies in my life;

> Anna K. Boschmann, my mother
> Lahla M. Selzer, my mother-in-law
> Priscilla S. Boschmann, my wife.

All are teachers, and all made the noble decision to sacrifice their love of classroom teaching in favor of the only greater calling: the full-time teaching of their own children.

Contents

Detailed Contents

Foreword

Ten Teaching Tools is much more than ten teaching tools; in fact it is many times ten. Erwin Boschmann has described in detail the many creative ideas that he has had about teaching, and it is pleasing to a psychologist to find that this skilled teacher has discovered many of the things that psychologists have derived from research on cognition and motivation. For example, the technique of explaining to another student who explains back to the instructor fits well with our concept, "elaboration." Laboratory research has demonstrated that concepts are much better remembered if the individual has done more than simply memorize them, but rather has made them meaningful by translating them into the student's own language.

Teachers who read this book will find many ideas they can use; they should not expect that all of the ideas will work for other teachers as they have for Boschmann. Each of us has his or her own style and own way of teaching. Some of Boschmann's ideas actually run counter to theories or to my own intuitions about what would work for me, but Boschmann obviously makes them work because of his own enthusiasm, commitment, and unique personality. Thus one comes away from this book with admiration for Boschmann as a teacher, but also with much to ponder and to try–a wealth of ideas that will illuminate and improve one's own teaching.

Wilbert J. McKeachie
Professor of Psychology
The University of Michigan

Introduction

My baptism of fire into the teaching profession was severe. Fresh out of graduate school, my chairman introduced me to the class of 120 eager souls–then left. That day I delivered my semi-memorized lecture, wishing I could trade places with the janitor down the hall. He looked like he enjoyed his job more than I did mine; and, I was sure, his mouth was not puckered and dry.

How was I to establish a professorial authority when many students were my age or older? How was I to know what to do with the student who came to my office crying–no one ever taught me how to counsel? How was I to know how to handle grade assignments–I had always been the recipient, never the giver of grades? How was I to know how to select textbooks–they were always selected for me? What was I to do with the beautiful young lady in the front row, who during an exam fell over–how was I to know when someone was on drugs? And how was I to deal with my own feeling of awesome responsibility at the news that one of my students had committed suicide? That first semester I frequently took walks in a nearby park, wrestling with the question of my calling. I found that I was least prepared for the thing I did most: teaching.

I am glad I did not give up teaching. The pain was severe, but rewards have been high.

This is a how-to book. Gleaned from the experiences of dealing with some 15,000 students over a twenty-year period, TEN TEACHING TOOLS is meant to help the new teachers and encourage those seasoned with experience. It is not a theoretical book quoting facts, giving references, or citing research results. Instead, it is a book which attempts to share experiences and give sound advice helpful to the teacher of adults and adolescents.

As a practical book it gives many details:

- How to develop a *caring* attitude.
- Forms and tables to facilitate *counseling, encouragement, evaluations*.
- Steps to good *lecture preparation*.
- Diagrams giving a glimpse into *human nature*.
- Appropriate bibliography for further *reference*.
- Details on the mechanics and emotion of *speaking*.
- How to develop and maintain *enthusiasm and positive attitude*.
- A minute-by-minute *sample lecture*.
- Interesting and helpful *facts* and findings about *teaching and learning*.
- Observations on *student performance* as a function of age.
- Suggestions for writing good *multiple-choice questions*.
- A technique for a quick check of validity of multiple-choice questions.
- An entire chapter detailing ways to teach *how to study*.
- Some *unusual uses* of the overhead projector.
- *Nonstandard* ways to prepare overhead transparencies.
- Time management by *self-supervision*.

- How to save time in the *management of things*.
- How to assemble a professional looking exam in just a few minutes.
- How to *assign grades*.
- How to *improve teaching* through evaluation.
- Sample *student evaluation forms*.
- Suggestions for *peer evaluations*.
- Preparation of a *teaching dossier*.

I acknowledge first of all the contributions the many generations of students have made. They have taught me. During my first years, I was on the mountain top giving detailed and carefully prepared instructions to my students down in the swamps: "Step on that stone, use the big branch to pull yourself up." During the next years I learned to go down to the swamp where my students were and throw ropes to them, encouraging them and pulling them up. But in recent years I have taken off my shoes, walked into the swamp, and together with my students we struggled out of the swamp onto the mountain top. My students have taught me, and I thank them.

I further acknowledge the encouragement received from my dean, Marshall Yovits, and the university environment which allows and encourages self-expression. I am grateful to Kendall/Hunt Publishing Company and its editors for their willingness to take a risk with my work. But a very special thanks goes to The Lilly Endowment, Inc., which listened to my lofty goal and provided a tremendous infusion of confidence by awarding me a Faculty Open Fellowship. May this work be a partial repayment for their confidence in my.

Indianapolis
February, 1987

PART I

THE SPIRIT OF TEACHING

Care
Preparation
Share with Gusto

Chapter 1
Care

"I touch the future; I teach."
Christa McAuliffe

Ours is not a routine profession. As teachers we do not produce, package, sell and deliver products or services as many professions do. We work with unknowns; we do not get good and fast quality control reports; and we are constantly challenged to work without the benefits of seeing the fruits of our labors. A student may respond to us years after he was in class, or he may never respond–at least not to us. It is this challenge of the unknown that makes ours an exciting profession.

Consider these findings. The average amount of time faculty spend on their jobs is about sixty hours per week. Along with MDs, college faculty report the least amount of dissatisfaction; along with air traffic controllers, they show the least boredom; those faculty who value students and intellectual pursuits over financial gain show the lowest heart attack rate; and those who have spousal support are among the happiest.

So what is the problem? There are many teachers who are unhappy, even fearful because of the unknown dimension of teaching, the mountain of work to be done and the limited amount of available time, not to mention low pay. This book is an attempt to help along some of these lines.

Consider our clientele, our audience, the students. Although our institutions are centers of intellectual endeavors, the students who seek the scholarly life are strongly feeling individuals. To recognize the student's problems and feelings is an essential part of being able to get through on the intellectual level. For the freshmen especially, school anxiety is often mountainous. The class size is intimidating; the experience of living away from home for the first time is new; the expectations and demands are many; yet the supervision is low. Professors are often considered with awe and perceived as unapproachable. The sheer appearance of the professor's office is intimidating.

Personal problems with which students are burdened are often such that I have come to believe that in comparison, mine is an easy, peaceful life. Caren, a student in our classes, learned during the semester that her infant daughter may not survive a terminal disease. During that same time her father passed away. She chose to stay in school.

Sometimes the problems are both staggering and border on the unbelievable. Consider this note we received:

Dear Sir:

I know this will sound unbelievable, but every word is true–this is an explanation for the late labs I will be turning in on Wednesday. You can verify this story by checking with anyone–parents, police, hospital, etc.

On February 13 I was in a car accident. The car was totalled. I was not hurt badly, but enough to slow me down. Next my grandfather had a heart attack. Next my Mom and Dad were in a car accident and my Mom was hurt. Meanwhile I was married on March 21, and we had wedding plans to make. Then the night before the wedding my new car was stolen. So, Dad loaned us his car for the honeymoon; it broke down on the way back and we were late getting home. After we were home I found out that my Dad was layed off from his job and transferred to Little Rock, Arkansas. So last week my family moved. Please accept my late papers under these circumstances.

Signed, Loni

As teachers we must understand that transmittal of knowledge is but a small part of our task. To bring together the student with the subject matter in a caring way is indeed a challenge. Knowingly or unknowingly, the relationships lacking in the home environment are sometimes looked for by students in the school setting. The Minneapolis-based Search Institute surveyed 8,000 adolescents and 10,000 parents. The study reveals that 53% of adolescents spend less than thirty minutes a day with their father; 44% spend less than thirty minutes with their mother. No wonder that Leo Buscaglia's books on love are best sellers. I work to let the students feel that I like them, that I am not here so much to correct as to work alongside.

The Marian Magnet states this philosophy in a meaningful way:

A STUDENT is the most important person in our business.
A STUDENT is not dependent on us–we are dependent on him.
A STUDENT is not an interruption of our work–he is the purpose of it.
A STUDENT does us a favor when he calls–we are not doing him a favor by serving him.
A STUDENT is part of our business–not an outsider.
A STUDENT is not a cold statistic–he is a flesh-and-blood human being with feelings and emotions like our own.
A STUDENT is not someone to argue or match wits with.
A STUDENT is a person who brings us his wants–it is our job to fill these wants.
A STUDENT is deserving of the most courteous and attentive treatment we can give him.
A STUDENT is the lifeblood of every school.

How can we portray this feeling of care to our students? Here are some ways that are helpful.

Show Care by Not Wielding Faculty Power

Some time ago I overheard a conversation in a faculty dining room during which one professor related to the rest an encounter with a student. Apparently the student had asked for an "Incomplete" in a course. The professor replied to the student "I'll give you this 'Incomplete' under one condition: that you never again enroll in any of my courses." I am not sure if the faculty member had the (legal) right to say so, but beyond legality, what was he saying to the student? In effect he was informing the student, in no uncertain terms, that power resides with the faculty, and that this faculty member, for one, will use that power.

Just as there is government by force or by the democratic process, there also exist the same two ways in which teaching can take place: by the stick or by the carrot method, with all the shadings in between. Which is best? To "educate," according to the Latin origin of the word, means to "draw out." This implies a responsibility both on part of the teacher and the student. Or better yet, we want to "educare." To teach by force will accomplish some learning. However, the student will do so against his will; he will develop a dislike for teacher and subject and will be anxious to leave such a setting, never to return to it. On the other hand, to educare will draw out the best of the student. It will show him the beauty of the subject, the noble feelings of the learning process and will instill in him a special kinship for the person who first brought the experience to his consciousness. Someone said that the successful teachers show kindness and sensitivity, have intelligence, and make the student feel significant–they are teachers who care.

A student came to me after an exam with a concern. "Sir, you spent a lot of time in class talking about electronic configuration, yet on the exam only one question was asked on the topic. Why?" The student obviously had a complaint. He knew the topic of electronic configuration but was not given enough of a chance to show his knowledge and improve his score. As a teacher, I can respond to his approach in a number of ways. Response #1 might be, "Well, what about it? Are you giving me advice on how to write tests?" This may have been the response I was feeling, however it is not conciliatory. So my response (#2) was, "You may be right. In looking at it now, I think there probably should have been a few more questions on electronic configuration. Sometimes it is really hard to know what to choose for test questions." Both responses give essentially the same information ("I have heard you. Right now, though, there is not much I can do about it")–but they do so with vastly different feelings.

Perhaps hardest to confront is belligerent behaviour by students. You can see it come, you can sense it by the fiery eyes, a voice that signals war, a speech that invites engagement. "There are no more books in the bookstore. I will wait only so long. Why did you not order enough?" or "I don't understand this at all. You're not explaining this right. It is your job to teach me."

My approach is to (force a) smile and then immediately acknowledge his right to anger: "I can see why you would be upset–I would be too." His challenge to a confrontation has been declined, and an invitation for amiable talk has been given. It is in my power to do so. That is the kind of faculty power I like to use. Only once have I been unable to handle a confrontation.

A young lady caught cheating on an exam accused me of racism. This was particularly hurtful to me, since I grew up in an environment where I was the minority and since I do live in an integrated neighborhood. The case was forwarded to the chairman, who called a meeting of the parties concerned. The case was dropped there, since she chose not to attend that meeting.

There are many other ways in which we can avoid wielding or instead use proper faculty power. During the first experience with computerized exams, students sometimes transfer a correct answer from the exam to the wrong spot on the scoring sheet. While we cannot correct these errors very often, we do so on occasion at the beginning, if the evidence is clear that indeed it is just a transfer error. It removes some of the coldness of the computer and puts just a bit of humanity into the process. The students are infinitely grateful–and usually very careful thereafter.

I like to give course evaluations at about halfway through the term in addition to the normal evaluation also given at the end of the term. Such midterm evaluations have definite advantages. They alllow for double student input; they provide an opportunity for midcourse corrections, which can still help the very class making the suggestions; and they give me an opportunity to present myself as a vulnerable individual. The evaluation results are shared with the class, with emphasis on those things that do need improvement and a request to the students for help in accomplishing these.

I have also used the concept of a Gripe Box outside the office, where students can insert suggestions and complaints. My students are encouraged to send notes to me (anonymously, if they wish), through the mail, or by placing them under my office door.

But perhaps the best approach has been our Student Response Group. After the second exam, a student is selected (perhaps the one with the highest combined score) and is asked to draw five names from a box containing the names of the entire class. This is done publically in front of the entire class; the selected names are then read; and the students are asked if they are willing to serve on this group. We meet once a week for the purpose of feedback. I encourage the members of the Response Group to be the "eyes and ears" out there in the halls, the labs, the lecture, and the recitation. These students make it a special point to be receptive to suggestions. The emphasis is on suggestions. If there is a complaint, it is hoped that the student with the complaint also has a suggestion for improvement. In this manner, we have been able to make such simple corrections as changing the color of the pen I use to advising the Teaching Assistant to be more aware of lecture topics covered before giving a quiz. All this can be done in a nonthreatening way. It reduces the image of faculty power.

Care by Placing Yourself in Student's Shoes

We all remember our encounters with people in positions of power. Depending on the behavior and subtle messages sent by that person, we either became comfortable or could not wait to leave. To many students, we as teachers are the persons in position of power and authority over them. How does the student feel and respond to my behavior? Do I build him up? Does he get the feeling that I'm on his side, that we're in this together, and that I'm here to help? Does he enjoy talking with me? Is he likely to return?

Let's place ourselves in the student's shoes. This can take so many different forms and be as simple as a physical motion. As we lecture, it may be helpful to displace ourselves mentally into the audience. How do they see me? When I describe a trend that goes from left to right and I sweep my arms to show that direction, do I sweep from *my* left to right or from *their* left to right?

Occasionally we have a student whose level of exam anxiety is far beyond the normal, to the extent that he or she perspires profusely, shakes, and obviously cannot function mentally. Placing that student in a back room or the office, where one removes the feeling of the large crowd, will sometimes alleviate the problem.

A good time to place ourselves in the student's shoes is when he comes to the office. To most of the students, a visit to the professor's office is about as pleasant as a visit to the dentist's office. They know a visit is necessary–but assume it will likely be unpleasant. One key to how the student will feel on first sight is the location of the desk. What is said (in unspoken words) when the desk is located as follows?

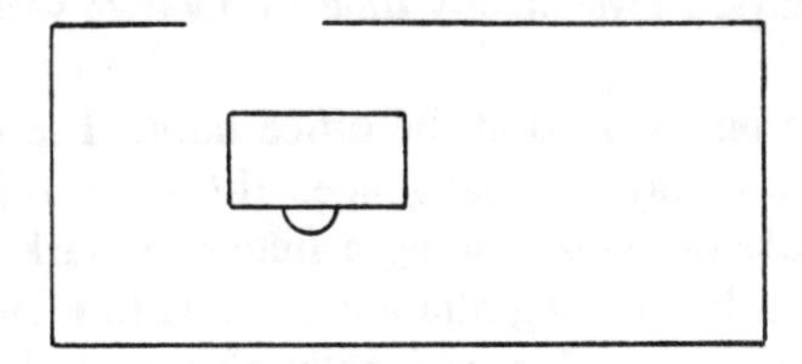

Does it not say "Come in, but stay on the other side of the desk. I'm the prof, you're the student."

What about this arrangement?

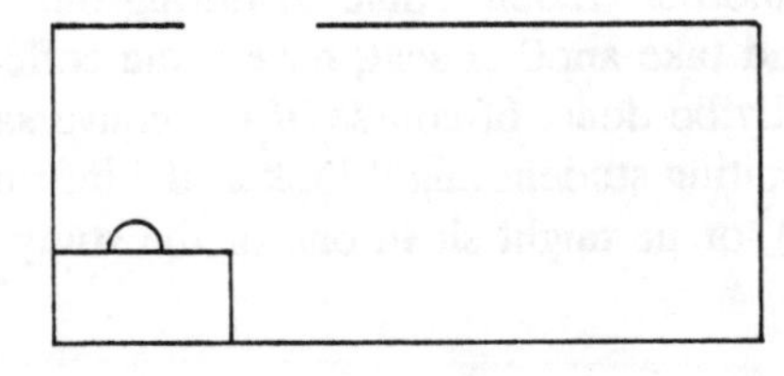

It says "If you need my attention, I'll turn around, but as you see, I am busy."

I like this arrangement:

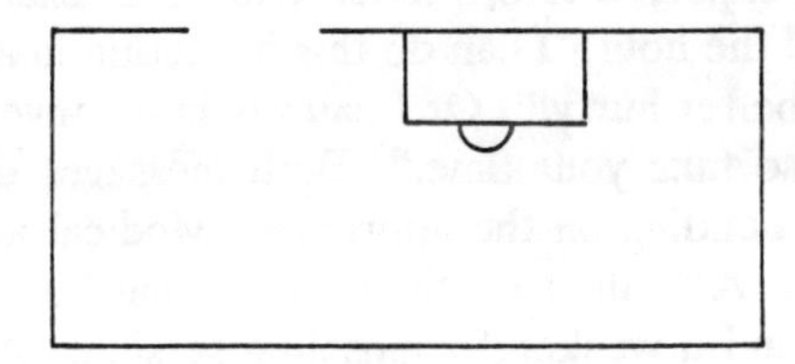

The desk is close to the door, facing a wall, so that there is no chance whatsoever of facing the student across the desk. In fact, when the student does come to the door, there is no other way to greet him than to do so on the same side of the desk. We are on an equal basis.

Let us go through a scenario of a student coming to the office. He comes to the door and asks "Are you busy?" (It is much like the question "I was not in class today, did you say anything important?") I always feel trapped with such questions. If I say "yes" to his question about whether I am busy, he is told, indirectly, to go away; if I say "no," he might wonder what I do all day just sitting there. What he really is asking is "Do you have time for me?" Of course I do. In fact, on Mondays, Wednesdays, and Fridays the office door is wide open all day long. On Tuesdays and Thursdays the door is closed, and students know that that is my time set aside for reading, writing, reflecting, and research. I may be in the office, or in the library, but unless a prior appointment has been made, I am not available to the students on those two days. This arrangement has been discussed with the students from Day One, and they know that on three days I give myself completely to them. It is quality time. Their coming will not be a frustrating interruption to my work. During my free time on the three days, I do routine work. On the two personal days, I give quality time to my own work–and students respect that setup.

Back to the student who just arrived at the office door. I've told him that I am available. How available I am will be told by my body language. If I was reading a book when he came in, do I continue holding the book, perhaps holding a finger to mark my place and ready to read on, or do I close it and set it aside, offering him a chair next to mine? As the conversation goes on and he keeps asking questions, do I occasionally glance at the watch, or even pull out a book, open it to a certain page and have it ready for when he leaves? If I do want to make myself a note, I'll tell the student "Listen, you just gave me an idea I want to write down." He has been informed and feels OK. Even if I do not have a lot of time, at least I like to pretend I do. Acting soon becomes reality; I forget whatever else it was I was planning to do; and I become more relaxed. Should another student come by during our conversation, I will often invite that student to come in and take another seat, have some coffee, or solve the puzzle laying on another table. This can only be done, of course, if the conversation is topical and not personal. In the latter case, the waiting student might look at the information on the bulletin board in the hall (updated routinely), or he might sit in one of the study chairs always available outside my office.

There are many other ways in which we can place ourselves into the student's shoes. I make available both my office and home phone numbers; when I leave the office a note always indicates my whereabouts and expected return time. During an exam, students often like a time signal at about five minutes till the hour. I can do this by stating in a slow and low authoritarian voice "Only five minutes left, better hurry!" Or I can say in a conversational tone "You have at least a full five minutes left, so take your time." Both messages do the job, but the last five minutes do feel differently, depending on the approach. Medical and personal problems often require special judgment calls. A student confided in me that his marriage was in trouble and that they had a chance to attend a weekend counseling session. Attending the session meant missing a scheduled exam. I did something almost unheard of; I gladly excused him from the exam.

Sometimes it is difficult to place myself in the student's shoes. A student gave his name as "Chie"; I asked for his last name, and he replied "Chie." I said, "Is that not also your first name?" He replied "Yes." I said "You mean your full name is Chie Chie?" "That is correct," he answered, explaining that he did not like the name his parents gave him. The university carried Chie Chie on its roster. Other difficult, though more sympathetic, situations involve handicapped students. We have had deaf students; blind students; quadriplegic students; wheelchair students; epileptic students; dyslexic students; students with severe allergies, on demanding drug prescriptions; (former) mental patients as students; and politically trapped students (during the Iran-Iraq conflict, a student was unable to function properly, worrying about relatives in the war zone). We have had asthmatic students, pregnant students, and lazy students. It is important that special cases be known to the teacher, that special procedures, phones, and medication be made known. Fellow students will almost always cooperate in a grand manner. Wherever possible, their privacy must be protected. However, at times it might be helpful to share with the class the struggles a particular student has. To this day, I do wish I would have introduced a special asthmatic girl to the class. She coughed routinely and did so, likely to the annoyance of some unknowing fellow students. She had to drop out and reenrolled the following semester, only to fail the course. This repeated itself, and it was not until her fourth try that she was able to successfully complete the course–with an average grade. Her accomplishments, however, would be considered far beyond a letter grade, and she would have deserved special recognition. Today I don't recall her name, but to me she is a hero.

Care by Providing Many Chances

After the first two weeks of a major league baseball season, newspapers begin to report the top ten batting averages. Typically, the leading batter after two weeks has an average of about 0.450. Yet no player in major league history has ever averaged 0.450 at the end of the season. Why? The answer, of course, is statistics. Given just a few chances of performances, the results will not show a true picture of capabilities. The initially high scores will often be unrealistic, as will often be the low scores. The more the chances, the truer the performance picture.

It is for these reasons that giving a mid-term and a final is a poor way of assessing student performance. Typically my classes are given six exams (lowest is dropped), one final exam, fourteen homework assignments, eleven experiments (lowest is dropped), and six quizzes (lowest is dropped), for a total possible of one thousand points. The high number of possible points has a psychological advantage, in that each item still carries ten to one hundred points, yet no one of these can ruin the record. In fact, it is possible to fail two exams and still earn an A in the course. There are other advantages of this system of many chances–many points. It gives the student a chance to practice the feeling of working under pressure. Furthermore, there never is much time in the term when something is not due, such as a homework, a quiz, an exam, a write-up, and so on. This places the burden of responsibility on the student. It is like a democracy, where one is free, yet shoulders responsibility.

Many chances are also given by making lecture notes available, by taping the lectures, by providing other texts on reserve in the library, and by making available old exams. The material can be learned not just through the lecture and the text, but also through the recitation, the office hours provided by the lecturer and the assistants, demonstration, films, experiments, via phone, student study groups, special help sessions, and computer-aided instruction. We have been fortunate to have access to PLATO (Programmed Logic Automated Teaching Operations) materials for a good many years. Based outside the home institution, terminals are hooked via direct lines to the main computer. Students have found the system an infinitely patient tutor, a system which builds confidence, one that is self-paced. All students are encouraged to use it for at least a few weeks and are then free to choose to continue with it or not. The system can now be easily replaced with self-contained microcomputers.

Providing many chances calls for much preparation on the part of the teacher. However, if done efficiently, a system can be developed to minimize the time demands. In any case, the students are worth it!

Care by "Letting My Hair Down"–Occasionally

The profession of teaching calls for a special relationship between teacher and student. It is not the relationship a business person has with a client, which tends to be a one-time interaction; neither is it a permanent parent-child relationship. As in the former case, we have but a limited amount of time for the interaction, but as in the latter, we are examples and models to the students. So, while we usually do keep a formal teacher-student interaction, it is nice too at times let down the guards and bare one's soul. Students have come to me years after their class with me and asked if I still climb mountains, or indicated a sense of appreciation for the lighter moments in class.

How do I "let my hair down?" Inasmuch as is possible, I do so by removing formality. This may at times mean sitting in the halls with a student chit-chatting, looking at his notes to see what he missed, visiting the recitations and laboratories, talking with students on campus, or at times wearing some very casual clothing. It has always been my contention that as a teacher I must dress nicely–not necessarily expensively or even stylishly–but in a pleasing manner. After all, I am being looked at during the lecture, and my body is 98% covered with clothing. Looking at me for an hour, when I am portrayed almost entirely by the clothing I have on, places a burden on that clothing. It reflects who I am, what I think of myself, how I feel about myself. Generally my students will find me an acceptable example in this area. Given this general practice, one can easily remove some formality by occasionally wearing a T-shirt. It signals messages such as "I too like to change," "I'm not different."

Excellent techniques to remove formality, aside from the manner of lecturing and body language, are such things as asking the class to stand if the atmosphere appears to be heavy, encouraging the students to write a joke at the end of an exam paper, placing several Kleenexes on the bulletin board along with the exam results, once per term bringing in donuts for all students, or mentioning that "a tradition has been established by the good classes in the past to take out the teacher for lunch on Fridays."

A good place to interact with the students on a truly one-to-one basis is the hall area where the bulletin board is located. Many faculty post exam keys and scores and then promptly leave. Here is a golden opportunity to find out what the students really think. Assume an exam key is just posted. The students just took the exam and are, of course, anxious about the answers. They have worked on every problem, their feelings are likely high, and they are ready for combat if the key does not agree with their answers. If someone asks about a question, it would be logical perhaps to invite the student to the office. After all, that is where the chairs are; there is a desk, paper, books, good light and so on. True, but it also is my turf. I prefer staying in the hall, tacking some scratch paper to the wall, and working right there where the students are. In this manner, I am on equal footing with the students–the hall belongs to all of us, other students can see what is being done, and the carefree interaction encourages other students to come up and ask. It is at these times that I get the most honest gut reactions from the most unlikely students. They will surprise themselves in challenging me, in confronting other students about answers, in thinking aloud–in short, these are glorious bull sessions which would never take place in the office.

But perhaps the best form of letting my hair down is when I let the students know something about myself, who I am, what I do in my spare time, etc. No matter how good a chemist I am or how good a teacher I am, if I am a model–not by choice, but by necessity–I might as well have a positive impact. To do so I must share of myself. On a tombstone in a cemetery in Showhegan, Maine, are chiseled these words:

> "Come stranger, let me counsel you;
> Where you are now, I once was too;
> Where I am now, you soon will be;
> So haste not on, come, follow me."

Below which someone has penciled:

> "To follow you, I'll not consent
> Until I know which way you went."

As teachers we are models, and we only have the choice of being good or poor models. We do not have the choice of not being a model. Before the semester is over I want my students to "know which way I went." They will know something of my values and beliefs; they know I come from an intact family where we do things together; they hear an occasional story about my wife or children. On one occasion, I mentioned that this was the day of my wife's birthday and that she would enjoy phone calls. Later that evening I learned that she had received dozens of calls. Students will know where I am from; they know that I like to live a clean, orderly life (it is surprising to students to learn that I never dropped a class–once enrolled, I remained committed). I reminisce about how I was taught, what I had difficulties with, and about learning that I do now. It is reassuring to the students to know that I recently took a course in a field completely foreign to mine, and that after following myself the advice I give them on how to study (see Chapter 6), I emerged with a successful grade. They know the frustration I experienced trying to learn to ski at age forty-three and the trauma I experienced in college, when taking a philosophy course where I just could not seem to grasp the concepts. The students know about the Organ Donor Transplant program which I believe in.

These are little vignettes of personal life that take but a few sentences on an occasional day but can have a lasting impact. This showing of one's humanity does signal to students that sharing their life with me will be received with dignity. The results are often surprising. Monica shared her desperate situation of being pregnant and being abandoned by her boyfriend. Worse yet, her parents demanded an abortion if she wanted to continue living at home. "Do you believe in abortion?" she asked me. Such are moments of uncomfortable responsibility but also unequaled opportunities. Monica followed her conscience to keep the baby, which meant moving out until a short while later reconciliation at home allowed her to move back.

The motive for letting my hair down on occasions is not to develop a "buddy, buddy" relationship with the students but rather to foster respectability worthy of emulation.

Care by Being Firm but Fair

During my first term of teaching, I was taught two lessons I still remember. The first concerned setting rules and schedules. After having set the examination schedule in my large class, there were, as usual, students with conflicts. I was approached about changing an examination schedule. Trying to please, I agreed and decided just to check with the rest of the students. What a hornet's nest I had walked into. First of all, some students could not have an exam on the proposed new date; others could if we would rearrange something else. After a few minutes of nightmare, I thought it best to go back to the old schedule. Not so easy. Now that students realized that the schedule was open to suggestions, many other proposals came my way. Lesson number one I learned concerned schedules; set and leave set.

The second lesson was more sweeping in its impact. It was taught to me by a mature student in the class. She had observed incidents like the one just described and noticed my utter vulnerability. I was forever trying to please all students. Students in the lower grade ranges wanted to do special papers to improve their scores. Accepting such, I found that students with a C or a B also wanted to do extra work to improve their grades. I was frustrated. One day she came to me privately and said "What I look for in a teacher is one who is firm but fair." I still thank her today.

My outlines, rules, and regulations are set and announced from Day One. Students are made aware that I have planned my work and that we will now work the plan. Figure 1.1 gives a sample outline. Its message is clear; students are welcomed, they are given proper instructions as to what happens when, they see many chances to prove themselves, and they know the grading pattern. This is care for the student.

I believe care is also shown for the student by firmly stating that no late papers are accepted (DON'T ASK!), that withdrawal dates are inflexible, that a written legal or medical excuse is needed to make up a missed laboratory, and that unfair student practices will be dealt with promptly. I further believe care is shown by giving increasing weight to homework assignment as the term progresses. It is a fact of human nature to lose motivation for a cause or an event as time goes on (Figure 1.2a), hence giving a higher number of points for each succeeding homework counters this trend (Figure 1.2b), such that on balancing time with credit, the level of motivation will hopefully smooth out (Figure 1.2c).

"Incompletes" are not issued unless one is physically incapacitated during the last two weeks of the term–and then only if the work up to that point is acceptable. I tell the students that we will deviate from this only "if the Emperor delivers a decree announcing that the city is being hit by the Bubonic Plague." The message is clear, but can also backfire. I well remember the time when a mother brought her ill daughter in to take the scheduled exam. Naturally, there are circumstances which call for special consideration. Generally, however, strict adherence to policies promotes a smooth running operation. Thus, of the 15,000+ students taught, we have had to issue fewer than perhaps a dozen "Incompletes."

Figure 1.1 Typical course outline.

LECTURE OUTLINE FOR CHEMISTRY C 101
Day Sections

Texts: Ouellette, Chemistry
Wells, Studies in Chem

Week of		Mondays	Wednesdays	Fridays
Aug	26	–	Introduction to course	1. Measurements
Sept	2	LABOR DAY	1. (cont.)	2. Classif. of Matter
	9	2. (cont.)	EXAM I	3. Structure of Matter
	16	3. (cont.)	3. (cont.)	4. Stoichiometry
	24	4. (cont.)	4. (cont.)	4. (cont.)
			No refunds after today	
	30	4. (cont.)	4. (cont.)	EXAM II
Oct	7	HOW TO STUDY	5. Periodic Table	5. (cont.)
	14	6. Bonding	6. (cont.)	6. (cont.)
	21	EXAM III	7. Gases	7. (cont.)
	28	7. (cont.)	7. (cont.)	8. Liquids & Solids
Nov	4	8. (cont.)	EXAM IV	9. Solutions
	11	9. (cont.)	9. (cont.)	10. Reactions
			To withdraw: W or F only!	
	18	10. (cont.)	I0. (cont.)	EXAM V
	25	11. Acids & Bases		THANKSGIVING RECESS
Dec	2	11. (cont.)	11. (cont.)	11. (cont.)
	9	12. Nuclear Chemistry	12. (cont.)	EXAM VI
	16	REVIEW FOR FINAL	–	FINAL EXAM

HOMEWORK ASSIGNMENTS

The way a student does homework assignments is indicative of the way in which the student will perform in the course as a whole. Keep that in mind. The problems are taken from the text problems found at the end of each chapter. Problems are due on the Mondays indicated. No late papers are accepted. DON'T ASK!

Due on		Points	Chapter and Problems
Sept	9	0	1: 3,9,15,17,27,31,35,39,43
	16	1	2: 5,7,13,18,21,27,29,33,35,43,51,53
	23	2	3: 5,7,11,19,21,27,29,35,41,43,45,47,49,51
	30	3	4: 7,9,13,17,21,23,27,29
Oct	7	4	4: 31,33,37,39,43,45,47,49
	14	5	5: 3,11,13,17,23,27,31,35,39,43,49,55,59
	21	6	6: 5,7,9,11,17,19,25,27,29,35,39,43
	28	7	7: 5,13,15,23,27
Nov	4	8	7: 33,35,39,45,51; 8: 5,9,II,13,15,19,27,29,35,37,43
	11	9	9: 5,11,15,19,25,27,29
	18	10	9: 31,35,49,51,53,61,63
	25	11	10: 5,11,13,15,19,23,27,33,35,37,39,41,47,51,53,55
Dec	2	12	11: 5,9,11,15,19,23,29
	12	13	11: 37,39,45,47,51,55,57
	16	14	12: 3,7,9,11,15,17,19,31,37,45,49,53,54,55

Figure 1.1 Continued

LABORATORY OUTLINE FOR CHEMISTRY C 101
Day Sections

Fall

Text: Wells, CHEMISTRY IN ACTION, 2/e

Week of		Experiment	
Aug	26	*	Check-in and Introduction to the Laboratory, p. 1
Sep	2	*	Simple Techniques, p. 17 (W and F sections only)
	9	1.	Scientific Measurements, p. 5
	16	5.	Occurrence and Isolation of Elements, p. 39 (We'll help with equations)
	23	4.	Scientific Observations, p. 27
	30	11.	Elemental Composition of Antimony Iodide, p. 85
Oct	7	8.	Periodic Trends, p. 61
	14	*27.	Molecular Models: Shapes, p. 163
	21	14.	Measuring a Molecule; Avogadro's Number, p. 109
	28	*7.	Boyle's Law, p. 55
Nov	4	19.	Physical Properties, p. 139
	11	9.	Solutions: General Studies, p. 69
	18		Kinetics (hand-out)
	25	*	Equilibrium (hand-out) M sections and those with valid Make-Up permits only
Dec	2	18.	Metal Ions in Rocks, p. 133
	9	20.	Acids and Bases, p. 147–Check out after experiment

*A required, noncredit laboratory activity. (-20 points if not done and handed in)

* * *

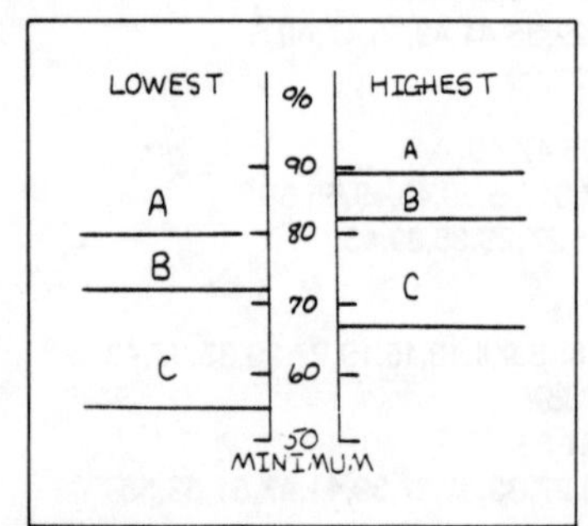

COURSE GRADING FOR C101

5 Exams (drop 1 of 6) @ 100 points	500 points
Final Exam	100 points
Homework	100 points
Quizzes (drop 1 of 11) @ 10 points	100 points
Experiments (drop 1 of 11) @ 20 points	200 points
TOTAL	1000 points

Unfair Student Practices. Any student found engaging in cheating, aiding in cheating, or any other unfair practice, will be dealt with promptly in a nonforgiving manner according to the rules of the IUPUI Faculty Handbook (Copy on bulletin board). See me if you need proof that we do make use of these rules if need be!

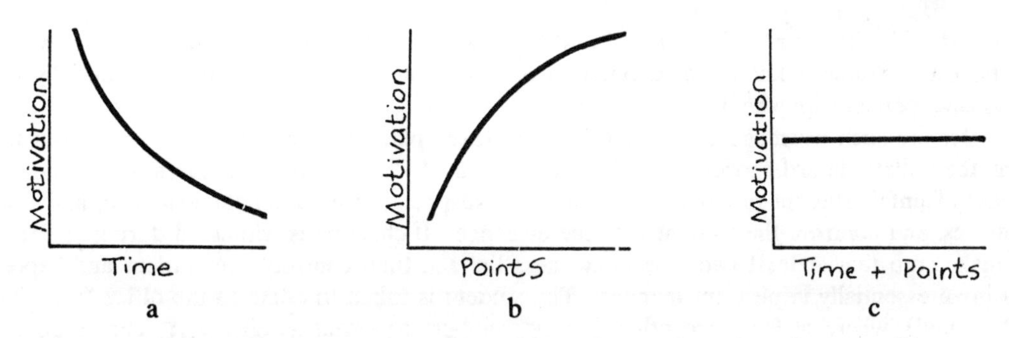

Figure 1.2 The level of motivation vs time (a); vs the number of credit points (b); and the combination of the two (c).

Class discipline–Fortunately, this is not a problem in most college and university settings. However, especially in large classes, it is inevitable that sometime or other a pair or a small group of students will huddle somewhere in the back and talk, mostly to the annoyance of surrounding students. It usually says something about the student. Left to themselves, students will, on the average, automatically seat themselves in a classroom in such a way that the A students sit in front, the B students behind them, and so on. In fact, we are told that students choosing to sit past row fifteen or so are essentially choosing to distance themselves from classroom activity. They prefer a feeling of disengagement and would like to avoid involvement. I believe students talking during class are giving me helpful feedback: "You are not speaking to us." So I must change the pace, stop lecturing, and relate an incident. Perhaps I can ask a question directed to their general vicinity; perhaps I can even stop talking, and the ensuing silence, accompanied by a properly focused look (stare?) will usually deliver the message. A colleague of mine solves the problem by lowering the pitch of his voice and speaking quietly and more quietly. The talking student's voices, by difference, become louder and louder, and usually fellow students will then solve the problem.

A couple of times when nothing seems to help, I have stopped my lecture, looked squarely at the students and stated "Do I have your attention now?" (The room has now become deathly quiet, and of course I have their attention.) Then I continue "I would like to remind you that in this setting we take turns talking. I will be pleased to have you ask or comment. If you can't agree with this procedure, would you please leave the room at this time." Impact? You bet! Laura was one such student who was singled out. A week later she came to me saying that she had never been confronted in that manner, nor for that matter had she ever been disciplined by her teachers or her parents. She said it had been good for her. Such drastic measures have to be taken only on very, very few occasions–rumors about your insistence on discipline will precede you.

Dishonesty–Much of the workings of this country are based on the honor system. The taxing system is largely dependent on the basic honesty of most persons. What is in the news is a small percentage on dishonest persons. The coins we drop in at the newsstand open a lid exposing a stack of papers, yet most persons remove only one paper. The roadside self-service fruit stands depend on the honor system. This is part of what makes this country both great and unique. There are not too many parts of the world where this can be done. Once a term I do mention to the students the precious aspects of this system and the fact that we rely on that same system in the course, since the laboratory reports and homework assignments are assuming honesty. Students know that a violation of this principle turns me into an essentially unreasonable person with whom to deal.

Despite such warnings, a cheating incident takes place here and there. Throughout the term, the bulletin board carries a copy of the exact faculty handbook procedures to be followed in case of unfair student practices. If cheating is suspected, we gather the evidence, assemble witnesses, and confront the student with the evidence. If cheating is witnessed during an exam, we make sure that at least two persons witness the act, then confront the student and expose him in an essentially unpleasant manner. The student is asked to come to the office (very formal setting!), where at least one other faculty member is present as observer. The student is presented with the evidence and given a mutually agreeable time to present his counter case. If there is remorse and an obvious opportunity presents itself for redirecting the person's life, we do so. Otherwise, the guidelines are followed. Of perhaps a handful of such cases in fifteen years, most were remorseful, citing family problems, professional anxiety, etc. It is not unusual for such persons to come back later and apologize.

Some time ago we were urged to watch a particular group of three students. Not noting any unusual behavior, we casually looked at the records for past exams, only to find that all scored the same. Fueled by suspicion, we investigated further and found that the computer printout showed not only that their scores were the same, but that the exact same questions were missed by all three on several exams. Obviously something was not right. Further searching revealed scoring sheets that had been erased and corrected to match each other, homework that was identical, laboratory reports that contained the same errors and the same phraseology, etc. Armed with the evidence, and in the presence of an uninvolved faculty member, formal accusation was made with the explanation of their rights. Two admitted to dishonesty; one did not. However, just a few days ago as of this writing, the third member suddenly appeared at the office. He explained that he had had an agonizing year and that he has learned a lot and wishes to start over. While one of the worst aspects of teaching is having to deal with cheating, one of the most exhilirating experiences is to be able to shake the hand of a remorseful offender.

Only twice, to my knowledge, have I been approached with offers of bribery, and one of these I did not recognize as a bribe until after the fact. A foreign student brought me a present–in this case, a beautiful wood carving from his native country. At the end of the term he received the deserved D and approached me saying "You gave me a D, what about the carving?" Realizing that this had been a bribe, I asked him to take the carving back. Despite my urgings, he left it but hopefully took with him a valuable lesson.

Care by Going the Extra Mile

As is the case with most computer novices, when I first began using microcomputers in my work, there arose many occasions of utter frustration and feelings of helplessness. I remember one particular time when the student records for an entire section seemed to be lost. Even the back-up disk, which I had carefully stored elsewhere, showed the same irretrievability. After desperate attempts on my system, I used the disk on other computers, but all efforts failed. The solution seemed to be the experts at the computing services office. However, the message there was that "this happens sometimes, you will have to redo all those records from the beginning of the semester." I related my sad tale to Mike, a colleague, during a casual conversation in the hall. He invited me to bring all the information in, and he spent the next hour searching for an answer, but to no avail. Finally, he made a careful analysis of the command printout both for the bad disk and a good one from a similar section. Noting an error message, he deleted that portion and inserted the similar portion from the good disk to the bad one. Bingo, the radical surgery had worked. I am taking the time to relate the incident because it is one example of going the extra mile. The important point is that Mike could have talked to me for a bit, made some suggestions, and then wished me good luck. I would have felt good about Mike taking the time to do so. However, for Mike to actually sit down and work with me left a lasting impression on me. Mike is my friend!

Students are in the underdog role, while faculty are naturally in the role of being in control. For the master to take the time and go the extra mile for the student is truly an act of service beyond the call of duty. This service can be done by such simple acts as lending a book to a student; having extra help sessions; taping the lectures for later student use; making lecture notes available; asking the student to reexplain a principle back to me right after I have explained it to him; giving a get-acquainted, noncredit test; giving weekly quizzes; encouraging students to study in groups; introducing likely study partners to each other; inviting students to react during lecture via questions and body language; sending grades by mail after the term is finished; posting any helpful hints on the bulletin board; even paying a registration fee for a needy student to attend a scholarly event; and, as I do routinely, sending a congratulatory letter to all "A" students at the end of the term.

Students will respond to such overtures by developing their own extra-mile efforts. It is not uncommon at all to see some of the better students help those in need, either in the hall, in class, or often, in more organized help session settings. I remember well when Dave, a brilliant young student, took the time, not once or thrice, but on a scheduled basis throughout the term, to help a struggling older student. I also remember John and his unselfish devotion to the organization and implementation of a weekly study session open to anyone wishing to come. The teaching staff, too, amazes me many times with offers of extra help sessions and handouts for the students.

Some instructors hire note takers so that students are free from note taking and can devote complete attention to what is being said. While there may be merit in that process, it has also been found that the removal of a sense of responsibility tends to lower the level of involvement. A passive observer ("the note taker will get it down for me") learns less than the involved student. It is perhaps much better to encourage the students to take sketchy notes and flesh them in immediately after class. If need be, it is always possible to use fellow student's notes or use the audiovisual recording of the lecture. The need of having to pay close attention, so that details can be filled in later, is a good learning experience.

Every term, after the results of the second exam are in, we encourage all students who received a C- or less on the two exams to come in for suggestions. At this time we go over the results of the Readiness Profile (see Chapter 5), which often indicate that the student will either have to do some remedial work, rid himself of some overcommitments, or have a change in attitude, or any combination of these symptoms. The student is asked to state a date and time by when he will have made the necessary adjustment.

Many institutions have honors programs. They take extra faculty time, but students appreciate the time spent in allowing them to enroll in the programs. We have also instituted

Speed Chem, an opportunity for those students who either are fast learners, or have a good background in chemistry, to advance at their own (faster) pace. These efforts take time, but the extra contact with students is worth it. Years later they remember the special projects we undertook.

Occasionally, I take personal time with and for a student. Students representing the institution in athletic events are honored to have their faculty show support by their presence. Eating with students has a unique way of removing inhibition. It was over lunch that Renee was given a chance to express her grief on the recent loss of a loved one. Utter care must be taken to ensure that such personal time involvement is not seen as showing favoratism by other students.

Certainly, one of the simplest means to go the extra mile is to learn the student names. If from a class of two hundred to three hundred students I am able to call someone by name, that is special to the student ("You remembered my name!"). For me this is not easy, especially if I do not see the students in the laboratory or recitation setting. One will automatically get to know some names; perhaps the outstanding students, the problem students, those with special features or characteristics. What about the rest?

There are several things I can do. First, I can go over the class roster and become familiar with the names, the spelling, and the sections they are in. Next, I make it a point to enter the names into the grade book system, so that the writing will emphasize the reading. Then I read the names aloud. Once a week, if possible, I go to the laboratory where the students work and, with seating chart in hand, I survey the class. This is a good time to associate name with physical appearance, making mental hooks to remember the association. As I talk with them, more mnemonics will become available. If I have a small class (fewer than fifty), I ask everyone to put on a 3 x 5 card their name and something interesting, unique, or unusual about themselves which will help me remember their names quickly. In this manner, I learned of a student who spent the summer restoring paintings in Italy, one who trains and shows wolves, or another who loves her red hair. Still another opportunity to learn students' names presents itself during office hours, when I like to keep a running log, recording the student's names and describing briefly something about that person. "Bruce, tall, works in an appliance store; Debbie has a limp, really does not study; Harold, happy disposition, good background; Mary, pretty, tiny features, will be satisfied with C." The acid test for these exercises is the use of the names. I call on them even at the risk of having the wrong name.

Spending time with students pays off. It gives a personal feeling of satisfaction, of service well done. It draws out the student; he will relate his general attitude about school, what is good and what hinders; he will relate his experiences with other teachers; but most of all, going the extra mile with a student encourages him to do likewise.

Polaroid photos, or brief video shots, where each student introduces himself, provide an excellent means of learning sources.

Building Student Self-Confidence

- Teacher to class on opening day: "Look to the classmate on your right, look to the one on your left. One of the three of you will not pass this course."
- A not-so-uncommon announcement in large, freshmen, so-called "weed-out" courses: "Fifty percent of you will fail."
- A feedback a class received after the first exam: "I hope none of you plan to go into the sciences, because you are too dumb."

These are not made-up statements; they are paraphrased quotes from actual teacher pronouncements to classes. What the mind is told over and over again, the subconscious will process into reality. Research proves this to be true in many different ways. Young elephants are kept in place by tying a foot with a heavy chain to a metal post sunk deep into the ground. However, mature elephants can be kept in the same position by simply tying a string around the foot and essentially laying it on the ground. The reason for the difference is simple. Years of experience have told the elephant that the foot is chained to the ground and that there is no freedom of movement. When eventually the chain is removed and replaced by a simple string, the assumption still remains, "I can't move!"

The very same thing works with humans. Zig Ziglar tells of a girl who was passed from Kindergarten on to first grade with the information that "Linda can't learn." Linda had all the disadvantages; she was frail, black, and retarded. The first grade teacher naturally saw that Linda couldn't learn and passed her on to the second grade with the comment that "Linda can't learn." And so it went for years. The world about her kept telling her that "Linda can't learn; Linda can't learn; Linda can't learn; Linda can't learn; Linda can't learn!" After Linda dropped out of high school, a kindly lady took her in and showed her how to do some things, and to her amazement found that Linda could do it. She increased the level of demand and found that Linda thrived on the challenge, because she indeed could learn. She eventually became accomplished enough to become a secretary at Goodwill Industries. Linda could learn!

Our accomplishments are more a matter of will and confidence than talent. There are three ways in which student self-confidence can be built up.

First, we build confidence via the teacher to individual student relationship. Positive feedback by the teacher to the student can come in the form of verbal comments, written statements on papers, or special mention after an unusually good exam. We all receive many papers throughout our schooling, most of which are eventually thrown away, whether they are good or bad. But the ones most likely kept are the ones with good teacher comments. Think about it! It takes just a comment to build self-confidence. I tell my students that there are no dumb questions, and that I assume all students to be "A" students.

Some techniques that help build student self-confidence revolve around explanations. After I explain something to the student privately or even in a small class setting, I often ask that student to reexplain it to me. Just the experience of hearing himself say the words and sentences of something new is reassuring. The encouragement he gets from me helps along. If he heads in the wrong direction, I might immediately interrupt and say "OK thus far, now let's think about it" in order to get him on the right track again.

I well remember being the recipient of this technique. Having just arrived in graduate school, I was enrolled in a chemical analysis course where the assignment was to analyze the components in a mixture of chemicals. While I remember with fondness the course itself as a great learning experience, I remember even better the sessions with the instructor. Dr. Richter had the uncanny ability to answer my questions by asking me the right questions until I had the answer. Typically, he would sit at his desk and I was placed by the blackboard, chalk in hand. "If you think you have chemical X in your mixture, how could you test for it?" I made a suggestion. "OK, now let's put the proposed testing agent on the board along with chemical X." After a pause he continued, "What do you see about the two that might be helpful? Do you really think there is no better way?" And so the session went until a clear picture had been formulated in my mind. These were grueling and exhausing, but infinitely helpful sessions. I almost looked forward to the agony of the next session.

When doing numerical problems either one-on-one or in the lecture session, I insist that the students do any necessary calculations. Involvement forces thinking and builds self-confidence.

It has been said that "teaching teaches the teacher." For this reason, I often ask my students who have just learned something to go out, find a student who does not understand it, and explain it to him. The experience of having to verbalize the thought process, and to do so in a manner helpful to someone else, is a tremendous learning opportunity. I try to make it very clear to the students that this process should not be viewed as building up the competition, but rather as a service to someone else and to oneself.

A second way to build self–confidence is through the teacher-to-class relationship. Smaller discussion settings lend wonderful opportunities. A student will ask a question. As I field the question, I will restate it and ask it back to the class as a whole. Answers will come, and after a bit I will return to the original student, asking if it makes sense. If not, it is helpful to ask a student who spoke up before to explain it to the student still in the dark. By this time the atmosphere is relaxed enough that all attention is on the explanation of the subject matter, and no time is left to worry about embarrassment to speak up.

"Do you realize how far you have come since the beginning of the term? Why, for example at the beginning of the term you did not know how to . . . ." Such a comment does wonders!

Setting small, attainable goals for the class to be attained in the next thirty minutes is useful. Everyone (who wants to participate) sees a definite target: ("By the end of today's class I'll know how to do this type of problem").

It also helps to stop lecturing, say, every fifteen minutes and ask the students to compare notes for a few minutes, to see if the understanding is the same. Questions will easily result from this technique. Furthermore, one can give sample pre-exams to build confidence, place old exams on file, and encourage students to work in cluster groups. I have also invited students to submit questions for the next exam. These are posted for all to see, and at least a fourth are used on the exam.

A more difficult technique is to build on student questions and try to maintain a thread, especially if these questions come somewhere out of left field. But it does build tremendous confidence to take a student's question and build upon it, use it for an example, use it as a bridge to the next topic, or refer to it again later in the lecture. The student can't help but feel "my question was a good one." If the question is just too far out or too advanced, it helps to say something like "You obviously have done some thinking on this and are advanced, how about if we talk about it after class?"

A third way of accomplishing self-confidence involves the student-to-student relationship, some of which has been previously referenced. Students like to hear from successful fellow students. After the first or second exam, it is wise to recognize the "A" students. Others will naturally seek them out for help. Students with a special twist or very special conditions are interesting to listen to when they speak. Once or twice per term such students are given five to ten minutes to talk to the class. Shelly spoke once about how she was successful in learning the material by making up her own exams, setting them aside, and then sometime later taking them under the same conditions as a regular exam. Leah related to the class her simple approach to study; make a schedule and stick to it. While she could speak with some authority since she took twenty credit hours and maintained an "A" average in all classes, it was the handicaps under which she existed that made her a worthy model for her peers. In addition to the twenty credits, Leah also worked thirty hours per week, had four children (two in diapers), had just undergone a divorce, slept only about six hours per day, was forced to ask for help from the Welfare Department, and had had no previous chemistry studies. She was later besieged by admiring fellow students, both to express support and seek help.

Finally, students feel a certain sense of comfort in hearing from former students who are now out in the field. It is good for the students to hear that the subjects learned actually do apply later in life. All such special talks are recorded and placed on file for later use.

As teachers we get what we give. The computer lingo for this is "gigo," garbage in, garbage out. If we are negative, students will complain, fuss, and argue, but if we are positive with a view to help, they will respond positively, not in one, but in an untold number of ways.

Care by Motivating

Motivation has always been a driving force in learning. In years gone by, it often was negative motivation, instilled by fear of the rod, that drove students to study. In the last century, the emphasis has been on positive motivation. Motivation is a dream coupled with energy to attain a goal. Every human being is motivated from birth. The teacher's task, therefore, is not to motivate but to channel the motivation. Since errors do erode motivation, one of the best means of channeling motivation in the proper direction is by providing a setting of a high probability for many small successes and reducing the possibility for errors. When errors do creep in, we can make them seem easy to overcome.

Motivation may be sparked by many factors. I like to point out the privilege of being able to go to school, the fact that we are in a comfortable room, with good lighting, the availability of so many good books. This is indeed a rare opportunity not enjoyed in many countries. The use of quotes properly applied and placed is occasionally a spark for motivation and so are tapes. My students have access to motivational tapes such as "How Chemistry Applies to Nursing," authored by a former faculty member of the School of Nursing, who made it a deliberate point to record all the incidents for a period of a week in her clinical practice where a chemical principle was used. It is done in a truly sensitive way, motivating to do better. Students also have access to general interest tapes by personalities such as Linus Pauling on "Vitamin C."

FACTS ON MOTIVATION

1. People are naturally curious, and curiosity motivates.
2. Learning and memory are closely tied to motivation.
3. Unexpected questions motivate most.
4. Motivation is highest when chances for success are at least modest.
5. A major source of motivation is the teacher's attitude and enthusiasm.
6. Grades, intimidation, fear and money are most commonly used yet least effective motivators.

W. J. McKeachie, Teaching Tips

Again, former students are a great source of student motivators. Tom qualified some years ago to be on the American bobsledding team for the Winter Olympics. When he spoke to the class on the attainment of excellence through practice, he spoke with authority and had complete student attention.

Roger Reynolds was a student who came to our class with a life experience behind him that is second to none. As a member of the Blue Angels parachuting team, he performed regularly at air shows with a particular emphasis on stunts such as releasing a chute, then cutting its strings to give the appearance of impending disaster, only to release a second chute at the very last moment. On one such occasion, after well over nine hundred jumps, the first chute did not open properly, and the second became entangled in the first, causing him to fall three thousand feet. Many things happened that saved his life. He fell sideways, reducing the impact; he landed on a soft spot in the back year of a doctor who was at home. Virtually every bone was broken, and recovery was slow, painful, and without the prediction that he would ever walk again. Through months and years of practice, determination, and willpower, he began to walk, eliminated a limp, started running, and eventually participated in and successfully finished the Boston Marathon, not once but numerous times. He also started jumping again and was able to complete his thousandth jump. The media soon made him a celebrity. When Roger spoke to the class about self-discipline and the lonely walk against all odds, the room was quietly filled with respect. An example was set; motivation had been attained. Though a below average student in high school, he successfully achieved admission to medical school.

During the last several years, I have set aside one lecture period for the sole purpose of motivating students. Usually given soon after the second exam, it is a talk on how to study, but hopefully also a stimulating motivator. All of our best efforts at teaching will be in vain unless the student wants to study. Judging from student comments, the time taken for this purpose is considered very useful and has become a vital component of my teaching. Not only are students challenged to channel their study efforts in a meaningful way, but they are also challenged to live clean, wholesome lives. For details see Chapter 6.

Care by Counseling

Mike came in saying that the computer printout of his midterm standing showed him to have an overall 49%. He knew that it takes at least 50% to pass the course and that at this rate he was in trouble. "I need at least a C-, what do you suggest?"

Here is a student asking for help. He is essentially looking for a formula, which when plugged in, will produce the desired result. Experience has shown that when students come and ask questions, as did Mike, or questions such as "I understand what you are saying, and I read the chapter three times, but when it comes to exams, I just blank out. What can I do?", they are really saying to me "If you feed me, I'll eat, but I don't want to take the time to learn how to eat by myself."

Mike and I went into the office and looked at the results of his Readiness Profile (see Chapter 5), which he had filled out at the beginning of the term. It immediately showed that his background and thinking level were quite appropriate, but that his motivation, and especially his personal affairs, showed some real problems. The next few minutes revealed the following. Mike, a nineteen year old, had received good grades in high school without studying; he now worked thirty hours per week stocking shelves in order to make car payments; he lived at home, had a girlfriend with whom he spent time on just about a daily basis, slept all Saturday and Sunday mornings, watched TV on at least four evenings, liked miniature golfing, and yet still found time to study one to three hours per week. While his parents did want him to go to college, there was no real effort to encourage, or a method of periodic checkups on performance. I began my suggestions by encouraging him to drop school immediately and become the best shelf stocker in the city. That suggestion did not seem too appealing to him and he wanted other alternatives. I continued my hard line approach: "You will get an F in this course–unless you are willing to do something you have never done in your life, and you have to decide to do it the minute you walk out of this door." Mike wanted to hear more. "You are going to have to go against your pattern, against the rut you're in. As soon as you leave here I want you to head for the first table, take out a sheet of paper, and make yourself a schedule of how life will be from now on. I want you to build in at least two hours of weekly study for each credit hour you are taking. Next I want you to call your girlfriend and tell her that from now on you will only see her once a week. I want you to show the schedule to your parents, and I want you to make arrangements with your employer to cut down on your working time to no more than twenty hours per week. When you study, you will have to do a lot of catching up of material you have missed so far in the course. I want you to study in the library, not at home. Finally, I want you to come in and check with me at least once a week."

I concluded my suggestions to Mike by saying that "I am not sure that you have the willpower, guts, and stamina to do all this, and you may still choose to become a good shelf stocker and I will wish you the best. However, if you do decide to follow my advice, I invite you to come to me three times a week for help and support, and if you try, I will drop everything and do my utmost to help, and I promise not only will you be successful in the course, but in the long run you will be thankful as well."

My counseling approach used to be one of reaction to a need; it was passive. Now it is more confrontive, aggressive, and where possible, preventive. Instead of reacting to an event, I like to act to shape events in the student's life. It is for this reason that all students with a C- or lower average at the end of the second exam must come to see me.

When I see my doctor, he has license to ask me all kinds of personal questions. He does ask these, not because he is snoopy, but because the answer will help him to help me. In the same manner, as a teacher I do have license to ask personal questions of my students. When warranted, I ask about their home life, whether they date heavily; I even ask whether they are on drugs. No student has ever refused to answer, and I have not hesitated to encourage students to drop a class or even to drop out of school. Often such drastic measures will shock the student into a realization that something is wrong.

Beth came in stating that she could not get a good score on the exams. A few short questions indicated that her schedule was likely overambitious. I asked her to fill out the counseling Help Sheet, which revealed some interesting facts (Figure 1.3). Though she only took ten credit hours (fifteen is normal), she was overcommitted. In looking at her schedule, a first sign of overcommitment is too much undisciplined time. She really is not up and functioning by eight in the morning. True, she does come to class at eight, but look what happens immediately following class: breakfast! When no early class is on she sleeps until nine in the morning!, and she "gets ready" and showers in midday. So, one of the time-consuming parts of her life is unplanned, lazy time. Another commitment is work, thirty-four hours per week, which is nearly a full-time job. It is virtually impossible to excel in school with that kind of demand. Next let's analyze her study pattern. She studies chemistry about seven hours per week, English five hours, and education two hours per week. This is far from the officially suggested three hours for every credit hour rule given by professional counselors. It means that, in order to be successful, she would have to devote fifteen hours per week to chemistry, nine to English and six to education. Five of the seven chemistry hours are in the afternoon or evening, when mental alertness is low and dropping. Five of the seven hours are also isolated hours, when it is much better to have larger (two to three-hour) blocks of study. Finally, she apparently has no fixed place of study, oscillating between three different locations. A last time commitment goes to recreation, a full twenty hours! Beth was encouraged to do some serious thinking about her priorities. She eventually chose to drop the class.

Not all counseling, of course, is shock treatment. Most students coming in are looking for minor adjustments in their approach. Based on schedules such as in Figure 1.3, I might suggest changing the study time from evening to early morning, or to divide too large a study block into smaller ones. I might suggest the use of tape recorders, study groups, self-tests, or on occasion it might even be the suggestion to aim higher.

Even in today's liberated times, at least in the Midwest, we still find a mentality among (especially female) students that stereotypes professional goals. Anita, a mother in her midthirties was returning to school to test the waters. She asked to sit in on class. She obviously was alert; her questions were on target; she was learning. I encouraged her to at least take the exams. Consistently she came out on top. Finally I was able to convince her to enroll as a full student. She spoke of a two-year nursing degree as a goal. I encouraged her to set higher goals in the clinical field: how about medical school? To gain ownership in the goal, I suggested she talk with her family about this (goals have a better chance if made known to others; it forces commitment), then I suggested that she talk with at least three female medical students, and finally that she visit with three practicing female MDs. Previously unheard of possibilities have a way of becoming reality. Years later, students such as Anita, now MDs, come back with glee in their eyes.

Counseling sessions often turn to very personal matters, such as family problems, personal medical difficulties, or extreme anxieties. In such cases I listen, help when possible, or suggest professional help, which is available on our campus free of charge to the students.

HELP SHEET

Name Beth [redacted]

List courses you are now taking:	Credit hours:
C101	5
Educ X 151	2
W 131	3
TOTAL:	10

Please fill in the schedule below giving all your activities for a routine week: biol lect, study chem, dinner, date, work, sleep, TV, etc... List anything that takes half an hour or more of your time.

	Monday	Tuesday	Wednesday	Thursday	Friday	Saturday	Sunday	
	sleep							
6 am	sleep	sleep	sleep	sleep	sleep	sleep	sleep	6 am
7 am	sleep	sleep	sleep	sleep	sleep	sleep	sleep	7 am
8 am	C101 Lect.	sleep	C101 lect.	sleep	C101 lect.	sleep	sleep	8 am
9 am	Breakfast	sleep	Breakfast	sleep	Breakfast	sleep	sleep	9 am
10 am	ready for work	ready for work	Study C101	laundry	Go over C101 lab	ready for work	sleep	10 am
11 am	work	work	Study X151 & C101	Study C101	Do C101 homework	work	ready-work	11 am
Noon	work	work	Study W131	lunch	C101 lab	work	work	Noon
1 pm	work	work	lunch	Go over W131	lab	work	work	1 pm
2 pm	work	work	X 151	shower/dress	Go home	work	work	2 pm
3 pm	work	work	X 151	laundry	Study C101	work	work	3 pm
4 pm	work	work	Go home-read/TV	Study-any	Study any	work	work	4 pm
5 pm	work	work	dinner	dinner	dinner	work	work	5 pm
6 pm	eat dinner	eat dinner	Go out	W 131	shower/dress	work	work	6 pm
7 pm	Study C101	Go out	recreation	W 131	Go out	work	Home/eat	7 pm
8 pm	Study C101	recreation	recreation	W 131	recreation	home/dress	Study C101	8 pm
9 pm	Study W131	came home	Came home.	Finish class/go home	recreation	Go out	Finish C101 hw	9 pm
10 pm	Study W131	Study C101 or W131	TV/read/phone	TV/read/home	recreation	recreation	Study C101	10 pm
11 pm	Bed	Bed	TV/read/phone	Bed	Home/TV	Home	Study W131/X151	11 pm
12 pm			bed		Bed	Bed	Bed	12 pm

Where do you study? the University Library, Warren Library, home.

Briefly, but exactly describe how you study. C101 - I read the chapter, do the homework + study/do problems from white workbook. W 131 - Read my chapter(s), do designated units, do journals, work on essay(s). X 151 - There really isn't too much I can do but read my chapter(s).

Figure 1.3

Justina had just received word that her brother was hospitalized as a stroke victim. That same week her son was involved in a car accident, and her daughter was reported AWOL. All I can do is listen.

Marie is a young unmarried mother of an eighteen-month-old infant. After a fight with her father, she had to move out, became ill, and could not study. We agreed to postpone her exam.

Donna is divorced and lives with her two small children, with her parents. But her problem is her total lack of self-confidence. Her mother takes over and mothers the children. As we talk she gains enough self-assurance to take two bold steps: to move out, and to enroll in an assertiveness training seminar. Months later she comes back expressing gratefulness.

Financial worries are often at the source of much anxiety. For many students it is a catch-22 situation where they have to work to be able to go to school, but work interferes with studies. Such a case was Jim, who worked as a maintenance man in an apartment complex in exchange for rent, but could not make ends meet. After a few minutes of conversation, it turned out that he spent too much on transportation, that the apartments were luxury units, and that he could work there without having to live there. A few quick calculations showed that he would be much better off spending one whole year at full-time work, saving every possible penny, and moving in with a lady who had an upstairs bedroom which he could have in exchange for help around the house. This arrangement, it turned out, would give him two full years of uninterrupted full-time studies without any need for work. Such a student, upon his return to school, is a good spokesman to other students about the need to watch overcommitments. He can give the best reasons why not to do it.

As a counselor, I consider myself a sort of compassionate uncle. In years past when the extended agrarian family was commonplace, counselors were built in. However, in the urban, nuclear (often split or merged) family, outsiders must take the place of helpers.

Care by Rewarding

When someone gives me a compliment and if, perhaps because it was said somewhat quietly, there is even the slightest possibility that the speaker might believe I did not hear what he said, I will eagerly ask "Excuse me, what did you say?" It has been said that praise does wonders for the sense of hearing. We all like to hear praise again and again. It spurs us on; it makes us want to do better and more. Maureen O'Donnell, Virginia's 1983 Teacher of the Year, says that the joys of teaching come by motivating, and she motivates by praising. There truly is sheer wonder and amazing power in praise. Praise is the verbal form of the general act of rewarding. What follows is a cafeteria of rewarding ideas found successful.

- Have all the top students stand after the first exam.
- At about midterm have the most improved students stand.
- Introduce students with a unique and interesting life.
- Put positive comments on papers, bulletin boards, and overheads.
- Bring donuts to class.
- Institute what a colleague calls "Miracle Grading," a sliding scale where the possible pointage on the final exam is the difference between the total points possible in the course and the points accumulated on all hourly exams.

- Involve students by asking questions, inviting them to read a section, or inviting them to explain something mastered.
- Provide opportunity for students to initial the examination key if they missed no questions or only 1, 2, or 3 (see Figure 1.4).
- Have (phony) newspaper headline printed: "Chem 101 is the best." Show to class after good exam performance (see Figure 1.5).
- Write up an interesting event pertaining to the subject of the course, but which has a touching human interest point. Run off on good parchment paper and give as holiday present (see Figure 1.6).
- Send congratulatory letters to top students.
- Have awards day toward the end of the term for
    - the most improved
    - the best study habit
    - the top student
    - the soundest sleeper
    - the most innovative excuses
    - the clumsiest in lab

You are invited to initial below if you missed only a few questions on the exam.

Number of questions missed	0	1	2	3	4	5
Initials						

Figure 1.4

★ EXTRA ★

HOME EDITION | **The Indiana Journal** | HOME EDITION

SECTION 1 | 10¢ | PAGE 1

IUPUI'S C101 "THE BEST"

Story on Page 3

Radiation Determined By Gadget

WASHINGTON — Doctors of the Army's Walter Reed Institute of Research have just developed a "whole man counter." It is described as an "electronic marvel." For the first time it makes possible complete determination of the radioactivity of a human being, both natural and acquired, from toenails to hair on the scalp.

"It provides," says a report "a fundamental research tool in the worldwide study of radio fall-out."

Ground has just been broken for a building to house a 50,000-watt nuclear reactor to produce various sorts of radiation.

Boats are being used to rescue stranded residents in flooded Fairbanks, Alaska. A boater arrives on the scene to remove a man and woman from a fire escape in downtown Fairbanks.

Battle Report

toward closing the postal revenue-expenditure gap.

About $24 million, the Post Office Department reports, was cut from obligations by:

- The Department's Nation-Wide Improved Mail Service (NIMS) Program, which involves 25,000 of the country's largest mailers in a continuing, cooperative effort to reschedule their mail to improve service for all postal patrons.
- A special Christmas mail program, which permitted the huge mail volume to be handled with thousands fewer temporary employees.
- Improvements in mail transportation.

Other savings the Postal service reports were the result of savings on contracts for buildings, equipment and machinery ($5.5 million); deferment to subsequent fiscal years some modernization plans ($6 million); adoption of uniform standards in the procurement of supplies and equipment ($5.5 million); and competitive bidding on mail

Think Orange Any Time Of The Year

Here are some of the oranges available now and during other seasons of the year:

—NAVEL—Medium to large in size, a thick-skinned orange, good for eating out of hand and also for serving sliced or sectioned. Has characteristic puckered appearance at bloom end. The peel crystalizes well and makes a good marmalade. In season from October to December although the California season extends from October to April.

—VALENCIA—An excellent juice orange, somewhat elongated vertically (a little egg-shaped), large in size and good in flavor. The sections freeze well. Makes a good marmalade. In season from March to July. The California season

USE OF WATER IS UP IN NATION

Industry Greatest Glutton Using Half Consumed

WASHINGTON — Americans are using more water than ever to keep cool, clean and occupied.

Water consumption by factories, farms and homes has jumped more than 12 per cent in the past six years. The United States gulps its liquid assets at the rate of 270 million gallons per day (mgd), says the National Geographic Society.

The greatest water glutton is not the hot tennis player or suburban gardener but American industry. Industrial cooling processes account for more than half the water consumed in this country. It takes 65,00 gallons of water to produce a ton of finished steel, 200,000 gallons for a ton of rayon, and no less than 600,000 gallons for a ton of syn-

Figure 1.5

HOLIDAY CANDLEGLOW

by Lois Leamon
Hilton U. Brown Library

Light has been a symbol of faith for eons. Earliest man used torches and beacon fires to dispel the darkness of night. Pagans built huge bonfires in winter to maintain the strength of their sun gods and to enable them to come back in the spring. In Old Testament times the light of the candle was often referred to as the symbol of spiritual light. In Psalms 18:28 we read "For thou wilt light my candle; the Lord my God will enlighten my darkness."

As the years passed, Romans burned candles before the altars of their gods and at the same time martyred Christians were using them to light the catacombs. In the medieval church the blessing of candles for liturgical and devotional purposes came into common use. These candles were traditionally made of beeswax; the belief being that bees came to earth directly from heaven.

Many, many countries have used candles as a symbol of faith at Christmas, but the origin of this use is probably in the Jewish Feast of the Rededication of the Temple (Hanukkah), also known as the Festival or Feast of Lights. This festival commemorates the victory of the Maccabees over the Syrian Greeks in 165 B. C. and restored Jewish independence. Hanukkah is celebrated today by the lighting of candles — beginning with one on the first day and increasing the number until eight are lit on the last day. During this time, in addition to the lighting of the ceremonial candles, gifts are exchanged and children play holiday games.

Christian candle traditions vary with the originating country. The Irish welcome the Christ Child and strangers by placing candles in the windows of homes on Christmas Eve. This custom was brought to America by Irish immigrants in the 19th century. Italians keep a lighted one before their creches. Spaniards place them over their doorways. Swedes, in honor of St. Lucy, wear them in a crown on her feast day (December 13). Bulgarians take a lighted candle and awaken the animals on Christmas Eve.

The luminaria is a lovely candle custom that has been used for hundreds of years as a symbolic way of lighting the arrival of the Christ Child. This custom originated in Spain and old Mexico when the first luminarias were bonfires of criss-crossed boughs built in three foot high squares. When colored wrapping paper was brought from the Orient to Spain, the Spanish people found it easier to use lanterns made from paper instead of the bonfires. Gradually the bonfires were replaced by lanterns that hung in trees or from wires around the house.

When the Spanish people emigrated to Mexico and our Southwest they brought the custom with them. The lanterns were set out on roads, sidewalks, steps, and rooftops. The Yankee traders who came down the Santa Fe Trail in 1820 introduced the Southwesterners to brown paper bags. It was then that paper bags replaced lanterns.

Merry Christmas! Happy Holidays!

Erwin Boschmann

Figure 1.6

The awards may be such things as

- books
- certificates
- buttons
- engraved pencils
- "pet rocks"
- apples
- half dollars
- plants
- SET A GOAL license plate

Figure 1.7

Of course, it is not the item given that matters, but rather the act of giving. I like to give something other than what is traditionally given. Most students have shelves full of trophies but likely have no engraved pencils or Chem 101 buttons. Students will come back in later semesters and talk about the behavior of their pet rock or the growing Creeping Moses plant.

With all these possibilities, it should be remembered that there is no substitute for the personal word of praise or a handshake. While the student response may not be telling at the time, the effort may make a difference for life. It should also be pointed out that research has shown that if rewards are given too early, they may have a dampening effect. Carrots can undermine student interest.

It is a truism that teaching rewards and rewarding teaches. The rewards to the teacher may come in the form of a greeting or in the most unusual and unexpected ways. George came to class late one day in what appeared to be underwear. I assumed he did not care much for this class and had his own way of letting me know. After class I expressed my "surprise" at his attire, to which he gleefully responded "But Dr. Boschmann, you ought to feel good about it, because I woke up late and did not want to miss your lecture, so rather than take time to get dressed, I came as I was. It shows what I think of your lectures."

Stuart was self-negligent, overweight, and sloppy in his mannerism and paperwork. He never spoke in class, but his disposition and facial expression told me, so I thought, that he certainly did not care to be in my class. At the end of the term Stuart came to me, expressing profound gratitude for an excellent course and for my caring approach to teaching. More than honor, I felt shame for prejudging. I have learned much from my students!

In his book How To Win Friends and Influence People, Dale Carnegie captures the meaning of the personal touch of caring. The following personal summary of his insights has for years hung in my office and on my bedroom closet door where I can see it first thing in the morning and before I retire.

This chapter has dealt with care for the student. Care is not felt immediately by all students. The art of caring is developed as the term goes on. At first it must perhaps be acted out, but soon, especially when students begin to return their care in manyfold ways, it will be a real act of caring for students. At that point I give much for my students. My whole being is devoted to them; they are my professional family. I think about them as I drive or take a shower; I think of ways of suggesting new study approaches; I think of ways of encouraging and rewarding. I find myself working intensely for my class; I protect them; they are mine; I am intensely loyal to them; and it is hard to let go. In fact, I have yet to find a good way of ending the last session, when my feelings for them are high, and somehow I would like to pass on that feeling in a meaningful manner. The days and weeks following the last class for me are filled with withdrawal symptoms. Even as I think longingly about the most recent group of students, I must let go, because there is another class full of fresh faces waiting for me. And what an opportunity awaits me to make a difference in so many new lives!

WHAT YOU CAN DO . . .

1. Listen.
2. Call students by their names. Learn five names per day.
3. Visit with students on nonacademic matters. Have at least one good personal visit per week.
4. Absolutely and completly insist on discipline and honesty.
5. Once a month do something nice and special for the students.
6. In all situations ask yourself: Would I like to be a student in this class?
7. Take a walk outside everyday.

Further Reading

Dale Carnegie, How to Win Friends and Influence People, Pocket Books, 1936.

Dale Carnegie HOW TO WIN FRIENDS AND INFLUENCE PEOPLE

The ability to speak is a shortcut to distiction.
The great aim of education is not knowledge, but action.

I.
1. It is foolish to scold. Criticism always returns home.
2. Give appreciation, not flattery.
3. Think in terms of the other person's point of view.

II.
1. Become genuinely interested in other persons.
2. Smile.
3. Remember people's names.
4. Be a good listener. Encourage others to talk about themselves.
5. Talk in terms of the other person's interests.
6. Do unto others as you would have them do unto you.

III.
1. You can't win an argument.
2. Forbear all direct contradiction. Instead say "I may be wrong. . . "
3. If you are wrong, admit it quickly and emphatically.
4. Begin in a friendly way. "This may, perhaps, be worth thinking of."
5. Get the other person to say "yes, yes" immediately.
6. Be modest. Let the others do the talking.
7. Let others feel the idea is theirs.
8. Try honestly to see things from the other person's point of view.
9. "I don't blame you one iota for feeling ad you do. If I were you, I would too."
10. Appeal to the nobler motives.
11. Dramatize your ideas. Use showmanship.
12. Take a challenge–for the desire to excel.

IV.
1. If you must find fault, begin with praise.
2. Call attention to people's mistakes indirectly.
3. Talk about your own mistakes before criticizing others.
4. Ask questions instead of giving orders directly.
5. Let the other man save his face.
6. Be hearty in your approbation and lavish in your praise. There is sheer witchery in praise.
7. Give a man a fine reputattion to live up to.
8. Make fault seem easy to correct.
9. Make others happy about the things you suggest. (Awards)

V.
Letters with results: Use do–me–a–favor psychology.

VI.
1. Don't, don't nag.
2. Don't try to make your partner over.
3. Don't criticize.
4. Give honest appreciation.
5. Pay little attentions.
6. Be courteous.
7. Know the sexual side of marriage.

Chapter 2
Preparation

I care not what subject is taught if only it be taught well.
Thomas Huxley

I remember the embarrassment to this day. As a young foreign student in college, I was asked to speak to a church group on Sunday. Having spoken to Sunday School groups on numerous previous occasions, I went with a come-what-may attitude, only to find to my surprise that I was the main speaker at the Sunday morning service, and I was not prepared! Somehow I filled in the time, speaking but saying nothing. My only wish was to get to my room, where I went to bed hoping that sleep would reveal that this had been a bad dream.

Humiliating as the experience was, it also taught me the need for preparation. Today I tend to overprepare to be sure.

The Subject–Dominate It!

Let's get to the bottom line of teaching. Is not the object of our teaching to allow students to learn and master the subject matter? In this statement we have identified three foci: The student, the teacher, and the subject. All three are necessary for a successful learning process; however, the interplay of the three will dictate whether teaching and learning are poor, good, or excellent.

Figure 2.1 shows several possible interplays between the three foci:

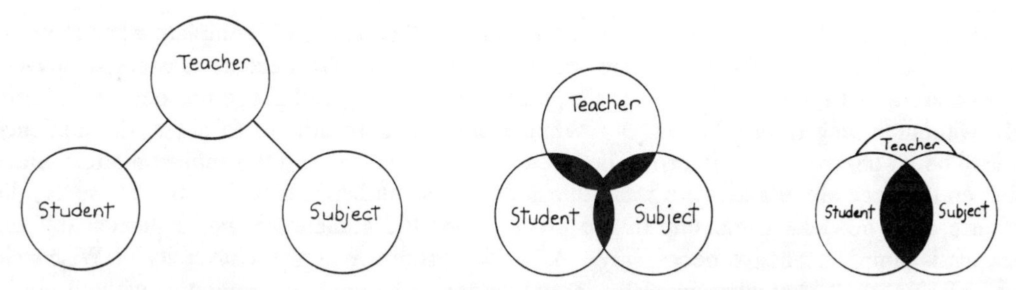

Figure 2.1 Interplay between student, teacher and subject.

In the first rendering, attention is drawn to the teacher. He is the one that controls the proceedings. He is the one that is the go-between of the students and the subject. It is only by looking at the teacher that the subject will be made available. Attention is drawn to the teacher. He may choose to make teaching an expected delivery process, or he may choose to make it a social event, talking about himself, sports events, or anything else.

The second approach shows an overlap between teacher, student, and subject. Of importance is the shaded area where student and subject meet. The teacher becomes a vehicle of this process, retaining, however, a fair amount of visibility.

The third diagram shows an increased student-subject overlap with the teacher's visibility essentially faded into the background.

Think of it! Teaching is a complicated interplay between lecture notes, the blackboard, overhead projector, demonstrations, the audience, and yourself as a teacher. Let's face it! Most of us can only do one, maybe two things well at a time, and if we are lucky, we can quickly change back and forth between two things. However, keeping track of more than two demands at a time is next to impossible. In teaching we have no choice but to be concerned with the subject matter, with the students, and with the delivery; three things to keep track of, which is difficult, if not impossible for most. The usual outcome is that the professor watches the subject matter and the delivery but then has no chance to interact with the students. My proposal is that we learn how to become very well adept at two of the three, students and delivery. We must seek ways to make the subject matter and the delivery one and the same. What I am advocating here is freeing the teacher of the lecture notes as much as is possible. Certainly, we will need some benchmarks to guide us, or even some details, if specific examples or problems are to be used. But in a course that has been taught more than once, we should be free from slavery to notes and devote all attention to delivery and student interaction.

There are two levels of preparation for a class. The first of these is simply preparation of the knowledge content, which usually is something we ourselves learned in school, obtained from books, journals, research notes, or other sources. It is our means to obtaining information on content.

The second level is the domination of the subject. Domination is complete when the subject matter and its best delivery become second nature to us. We become masters at delivery when we are able to sense the audience's level of understanding and gauge our delivery accordingly, without having to refer to notes. When I am having to adhere to notes, the audience tends to be an observer of an interplay between myself as teacher and the subject matter. Since I happen to speak aloud and write some things down, the audience can observe. However, the audience does not take ownership in the proceedings; the audience is not a participant; the audience is simply a passive beneficiary. A biology professor at the University of Wisconsin goes so far as to say that when he walks into a classroom he does so completely without notes. He feels that the thorough preparation he undertook beforehand will serve him well, and that if he does forget something, it must not have been very important.

To me the lecture is the most important event for the day. I live for lectures. I've planned a scenario and am now eager to deliver it. I can't wait to participate in the event. It really is a time when I forget whatever troubles there may be in my life. In fact, for me teaching is therapeutic; it helps me have a better day. In a sense I become so totally absorbed in the subject that I really forget about myself, and inhibitions, such as being observed by visitors, really fade into the background. A lecture should be a memorable experience; it should be hard work as evidenced by a goodly amount of perspiration, but it should be fun.

Recently a student came to class with a walkman and earphones on his ears. The obvious message was that he was here to put in time, but his interest was elsewhere in the stratosphere.

My first reaction was to ask him to remove the competition and pay attention to me. I decided instead to take on the challenge and compete with the electronics for his attention. Fortunately, a number of demonstrations were planned. As I worked, showing enthusiasm, living the topic and radiating a feeling that the subject matter is both deadly serious and fun, I eventually won over the earphones.

There is sheer magic in a prepared presentation. Emerson White said it well nearly a hundred years ago: "The fresher the teacher's knowledge, the livelier his interest. The livelier his interest, the keener the student's interest. The keener their interest, the closer their attention. And as a result, the easier their mastery of what is being taught."

William James talked about good teaching when he said that he had been "listening to someone think aloud in the presence of a class." Such freedom to think aloud can only come when one is free of adherence to lecture notes, can deviate as conditions may demand, can react to and use student input, and with ease can interrupt the lecture flow to give the mind a rest. Such freedom must be earned, and it can be earned only through hard work in utter preparation to truly dominate the subject.

Know the Student Profile

In order to prepare a lecture properly, most important are considerations of the student's intellectual and tolerance levels.

In a conversation with a student about the effect of altitude on the boiling point of water, we talked about cooking a three-minute egg. It was clear to him that at higher altitude the temperature of boiling water would be lower than under normal conditions. However, when talking about cooking the egg, it became obvious that to him cooking and boiling meant the same thing. As the conversation drew on, he realized that boiling a three-minute egg assumes that the boiling takes place under normal temperature conditions and that the cooking process of the egg is temperature dependent, so that the egg would have to boil longer at high altitudes to attain the same cooking effect. Piaget's classification would categorize the observation of boiling as a concrete process, while the deduction of cooking is abstract.

Knowing where the students are on an intellectual level is vital to lecture preparation. In the above case, the insight might lead me to spend more time using concrete props to build and eventually graduate to abstract concepts.

Story ~~Study~~ problems in the sciences are good gauges as to the student level. Many students will confess at never having mastered story problems: "The one thing I could never do in high school." Story problems are essentially mathematical relationships hidden in a sentence structure. The relationships must be discovered by removing the English and substituting it for mathematical equations. It is an abstract process where concrete props are such things as knowing formulas, watching units, or following a routine.

A second consideration in lecture preparation is the student tolerance level. All cycles of human events have their ups and their downs. Whether we consider a presidential term of office, a vacation, a class term, reading a chapter in a book, or giving a talk, all have their high points and their low points. This is due to physical exhaustion, the need to move about, monotony of the process ("I know what he'll do next"), boredom, etc. In many cases, tolerance highs and lows are directly related to the attention span. If attention and anticipation are high, so is the tolerance level. It is for this reason that usually the beginning of a cycle shows a high followed by a general drop. Research shows that for a typical class period of fifty minutes, the attention span looks as shown in Figure 2.2.

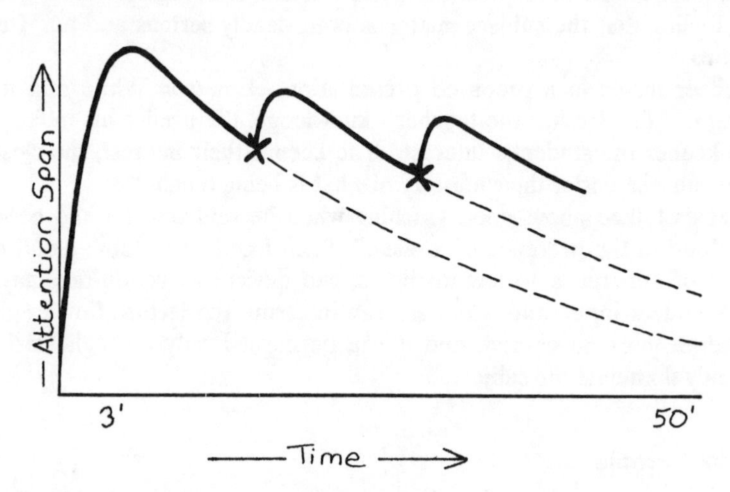

Figure 2.2 Attention span as a function of time. See text.

Knowledge of this fact tells us several things. First, it tells us that for most cyclic events there is an initial low in the attention which must be overcome. This simply is the noise of people coming in late, the talk among the audience, the shuffle of books and papers. It takes an attention getter to start the attention curve. This may be the simple act of beginning to talk ("may I have your attention, please"); it may be the dimming of lights; it may be an unexpected demonstration; or, for the first lecture in a term, it is the simple appearance of the professor. But note that this is a very brief investment of time, and the very highest attention is ours.

The second observation is that after the first inertia is overcome, the first few minutes are terribly important, and this time must be capitalized. These are likely the minutes where highest attention is lent, so this should be the time to state the key points to be elaborated upon later; or this may be the time to set the stage using an interesting example, creating a controversial situation, posing a puzzle, or spiking interest which hopefully will sustain through the period.

The curve also tells us that if indeed the attention level will drop off as shown, the point indicated by an asterisk might be a good one to stage a disturbance, to perk interest, and essentially to destroy or derail the curve and allow it to begin anew. Such disturbances can be created by giving the mind a rest from the heavy material through an example, a human interest story, a news event, or a joke. It is a time that will say "relax for a bit, laugh, and then work again."

This leads to a fourth lesson to be gleaned from the curve, which is the realization that a fifty-minute lecture should perhaps be divided into several fifteen to twenty-minute mini-lectures. The intent, of course, being that such a maneuver provides several highs with the ensuing opportunities to make key points stick. This is a lesson that we can learn from the world of radio and television, where an event is broken into small segments for commercials. The media are the pros and know minisegments to be better than, say, running a show for forty-five minutes and then having fifteen minutes of commercials. For most persons the short attention span is greater than the demands of a sustained long-term attention span.

The implementation of what the curve tells us is indeed an art. Only much practice and experimentation will bring about perfection. However, the best aid in shortening the learning time is to watch others. I have made it a practice for many years to visit colleagues in action. In larger classes this can be done essentially unnoticed, in smaller classes prior clearance is a courtesy. I do this not only at my institution, but anywhere I go, and while I often seek out what are known to be the better teachers, I also benefit from observing the average teacher–if nothing else, to see what I definitely do not want to do.

Let us leave this section with one final thought. The mind thinks about three times as fast as the average tongue can speak. Think about this in lecture delivery. Is it not true that the chances for the mind of the listener to wander off are indeed great during a lecture session? To overcome this we must engage the audience, make them part of the process, challenge them, involve them so that they feel ownership in the proceedings. To do so means to speak at a good rate (I would rather repeat a point several times than speak too slowly), and with utter preparation, so that we do not need to fumble about trying to find our place in the lecture sequence. Nothing is more disconcerting than to watch somebody try to reorient himself with his notes. We must, at all costs, avoid what actors refer to as "white spots"–unplanned times when nothing happens, when the lecturer is at a loss, when he needs time to find out what is going on. White spots are great invitations for the mind to take a walk. Once on a walk, its return is delayed, if not impossible. We can use exercises that truly involve the audience: "In a few minutes I will be asking a question," or "Every five minutes one salient point will be made. Watch for it!" Obviously, the message is that the following material will have bearing on upcoming questions. Chances are that a higher level of attention has been attained.

The Big Picture

It is the first day of the term. You are sitting in the class waiting for the professor to arrive. Right on the hour, he comes in the side door, pushing it open with a foot, one hand holding notes, and the other a coffee cup. He places the coffee in a carefully chosen spot and drops his books and papers onto the table. The heavy fall of the papers drops the ashes off the cigarette hanging in his mouth. He blows these off his papers in the direction toward the class. As he organizes the papers, he sips coffee and finishes the cigarette, extinguishing the butt on the floor with his foot. He then tucks in his shirt, straightens his hair and looks for some chalk. At about three minutes past the hour, he acknowledges the presence of the class: "This is Entymology 101, right?"

Half the students probably wish they were in the wrong class. We are told that the first impression is the lasting impression. As we think about the big picture, we want to identify our philosophy, what is ultimately important, and the means by which those important items are to be shared. The way we appear says a lot about the way we are in our professional life. If I dress properly (not necessarily expensively), I send a message that I do care about myself, and what I am about to do is terribly important to me. That message is fundamental if I expect the students to care about me and the subject I teach.

The way I conduct myself will soon reveal whether I asked myselff some rather important questions beforehand: Why is the topic important? What is the purpose of the talk? Who is my audience? When and in what environment is the talk given? How would I feel in the audience? If suddenly my lecture was cut short, could I make a good three-point summary? In other words, these questions ask whether I have planned. Have I planned the term, the week, the month, the day, the hour? Is it obvious that I have planned my work, and now I am about to work my plan?

I like to prepare the course outline at least a month or so before classes begin. It takes time to plan. Once a plan is in rough form, I set it aside and reconsider it later, perhaps from a different perspective. "What effect will an exam on this date have on the laboratory sequence?" "Is the homework well synchronized with the lecture and exam schedule?" I like to design my teaching so that the students are given many chances for correct input–a feeling of accomplishment. I like to provide student access to audio and videocassettes of eminent scientists and topics, provide for guest lectures, plan bulletin board use, reading assignments, etc. I want to make sure that students are challenged enough. If they see that I am doing my very best, they will accept challenges and do their very best. A student indicated to me some time ago that challenges are really welcome.

My daily outlines are prepared immediately after the previous lecture. That is, of course, the best time, because the mind is still working on the material, the exact beginning and ending places are still fresh in mind; but most importantly, the feeling with which students and I left the class is still clear. That is a good time to think of different approaches and new examples.

So what is the big picture? It is my attitude, my preparation, my devotion to the task and to the students. My attitude will determine what my physical appearance is in dress, grooming, and facial features. It is my attitude that will soon be mirrored within the students.

Preparation through Details, Details, Details

Think of some of the books you own. A few you treasure as truly good books, others you have forgotten. Such sweeping statements can be made about all books, and what makes this true are the many details that make up a book. Books have titles, tables of contents, chapters; chapters usually have subheadings and paragraphs. Each paragraph in turn is made up of sentences, words, and letters. Someone had to pay attention to the paper to be used, the binding, the ink, the letter type, the cover design, and overall size. All of these details contribute to our judgment, but even more important, of course, is the content of the book: what does it say, how does it say it, how do I feel about its message? The author behind the book thought about infinite details in sequencing events, style and grammar, choice of words, changes in mood, use of examples, etc. It is these details and their artful interweaving that make for a beautiful total. The same care for detail is necessary in the preparation of a new term or a class lecture.

In thinking of the term as a whole, it is our first task to decide on the eventual goal we are setting. Should the experience be a survey of the topic? Should it be treated mathematically? Should there be a laboratory component? If the goal is firmly set by (or often for) us, we then need to devise a means of accomplishing that goal. Objectives are the stepping-stones toward a goal. These are the day-to-day specifics which will eventually culminate in the attainment of the goal. I write my objectives down, for my own and the students' benefit. They are yardsticks by which we measure progress; they are my expectations of mastery from each chapter. While many texts will include objectives as part of the chapter, it is an enormous help to the students to have the instructor provide his as well, even if in many cases they duplicate the text's expectations. They will tell the students what they should be able to do when and under what conditions. It is, however, a fact of life that selection of objectives is easy, while maintaining them is not.

From among the many publications on objectives, two appear to be classics:
Benjamin Bloom, *Taxonomy of Educational Objectives* (1956)
Robert Mager, *Preparing Instructional Objectives* (1962)

A second task is a clear statement to the class concerning the rules under which the class will be conducted. Verbal announcements may be sufficient for small advanced classes but generally are not sufficient for large undergraduate classes. I have found that a distribution of written announcements and rules, coupled with an occasional verbal reminder, is helpful; yet not everyone takes the time to read cold, businesslike material, and a humorous approach may help.

Let us approach the subject of preparing for a class session. The table lists the various instructional methodologies we can choose from in our teaching.

Table 1.1 Instructional methodologies.*

Lecture	The instructor informs students orally through an organized format. It allows conveyance in minimal time to large audience.
Lecture/ Discussion	A brief lecture is followed by discussion. Proovides good opportunity for questions. Assumes prior reading, and small class.
Demonstration	Physical principles are illustrated through both process and result. Enhances understanding and memory. Most common in science classes.
Experiments	Students manipulate variables under controlled conditions. Provides exposure to tools and trains observation and generalization.
Field Trips	On site observation of profession in action. Theory and real world practice are blended.
Games	Small groups compete to accomplish a certain task. Has strong motivating element. Pretends a real world.
Independent Study	Student works individually under periodic guidance of instructor. Assumes self-discipline. A paper is usually expected.
Research	Student conducts research according to accepted data-gathering techniques. Close guidance is a must.
Computer Aided Instruction	An interactive means of instruction where the computer provides alternative responses dependent on student input. Students learn at own pace.
Programmed Learning	Student uses written materials specially developed for individual study. Often used in conjunction with lecture and text materials.

*Adapted from Marilyn D. Jacobson, University of Illinois, Chicago

Group Discussions	Single topic is proposed for discussion. Brainstorming often results in good conclusions. Analytical and problem solving abilities are sharpened.
Presentations by Students	Assigned talks to class by students on findings from research, readings. Sharpens public speaking and independent work. Good as thesis preparation.
Role Playing	Parts are assigned to students to portray actors in an event. Provides good understanding of problems.
Case Study Method	Carefully developed profiles of a process, event are used to stimulate. Increases analytical powers, promotes thinking. Written report is expected.
Study Carrels	Lectures are recorded on cassettes and/or slides or video. Excellent means of review.
Cooperative Programs	Students spend specified time as employee of business. Great practical extension of class. Must be monitored.
Simulation	A problem is outlined which illustrates a typical situation. Students become participants and propose solutions. Improves analytical skills.

In most settings the lecture format is by far the most common. When preparing my lectures, I draw upon four different files.

Text material–First, the text material is composed, naturally, of the text currently in use. It gives a feel for the emphasis the author places on different topics; it guides the sequence of topics that I will use; it allows me to refer to illustrations, diagrams, graphs, pictures, and examples. I use the text strictly as a guide, not a hitching post. In fact, I jealously avoid using examples from the text or particularly the method of explaining a principle. To me, the text is a separate item in the student's learning process. In fact, I must confess, that I usually don't read the text at all, except, as mentioned, for sequence of topics, illustrations, and examples.

In addition to the text and its ancillary materials, I have my own text material files which are divided according to the chapter sequence given by the text. Within each chapter heading I have two folders of different colors; one is for actual lecture material: ideas of explanations, different approaches, good examples and analogies. The lack of concrete examples is the most common lecture fault. The other folder in each chapter sequence contains clippings of supporting material, which is constantly updated. Using all of these available materials, I determine the best sequence to use during the next class period. By judging the approximate time I have, I normally plan one or two topics beyond what I think I can cover. These topics will end up on the day's outline shown on the outline transparency and thereby give the students an idea of the day's coverage, as well as what to expect early in the subsequent lecture.

Demonstrations–Ronald, an arson investigator in my class, was called to investigate a fire in Colorado. It was suspected that the apartment complex fire was related to a union dispute. Upon studying photographs of the fire, Ronald noticed intense white heat at the *bottom* of the fire, when common fires result in intense heat away from the floor. He suspected, and later confirmed, magnesium as the source of the fire. A demonstration in my class brought this to his attention.

I am a firm believer in demonstrations. They serve valuable purposes. First, they will often dramatically illustrate a principle; second, they are always of concrete nature and allow the students easier access to abstract thinking; third, they provide a break from routine lecturing; and fourth, they are usually action laden, and action draws attention. Whenever possible, I use demonstrations which can be shown on the overhead, simply because of class size but also because details do show up so very clearly. In a cabinet I store many gadgets for hundreds of demonstrations, which include chemical reactions, models, and ideas (when discussing rates of reactions I use an apple, bite into it, and allow the class to observe the slow browning). Many of the demonstrations are adapted from the ideas provided by the dean of undergraduate chemistry teaching, Hubert Alyea, Professor Emeritus at Princeton University, including the construction of a device which, when placed on normal overhead projectors, allows demonstrations on a vertical, rather than just a horizontal scale. This permits the display of test-tube reactions. It is a spectacular experience to see a test-tube reaction projected onto the screen where bubbles rise and colors change on a grand scale. Indeed, this is the only place I know where the professor can actually walk into the test tube and point out the different features of the reaction in progress.

Ideas for demonstrations come from everywhere. I find that when I constantly search, my mind is open to ideas that flash by while paging through a magazine or book, while watching someone else, or seeing a coincidence while driving down the street. Workshops and conferences are excellent sources of idea seeds for fertile minds.

From this pool of ideas, a selection of one to three appropriate demonstrations is made to illustrate key lecture points. Demonstrations have a way of translating abstract theories into real world situations. In nonscience fields, demonstrations are replaced by simulations, games, in-class exercises, etc.

Transparencies and slides–Again, virtually everywhere one looks there are ideas to be found for slides and transparencies. Magazines and ads often have beautiful drawings suitable for photocopying and subsequent conversion to transparencies. In every single lecture I use numerous transparencies, and my total file probably goes into the hundreds. These are also stored, by topic and chapter, in a separate file. I have fewer slides than transparencies. The reasons are that the former are more time-consuming (and expensive?) to prepare, the display in class calls for special setup, and I am not free to draw onto them as I can with transparencies. Nevertheless, they are very nice, especially to show dramatic colors, to show a sequence of events such as a nuclear reaction, and they allow for depicting what virtually is motion through the use of lap-dissolve projection. When accompanied by a sound track, they indeed are impressive, though time-consuming. It is often said that, due to budget and technical limitations, teachers really can not compete with television in the display of dramatic events. This is true; however, I believe we can't afford not to try.

Yellow sheets–Over the years of teaching I have compiled what my students have come to call "yellow sheets." Written on yellow paper, it is a collection of anecdotes, stories, human interest events, newspaper clippings, jokes, incidents, anything that will somehow break monotony, yet tie into what is being done. It may be the story of Fritz Haber, who was driven to the brink of insanity by the guilt feeling of the misuse of his inventions; or a newspaper clipping of a grain elevator explosion, illustrating how the speed of a reaction is increased as the surface area is increased; or the classification of chemical problem solvers into five categories:

the student who is classified as the asteroid type who gazes off into space hoping for Divine Guidance; the adrenaloid type who specializes in emotionally energetic action; the ulceroid type who worries about the problem; the adenoid type who screams about it; and the hemorrhoid type who just sits on it.

While the collection and selection of such proper inserts does take considerable time, their actual use takes but seconds. On the average, they demand less than thirty seconds, yet the use of only two or three of these per lecture period are as soothing as a cold drink on a hot day of work, both to the student and the instructor. The students know that these are mind relievers meant to serve as a breath of fresh air, and that as soon as they are over, it will be time for hard work once again. It is important not only to avoid repetition but also to avoid overdoing them. A carefully balanced diet will pay off.

These incidentals are available everywhere to the person who looks and selects carefully: newspapers, professional journals, books, television, radio, friends, conferences, lectures, etc.

Aside from textual material, demonstrations, transparencies, and incidentals, special events occasionally also are built in. These include films, guest speakers, visits, etc., but are kept to a minimum, since they have a tendency to break the thread of a continuous class.

Having selected the appropriate materials from each of the four files, it is now time to sequence these. The lecture flow will usually be dictated by the sequence of topics in the text. Topics are written down on a sheet of paper, and the key topics are also itemized on a transparency, which serves both as an outline for the students and a guide for my lecture. In a sense, it serves as my lecture notes. (More on this later.) Built into this planning is also the experience from the previous class period. It may be the realization that something was omitted, an error in the text must be pointed out, or judging from after-class questions, it became clear that a point was misunderstood. A good way to keep track of such points is to ask a student to be note taker ("Jim, would you keep track of my bloopers, so I can fix them next time?" Jim loves to do it!)

Once the topical sequence is established, the demonstrations, slides, and transparencies are organized in the same sequence, and reminders are noted on my lecture notes using different color ink, marginal signals, or a separate sheet altogether. A demonstration may precede the discussion of a topic, as a teaser, or be given during or after its presentation. The "yellow sheets" are prepared in the same topical order, if possible. However, most important here is the timing of delivery. They should be delivered in spaced sequence every ten, fifteen, or twenty minutes. Again, reminders are placed at the crucial places on the lecture notes. The mood of the class during the lecture will often encourage a change in plans, not just for the use of the Yellow Sheets, but the placement of the demonstrations as well.

The lecture sequence has been laid out. The overall topic and key points now come into focus, and it is time to zero in on the most important time, the first few minutes. The proper opener sets the stage and will alert the students to things to come, create curiosity, or stimulate interest. Here are a few examples of openers, usually taken from the file of Yellow Sheets.

- Major human successes and failures in the 20th century
- The story of DDT
- Methyl Isocyanate and the Bhopal incident
- Major chemical disasters
- Problem of detecting a counterfeit coin from among eight coins using only two weighings
- Display samples of sulfur, copper, water, and dirt. Ask for differences
- Cartoons, anecdotes about the metric system
- Clipping: God moves in mysterious metric ways
- Roman Times, a Roman (?) newspaper reporting atomic theory
- Readings from Salted Peanuts, a collection of 1800 facts and figures
- Exploded tin can and the gas laws
- Greenhouse effect
- Clipping: Monsanto vs. EPA controversy
- Talk on honesty
- The scientific method and the story of Dr. Semmelweiss
- Water–so very common, yet so very unusual
- Metal ions in the environment
- Detergents
- Invitations to join the American Chemical Society or the chemistry club
- Physiological effects of alkaloids
- A coded telephone conversation announcing the first nuclear test
- Dioxins
- What do Cleopatra's Needle and the rain in Amsterdam have in common?

All selections have been made, and the class has been planned. At least five minutes prior to the beginning of the class period, the students will see two transparencies displayed on the front. For example:

OUTLINE

March 13

Review
Chapter 6 (cont.)
  kinetic molecular theory
  pressure vs. amount
    (see text p. 147)
Boyle's Law
Charles' Law
absolute temperature
  conversion formula
ideal vs. real gases
combined gas law

Used with permission.

The transparency on the left will remain displayed throughout the period. It is the guide for all of us; it is an expected reference point, a security blanket, which in the depth of a discussion provides orientation, tells us all where we are and where we're heading. It essentially ties three lectures together. First, it reviews the materials from the previous lecture; second, it gives benchmarks for today's lecture; and third, since it usually cannot be completed, it means that the last item or two become the first items on the next lecture.

The display on the right calls attention to some feature in today's discussion. It will be removed when lecture begins so that this projector can become center stage for lecture activities. This is where the action will be in terms of displays, demonstrations, and notes.

My preparation for a recitation (help) session is completely different. I walk into the class without any materials, but I am utterly prepared to answer questions. Recitation is a time when the students set the agenda via the questions they pose. It is my role to lead the discussion, to draw out nonparticipating students, to help everyone find the solution. If a period of no questions occurs, I have an agenda in mind which I can propose ("What would you do if . . ." "What do you think about . . .")

Walk the Track

It has been said that Napoleon never won a battle on the field which he had not first won in the mind. Whether it is a small fix-it project at home or a large undertaking involving many people, the smoothness of the operation is directly proportional to the time taken to realize the project mentally before its actual execution. I have watched repairmen constantly run between the job and the supply store to obtain this part and that measurement. But I have also observed seasoned craftsmen work on a project by taking time to simply sit and think. In their mind, they go through all the steps necessary for successful completion of the project. Each important step or requirement is written down. The reward is the need for only one trip to the supply house, the early completion of the project, preventing exhaustion, and the satisfaction of having done something right. In the same manner I like to "case the joint" by mentally walking through the lecture, both in terms of physical facilities and of process.

You have experienced it many times. A speaker gets up and checks the microphone, saying "Is this on? Hello, can you hear me?" Observe the professionals who will never do this. To me it is an unnecessary interruption. I am at the meeting for a particular topic; my level of attention is high; the main points that can be made will be made during the first few minutes. If this time is spent on something that should have been checked beforehand, I do feel cheated. It is the job of the speaker or his host to see to it that such audiovisual theatrics be prevented as much as possible. In the classroom setting this is something routine and generally needs no prior checking. Nevertheless, I almost always arrive at class beforehand, in part to check on the physical facilities. I make it a point to establish good relations with the support staff, which may simply mean a "hello" or a chat. Their lives are interesting, and their help and willingness will at times be crucial for my work, when I need their help.

If the setting is new, it is an absolute must to check facilities beforehand. For me it is not uncommon to walk the track in the new setting two, even three, times. On one such occasion, I hosted an actor portraying Albert Einstein. We had checked the facilities in detail. After my introduction, I failed to turn off a tiny podium light, and as he walked in he attempted to find the switch. (He had wanted the room to be dark for his entry.) Two things happened; not only did he not find the right switch, but in the process he was visible to the audience in a setting completely unrelated to the theme. Oversights will be minimized, though not necessarily eliminated, by carefully walking the track.

The second area of mental checkout is with the process itself. I like to actually go through the lecture (in my mind); I like to visualize the audience, anticipate reactions and questions, test different approaches. This is a time when I search for opportunities to insert stories which might instill integrity, values, and beliefs. These shuld be a natural outgrowth of what is being done–planned spontaneity.

This is also a good time to search for good analogies to bridge the gap between the abstract and the concrete. Sometime ago I was preparing to lecture on the "mole" concept, a collective name like a dozen, or a ream. My attempt was to make clear to my students that atoms and molecules are so small that no balance can weigh these individually or even in hundreds or thousands, but that instead huge numbers are needed for even the most sophisticated balances. On the way to the University I, as well as many students, drive past an elevator where farmers deliver truckloads of corn. I used the concept of weighing one kernel of corn on the truck scale, which clearly is an impossibility as realized by everyone. However, a huge collection of kernels eventually will make a difference. Our most sophisticated balances are to atoms and molecules what truck scales are to individual kernels of corn.

The basic elements of a good analogy are that (1) there must be one or more points of contact within the real world of the student; (2) the analogy must feel good, illicit in the student an "ah, I see, that makes sense!" response; and (3) there must be a connection between the point of contact and the idea discussed.

The homework for the lecture is done, and we are now ready for delivery.

WHAT YOU CAN DO . . .

1. Think.
2. Prepare the next session immediately after a lecture.
3. Prepare at least triple of what you can use.
4. Use a well-organized filing system for all lectures, ideas, and ancillary materials.
5. Prepare the mind. Take time for yourself.
6. Go watch a good teacher at least once every two months.
7. Get to know and interact with a worthy model twice a year.

Chapter 3
Share with Gusto

Teaching is a red-eye, sweaty-palm, sinking stomach profession.
Peter G. Beidler

Some years ago I was privileged to visit both sections of a class on Greek Mythology taught at the University of Illinois at the Urbana-Champaign campus. The two sections of the class were offered by two different professors; one met in a standard room with an enrollment of perhaps twenty or thirty students, while the other met in the University auditorium with an enrollment of well over a thousand. Why the difference? The professors and their respective teaching styles, of course! The seasoned professor teaching the large class produced magic and excitement about the topic. His students did not want to miss being part of it. About fifteen minutes before the session was to begin, he prepared the atmosphere of the room. The lights were dimmed slightly; two projectors were set up, each displaying a picture appropriate for the upcoming discussion; and over the sound system one could hear heavy Wagner music setting the proper mood. The professor continued to get ready for the session, stopping occasionally to talk with a passing student. Students filtered into the room and assembled with remarkable quietness. As the session began, the music was replaced by the excited voice of the professor launching into an eloquent description of the gods of the Greeks. As he spoke the slides were advanced alternately, and he literally walked into each of their projections, pointing out various details of note. Suddenly he paused and asked a question. Looking intently at the mass, he nodded approvingly, acknowledging a supposed correct response. As the minutes flew by, I suddenly felt myself transported into ancient Greece; I not only watched, but actually participated in life some two thousand years ago: I could feel the devotion to a God; I trembled at their demands; I sensed the terror of war. The professor had allowed me to live Greek mythology.

What is the difference? Why do some teachers "have it" and others do not? Is it not true that we all have at our disposal the three basic colors, the seven notes, the twenty-six letters of the alphabet, and the ten basic numbers? But it took a Michelangelo, a Mozart, an Apostle Paul, and an Einstein to make something beautiful with these basic ingredients. While not all of us are great talents, the art of teaching can be learned by those truly willing to give time, devotion, and care to the task. This chapter will help the committed in the task.

Effective Communication in Teaching

Communication has all conditions for failure because it is so complex. There is the sender, the encoder, the decoder, the receiver, the context, and the interference, both external and within the system. Even the experts are not immune from failure to communicate. It is not uncommon for professors of speech/communication to break the very rules they teach.

It is a known fact that student evaluations give lowest ratings when the students are freshmen or sophomores in large classes and are rating a required course taught by a faculty member in the lower ranks. Certainly, a good portion of the ratings must be due to faulty communication.

Consider the following exercise. A line drawing is given to someone with the instruction to describe it to the class, so that students can draw it based only on the description given. Each description can be given only once, there shall be no questions asked, and the students are to work independently.

Now the same drawing is described to another class for reproduction; however, in this case the students are free to ask questions and may even consult with one another. Certainly the results will be quite different for the two groups, with the first likely showing a whole assortment of drawings, while the second class, on the average, is much closer to the true picture.

In the first case the person describing the drawing is in total control; he takes no risks, and there is no interaction. It is a high efficiency process, but yielding a poor product and leaving the class with a feeling of isolation.

In the second case the communicator is under constant pressure to do a good job; the process can be very time-consuming, but the product is far superior to the first, with the class having a sense of accomplishment through community spirit.

While communication has all the parameters for failure, it also has the potential for powerful influence. As teachers we have no choice but to learn the basics of communication. Since a large portion of the teaching aspect involves verbal communication, we will consider two aspects of speaking: the mechanics and the emotion of speaking. We will apply speaking in its broader meaning: a picture can speak; a facial expression can speak.

The Mechanics of Speaking

It is often said that not only guns, but words, can kill. In the same manner, a speech can be destroyed by body language or faulty staging.

Body messages–The body constantly sends off signals. We instantly know whether a speaker feels comfortable or is nervous by the way he walks, smiles, or uses his arms. The body can tell us that the speaker is inviting, is in charge, is serious, gives us a feeling of participation or rivalry. As teachers we must remember that our bodies, our facial expressions, or voices are messengers that will tune students in or out.

As I was writing this section in the library, two students in a nearby section were talking. The conversation persisted and I became irritated. After all, they should know that the library is a place of study, not talk. In fact I had left my office for the library just for that reason. I needed a quiet place to reflect, and now this. I decided to wait just a few more minutes and then I would get up and tell them to "shut up." When the self-prescribed time was past, I got up. But as I walked toward them, I suddenly realized that here was an opportunity to practice what I was just now writing down for others to read. So my walk became less firm and more gentle, I smiled to myself and my frame of mind became conciliatory as I put my hand on the shoulder of one of the students. To my great surprise here were two of the students from my class practicing what I had taught them; one was helping the other. After a few minutes (yes, we too talked), I suggested that perhaps the far table back in the corner might be a better one for tutoring. We all parted feeling good.

Speakers who bring with them a cup of coffee, who smoke during class, or who sit down, send off the message of self-service. This is particularly tempting in laboratory settings where informality is the norm. It is so easy to sit down at the desk and let the students come to the teacher, when there are so many excellent opportunities to observe and help the students by constantly floating in the laboratory. Many insights of student understanding can be gained by talking with students as they are doing the experiment. In the long run, time will be saved by catching potential mistakes early.

Figure 3.1 is an excellent summary of distracting classroom mannerisms.

The most common offense is the foghorn where the speaker will start with a resounding "uh," and thereafter punctuate every pause or breath with "uhs" or "ums." One cause for this particular mannerism is the feeling that as a speaker the time must be filled with sounds. The first step toward cure is to recognize that pauses are natural and are even means for powerful dramatic effects. It helps to have someone in the audience be an assigned "uh" counter. Other common mannerisms include the tendency to speak to one section of the class, or perhaps even to just one person, to use only one area of the blackboard, to avoid total eye contact by either constantly looking down or above the audience onto the back wall, and to use arm and hand motions for the speaker rather than for the audience, such as left to right motion or outlining a graph by showing, say, an upward trend.

FIVE WAYS TO BLOW IT AS A SPEAKER

1. Imitate another speaker.
2. Project lack of confidence through posture, monotone, or wrong gestures.
3. Speak down to the audience (use jargon).
4. Do not prepare.
5. Lack a dynamic opening and closing.

by Rob Tucker
Toastmaster International

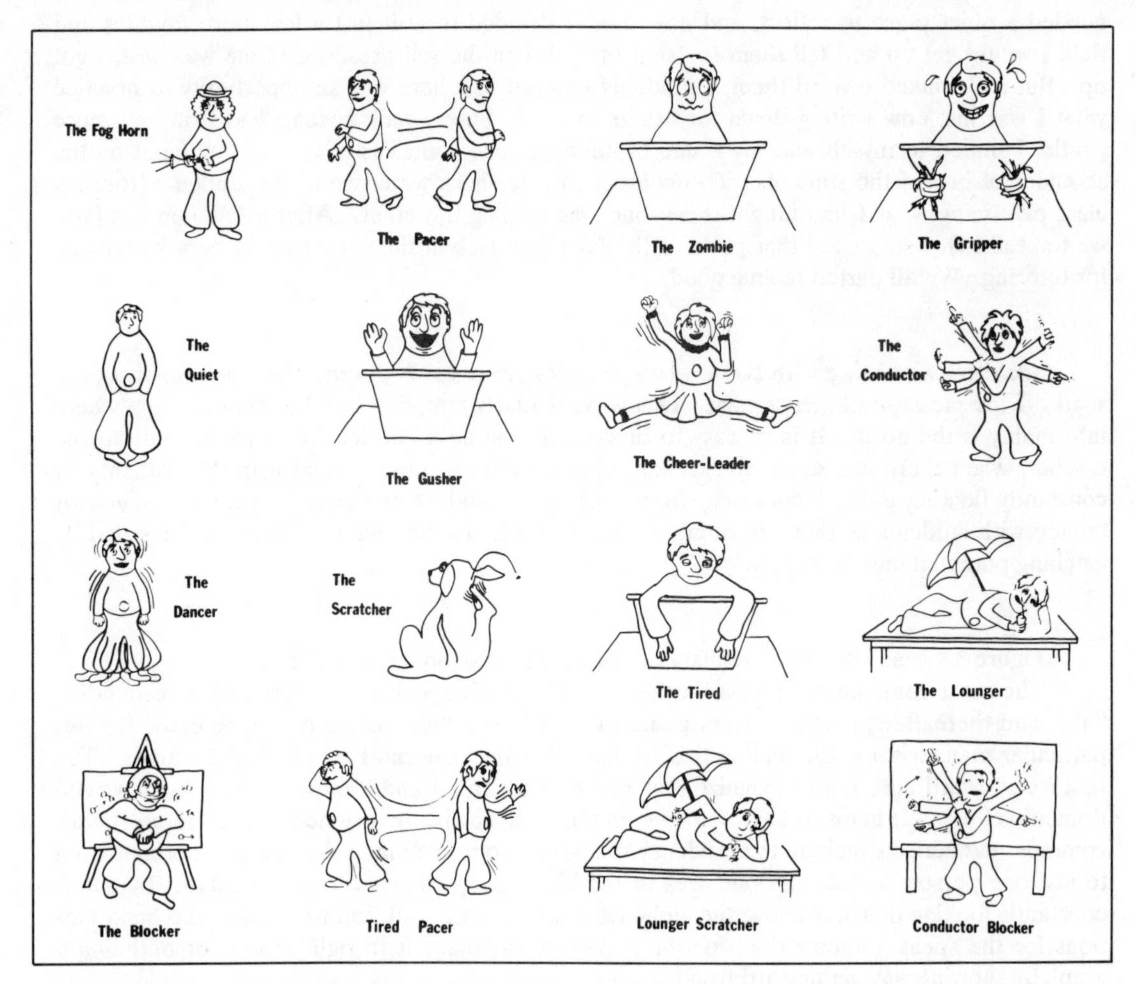

Figure 3.1 Distracting mannerisms. (Used with permission from the authors, Arthur Mirsky and J. Geol. Educa., 25, 157 [1977].)

Stage messages–Clean? dirty? dark? lit? orderly? prepared?–each gives its own message. We are told that a first impression is a lasting one. The first thing students will naturally look at when entering a class is the front of the room, and the impression for the day is made. It is for this reason that I prefer arriving well on time to check the surroundings. I prefer that upon entering, my students see something concerning the day's lecture content: an appropriate cartoon, an outline, a demonstration apparatus, or me, the teacher, getting ready for class.

It is my preference to use overheads rather than the chalkboard. The reasons are manyfold. The chalkboard cuts eye contact; unless a microphone is used, it reduces the sound level; it often results in writing that is too small; it is limited in its capacity, whereas the overhead projector usually has a continuous feed acetate which allows easy retrieval of earlier material. The chalkboard also forces the teacher to move about much more when referring to displayed material, thereby often blocking what should be seen. (Besides, the use of chalk makes the hands dirty.) The overhead allows for normal sized handwriting which is automatically magnified; it allows easy preparation of display material before class begins; it allows for very easy use of colors, for erasures, and for any demonstrations that are transparent. This latter advantage is particularly useful for large science classes when a demonstration cannot be done unless it is displayed in magnified form. In fact, a chemical reaction can be performed in a small glass dish on the projector platform and projected in magnified form onto the screen, thereby allowing the instructor to literally walk into the reaction, pointing to developing colors, evolving gas bubbles, and fading strips of metal.

A mistake often made, whether using chalkboard or the overhead projector, is the writing of titles and key words rather than complete phrases. Students tend to copy what they see, and words will later become puzzles simply because they are not shown with the needed connecting verbs. Thus to write "Chicago, Madison, St. Louis" does not give the intended meaning of "Midwestern cities are Chicago, Madison, and St. Louis."

Discussions in large classes have their special challenges. They tend to be much more infrequent than in smaller classes, both because of physical limitations (hard to hear) and due to the psychological inhibitions naturally present in a large group. However, when a discussion is taking place, two things are especially important. First, the instructor must remember to always repeat the question or comment made by a student to make sure the entire class heard it; and second, he should not give (unconscious) preference to the high hands, those up front, or those hands accompanied by verbal attention getters, thereby missing the shy one at the far extreme of the room.

Audience messages–There is a story about Abraham Lincoln, who was given the name of a person to be considered for a cabinet post. Lincoln's response was that he did not like that person's face. "But Mr. President, he cannot help the looks of his face," the advisor objected, to which Lincoln replied, "Oh yes, anyone over forty is responsible for his face." We are told that the face is the mirror of the inner person, and in a similar fashion the class is a mirror of the lecturer and the lecture. My behavior, my voice, my mannerisms are mirrored back to me by the audience. This should be a very comforting thought, because we can control what goes into that mirror; we are able to adjust the audience messages.

One of the best ways to be in control of those audience messages is to recognize that all things in nature come and go in cycles. There are the waves of water; we have radio, sound, light, laser, and electrical waves; there is the sine wave–all of these are cycles of change. Nature is teeming with life, in part because it works in seasonal cycles: spring, summer, fall, and winter. As human beings we also function in cycles. Why is television so engaging? Professionals have learned to use sight and sound variations. Professional speakers know that the attention span for the average person is about nine minutes and, therefore, they use jokes every nine minutes. These professional "interruptions" take only twenty-two seconds but have the powerful effect of causing a cycle to begin anew. Avoiding a monotone by voice inflections, tone, and volume are other effective means of cycling. Good, clear speaking can at times be altered with a rapid burst of phrases.

A helpful tip on effective lecturing is the recognition that nervousness on the part of the speaker is natural. It may be a sign of lack of experience, or it may be a form of humility, but it is expected. My father, a veteran teacher and speaker, told me in my teenage years that if my knees did not shake just a bit prior to a speech, then there probably was something wrong.

Familiarity breeds comfort. Time after time I may be totally at ease speaking to my class of hundreds of students, but when asked to give a single talk to twenty of my peers, I may become nervous. This can be overcome by much exposure to such situations where one eventually simply gets tired of being nervous–it takes too much energy. Nervousness can also be overcome by enthusiasm (more on this later), by memorizing a short opening to allow time for establishing audience rapport, or by quickly breaking the flow of events. Recently I was asked to give a presentation on teaching to a group of faculty. Although I have given such talks many times, and I felt well prepared, this particular time I found myself becoming unusually nervous just a few minutes into the talk. I quickly decided to break this undesirable flow of events by stopping and turning to my host, asking for a glass of water. The short rest, the ensuing informality helped, and soon I was on my way.

A final tip for effective lecturing comes from Ivor Davies, who states that slickness dilutes authority, but that slow speaking and lowering the pitch of the voice demand authority.

The Emotion in Speaking

If we have said that the physical aspects of speaking are important, it is no understatement that the psychological environment is life determining. The mechanics in the classroom is a mere vehicle for the feelings radiated therefrom. My early schooling took place in a one-room schoolhouse, where one teacher supervised six grades. My grade had only three students. I have many fond memories of those days, but a wound was also cut, the scar of which is still very much in evidence. While most children could sing reasonably well, I could hardly get by. During one of our singing sessions, the teacher came walking through the room putting his ear close to each student to assess the voice. Hearing my monotone, he said quite simply "Ah, you can't sing." Many decades later the pain is still there. I knew I could not sing, but I certainly would have liked to learn something about it. Today I am blessed with a musical wife, who plays several instruments and has a most lovely voice, and who has taken the time to teach each of our children the basics of music. To some extent I have resolved my feelings by enjoying what they are doing and by finally being able to speak openly about my handicap, even make light of it. But a small hurt is still there. It takes a hundred praises to undo one demeaning remark!

While feelings are radiated every time we face a class, they are usually not as personal, but rather more global feelings felt by a class as a whole. Do I show respect for the class as a whole, as well as any individual in the class? Does the class perceive me to be at ease? An audience desperately wants to see its speaker at ease, else it will suffer along with the speaker, watching his mannerisms more than the content of the speech. If the atmosphere is anxious, each person in the audience is tense and feels a grinding stomach.

One of the best ways to accomplish positive feelings is to be totally true to oneself. Do not try to adapt someone else's style; it will be spotted immediately by everyone. Students know when you are doing your best. The classroom is a place where we are compelled to be obedient to truth.

A most comforting thought is that while as teachers we do radiate feeling messages to the class, it is just as much in our power to change those messages. Even more comforting is the fact that, except for major happenings, most people's moods and attitudes are not fixed, they are flexible. We have a chance to change, affect, move, guide, and direct them toward wholesomeness.

I attempt to build a positive atmosphere by including students, by asking questions, by encouraging questions from students at any time and in any place, by spontaneous humor, by laughing at myself. However, the best promoter of goodwill is to build a comaraderie, an "esprit de corps" for the subject. Students should want to come to class; they should want to do the assigned homework, the laboratory report, the paper. This feeling was illustrated in our home, where we had an agreement that the dishwashing was to be rotated among the children. It seemed that forever there was confusion as to whose turn it was. At one point, we proposed to do away with the assigned rotation and instead just volunteer to do the job whenever possible. Heavy school homework assignments for one would be considered by the next. After a few examples from us as parents, the spirit of the approach soon became commonplace.

I have been most impressed how goodwill feelings are returned in untold ways. Excitement and enthusiasm for the subject, going the extra mile for the student, working more than one is paid for, all do pay off in untold and surprising ways; when student gratitude pours in as gifts and comments, when grants, consultantships, and writing contracts are offered, when unexpected awards are received, when speaking engagements come, etc.

Enthusiasm

The setting is a fundraising event for charity. An auctioneer encourages the crowd to bid and to bid high. He is highly enthusiastic, even if it is just a five-dollar item being sold. He thanks each bidder profusely and is wild when a sale is made. When an item has difficulty going, he will himself bid, and if need be, buy it. As he accumulates a number of small items, he uses them to further engage the crowd. As a token of appreciation for someone's courageous bidding, he gives that person an item from his collection. At another time he stops and looks at a lady in the crowd, saying "Now, Ma'am, your smile really is contagious and encouraging. Here, allow me to give you this item I just bought." Not only is he enthusiastic, but he radiates a feeling of integrity and total commitment to the cause. It did not take long for the crowd to respond in appreciation.

It has been said that enthusiasm paints life with color. Those who express enthusiasm enjoy their work and get more done. They also stay young longer (which must mean that if we'd have to do it over again, there would still be time).

A first lesson for effective lecturing is to communicate enthusiasm. It has been shown that while teaching itself does not seem to make much difference to student outcomes, teachers do. It certainly is true that I teach best not what I know, but what I *want* to teach. I want to teach when my insides say "Look what I've found." This leads to the conclusion that there really is no such thing as bad students, only bad professors. A "C" or "D" student who has tried and done his best is a good student. If a student does not try, it mirrors the teacher.

A delightful byproduct of enthusiasm is that it promotes boldness and the willingness to take some risks. When enthusiastic, I am much more willing to do what is innovative, threatening, daring. Reginald had been in the office, struggling to understand a principle, and was sparkling with glee when the light did come on. The next day during lecture, someone asked to explain that same point. Though I did my level best, the eyes of the querying student were as blank as before my answer. As I launched into another attack at explaining it ever so eloquently, I caught a glimpse of Reginald's sparkling eyes. I stopped and took the daring risk. "Reginald, would you come up here, please." As a surprised Reginald made his way to the platform, I mentioned to the class that just yesterday he had explained it back to me, and that he did so beautifully. I gave Reginald the pen, a clean overhead surface, the microphone, and stood back in awe as this nineteen year old stood in front of over two hundred of his peers and made the task seem so simple.

No risk, no gain.

I also find that after an exciting and enthusiastic class session, I am much more willing to do hard and unpleasant things unrelated to my students. After having written, then digested, changed, refined, and polished the poem "Honora Becker" many times, I had yet to show it to someone. It was after one such beautiful class session that I took the poem and decided to show it to the foremost poet on campus. To my complete astonishment, he asked if he could read it at a meeting of amateur poets!

How does one generate and maintain enthusiasm? For me there are at least four props.

The first prop for enthusiasm is to keep active. Both physical and mental muscles grow limp when not in use. Exercising, reading, listening, tackling hard things are growth promoting. For a lecture class, this may translate into preparing many handouts, good outlines, thinking of new ways to explain and demonstrate. Any nervousness can be overcome, and enthusiasm can be generated through the physical motions involved in doing a demonstration in class. It is interesting that students do prefer demonstrations over films, even though a film might depict the same thing in a flawless manner. Whereas a film is known to be perfect, the human element in doing a demonstration provides the possibility for error and the resulting need for investigation, which students can identify with from their own experience.

The second prop is to engage the audience. A powerful verb–to engage means to attract, to hold fast, to please, to become involved with, to interlock. Think of these meanings in regard to public appearances. How is an audience successfully engaged?

The obvious approaches are to ask questions, to hold a discussion, to maintain eye contact, to provide for mental breaks. A more advanced technique is to ask questions of the audience, then provide the answer. "I ask you what was Napoleon's downfall; and you say 'Waterloo.' But, what were the background factors that led to Waterloo?" The audience, while not actually responding, has been engaged.

I like to engage the audience even before class begins. In my classes, things are happening well before the scheduled 8:00 am starting time. Any needed materials are arranged, the lights and sound system checked, transparencies displayed, demonstrations tested, and so on. But most importantly, the minutes before class give me a chance to talk with the students. Audience engagement takes place on a very personal level.

A particularly interesting way to engage the students is for me to play the role of student. If a test has produced an unusually large number of questions on some items, I may ask an assistant to take my place as instructor, while I sit with the students. The assistant will then open the discussion about the previous test, which gives me the opportunity to ask all the questions the students had. It gives me a chance to do as students did on a one-to-one basis: question, argue, and complain. The audience is engaged.

Participatory exercises, such as having a student explain something to the class; encouraging a debate between two students who responded differently to a question; stopping the lecture and asking students to compare notes; always asking students to use their calculators to obtain answers to problems I do in class, rather than my bringing the calculator; asking students for matches needed for a demonstration all lend themselves to promote a feeling of helping and participating.

A helpful third prop for enthusiasm is to allow my humanity to be shown. There is nothing more monotonous than to watch and listen to someone who appears to be a machine. Studentss need to know that the teacher is human and vulnerable. It is comforting to know that the teacher will not be thrown by an unexpected turn of events. It is good to laugh at myself and my mistakes. Occasionally, I get stuck while trying to solve a problem with the class. A comment such as "OK, Boschmann, don't get nervous now," will display my vulnerability and, at the same time, rally the students to my rescue.

The final prop for enthusiasm is acting. Perhaps with a trifle of jealousy, a teacher may comment on a colleague's teaching success as being due to showmanship. Indeed some research has been done in this area by presenting an unsuspecting class with "Dr. Fox," an actor. However, in teaching, I believe that we have no choice but to do at least some acting. As one of my colleagues puts it, "in a sense we have to put on a show." The simple fact of being in front of people calls for a different behavior than what is otherwise normal.

I recall the euphoric feeling with which I was overcome many years ago, during a presentation to a group of school children, in which I attempted to illustrate foreign customs. The presentation was effective because it was somewhat dramatic, and many successive invitations resulted.

Acting, or pretending, has, for me, another very redeeming feature. It is a training for desired behavior. When I do not feel good, but am faced with a class, I might pretend a happy disposition. Lo and behold, the longer I pretend, the more I actually feel happy, and soon I am unable to distinguish between acting and being. This applies to times when students are not interested in the subject matter; as I lecture, pretending that they are, they soon do become interested. This also applies to a shy and withdrawn personality; as I go out and meet people, smile, and begin a conversation, soon I observe myself as comfortably outgoing. Most students appreciate the process; one did not. In her evaluation, she thought me to be a fake. Of the hundreds upon hundreds of positive evaluations received over the years, this one caused me much consternation. After talking with others and reading on the subject, I have come to the conclusion that acting is a needed process. While I may pretend at times, I truly come to live my act. On this subject Bernard Beck says:

"I believe that a large part of a teacher's activity is determined by temperament, and that my own practice is more a product of emergent style than rational intention. Nevertheless, my teaching style is not always a reflection of my personality in other settings, and I sometimes have to handle spontaneous reactions in myself which are at odds with my ideas of how I should behave in class."

It is possible to entertain without teaching, but it is virtually impossible to teach without entertaining.

Positive Attitude

Oliver Wendell Holmes once said that a person's education should begin at least one hundred years before he was born. And so it is with attitude; it must be practiced early and often. I cannot afford to get angry with a class; it just does not work. When there is a need for change, I must find positive means to encourage change. There are six things I do to build a positive attitude within myself.

Feed the Mind

Like a garden, what you plant you will reap. This is not a recent discovery but ancient wisdom. There is a verse in the New Testament, "Whatever we sow, we reap," and the Book of Proverbs advised us long ago, "As he thinketh in his heart, so is he." We really have no choice in this matter. Just as the gardener has no choice about the outcome of his planting; if weed seeds are sown, weeds will appear; if wheat seeds are sown, wheat will appear. It is that simple. Our minds are like gardens; what we sow, we will reap. In the garden, weeds grow easily and unattended, whereas produce must be tended and nurtured. There is absolutely no difference within the mind; the good and positive must be fed and nurtured, lest the weeds take over.

On my desk at home, I keep a calendar of daily quotes taken from the collected wisdom of humanity. In my car I have a flip chart of quotes. The car cassette player either plays soothing music (it must be music with low-beat number) or motivational speeches. I like to listen to Norman Vincent Peale, Earl Nightengale and Dennis Waitley. The minutes spent driving and listening to upbeat materials will pay off for the rest of the day. On my desk at the University, I have a copy of the Bible and a collection of poems by Robert Frost. While I do not have much time to read these at the office, an occasional reference is all that it takes. By my bedside is a collection of perhaps one hundred fifty books to choose from as a last feeding before the conscious goes to sleep and the subconscious takes over. Norman Vincent Peale's *The Power of Positive Thinking* is an absolute must. It is my good fortune to know Dr. Peale personally. His teachings and beliefs radiate as strongly from his writings as they do from his person.

Here is an interesting finding to keep in mind: we are told that reading aloud has unequaled power to influence the subconscious mind.

Exercise the Mind

FDR collected stamps, Ike played golf; you may collect antiques, refinish furniture, raise wolves, or have a small side business. Do something which you enjoy and which taxes your mind, something active, not passive (like watching TV). The mind does really not need a rest as much as the body does. In fact for most of us, it is the body, not the mind, that wears out. For most persons the mind only rusts out. We are told that only about ten percent or less of the mind's capabilities are used by most of us. Look around you and observe the successful people. As you check into their doings aside from the profession, you will find that they are deeply involved in something that absorbs them completely, something they can get lost in, something they enjoy and use their mind in.

I find that people who come to work exhausted on Monday morning do so because their minds have been on a standstill all weekend; nothing has challenged them. On the other hand, those who did something hard, something risky, something challenging which engaged their minds, those are the persons who look forward to Monday morning and who are most productive, even after a mind-taxing weekend.

Exercise the Body

At times when negative attitude threatens the mind, when perhaps even depression sets in, we need quick treatment. Depression can be overcome by physical exercise. There is nothing quicker or cheaper. No need for athletic club membership or strenuous competition, just move the body. Muscles not used will go limp. Swim, jog, or do routine, daily exercises in your room for fifteen minutes. It stirs the blood and clears the mind. There are many books on the subject.

Be Creative in Your Field

For those of us in the teaching profession, creativity means research and/or writing. Projects can be large undertakings or small personal ventures. Some time ago we became interested in the pattern in which students turn in their examination. Do the "A" or the "D" students hand in first, or is there no distinction? It took some planning and some work to do the research (Finding: there is no pattern). On another occasion we studied the performance of day vs. night students and found, in a sampling of about a thousand students, that the night enrolees outperform the day students by half a letter grade and that the most successful grade performer is the female student, age twenty-six, who enrolls at night and has a job (Chapter 5).

I always have projects going. These can be major ventures such as grant proposals, basic chemical research, writing a book, organizing a symposium; or smaller ones, such as writing new experiments, designing a novel learning tool, attending meetings, or coordinating Tuesday luncheons among faculty to share ideas on how to teach large classes, small classes, research classes, how to grade, or how to teach a particular topic.

Be Alone

I believe that to build a positive self-attitude, we must give ourselves time to digest and reflect; we must be alone. For me this is the time before I meet my 8:00 am class. I insist that the thirty minutes before class time is my time. I close the door. I see no one. The students know and respect this time. This is the time when I prepare myself from within. The lecture material has long since been prepared, all needed demonstrations are available but now I do internal adjusting so that when I walk into that classroom, I am a worthy model. I close my eyes and go over the topics; I check the connection between topics, the different illustrations, the examples and demonstrations, the difficult passages, and the times that the class will need mental relief. Paul Gauguin said "I shut my eyes in order to see." I visualize the class in my mind's eye; I anticipate questions; I even like to "see" the glow of the eyes that says "I understand." This is a wonderful time to come up with good analogies and illustrations. This is a time to read something good, so that when I walk into that classroom, I do so with a positive attitude. My challenge out there is a group of students who are not chemistry majors, who are taking a required course, for which many do not see the need. It is a group of students who may have had traumatic experiences with past chemistry attempts; it is a group of students who has come for an 8:00 am class when, during winter months, it is still dark. If I walk in gloomy and tired, they will feel a long hour or day ahead; they may even get cold, or hot, and wish they had stayed home.

Be Early

There is wonderful therapeutic magic about being on time, or better yet, being early. When you get to a meeting just on time, it takes several minutes to get all body functions calmed down, to get the mind into the atmosphere of the meeting subject matter, and, if slightly late, it takes several more minutes of wondering what was missed.

Particularly as a teacher, I set the mental stage by being early. It gives me time to adjust, to set up, and answer questions, and still have time to walk into the class and visit. It gives me time to promote a positive attitude even before class begins. If the students can walk into the classroom and see prepared materials projected, they are invited to prepare the mind for chemistry. On the other hand, if they see me serving myself by sitting down, sipping coffee or smoking, they will do likewise and say to themselves "Boy, I'm tired." But if they see me in nice clothes, scurrying about and getting ready, being excited about what is about to happen, their physical and mental metabolism will pick up as well. I am a model; what I do will come right back at me.

There is a simple test for positive attitude. Who is the first to come and the last to leave the classroom? Think about it!

Preparing a positive attitude is a service to my class. The attitude will show up in what I say and how I say it. When I announce the scores from the last exam, do I mention the ten Fs or the twenty-one As? Do I make mistakes seem easy to fix? Do I approach difficult subjects as major problems or as exciting challenges? When I am in the wrong, do I admit so quickly, openly, completely, and without hesitation?

Have Fun!

A wise old teacher once said "No teaching is important unless we have an opportunity to laugh together." This truism, more than anything else, is likely responsible for my lukewarm

feelings for special speakers that came to campus during my college days. They often displayed absolutely no fun and excitement, and certainly my personal teaching style is, in part, a reaction against what I saw. Fun and laughter are human needs which should be satisfied much like other needs. The popularity of cartoon strips proves this fact.

My classes often begin with an appropriate cartoon, which in some manner speaks to the upcoming topic. The cartoon draws attention, it focuses on the subject, and it allows us to smile, thereby preparing a wholesome frame of mind for the upcoming class session.

After solving a difficult problem and coming up with the right answer, or during a good demonstration, I will sometimes ask "Isn't this fun?" Or I might inquire of my nonmajor students, "OK, now how many chemistry majors?"

During a time when topics are covered in rapid succession, a side comment such as "If you think we are going fast, it probably is because we are" will at least acknowledge that I realize the speed with which we are going.

A way to introduce the need for studying is to hold up a dollar bill and ask "Who wants this dollar?" Many hands will go up. I continue holding the dollar and repeat "Who wants this dollar bill?" Hands are higher. "Who wants this dollar bill?" You continue this a few more times, and, if fortunate, a timid soul will come forward and get the dollar. Then the point can be made. Everybody talks about studying, but nobody does anything about it. If somebody did come up to get the dollar, it illustrates that while many talk, a few (or just one) did something about it.

There are exciting ways to involve students: check labels of goods for chemical content; write a letter to Congressmen regarding an issue of concern. During an experiment on analysis of calcium, a student brought in her baby tooth to check the calcium content. By comparing it with an adult's tooth, she was able to confirm the fact that the calcium uptake in baby teeth is much higher than in adult teeth. For several years, I have challenged my students to invent a totally transparent calculator for use on the overhead. "You could make a million! I'll buy one."

Exams are a good place to let creative fun juices flow. Drawings or cartoons, the use of alternating red and green sheets during the Christmas season, or the title, Let There Be A Miracle Exam, all have a way of reducing examination tension just a bit. I have used what students know as "football questions." In an effort to give all students a chance to at least have one correct answer, a question has an arrow pointing to an answer with the notation "This is the right answer."

We share a good laugh hearing some of the clever excuses used by students.

Remember, all such sidetracking takes place for a few seconds about every twelve to fifteen minutes, for the purpose of establishing a break and then, with a refreshed mind, return to the task at hand.

Of particular success are repeat situations where students anticipate the outcome. This may take the form of yet another reference to my bad handwriting, which I myself can't read: "Does anyone know what this says?" Or it may be a particular student I routinely "pick" on, much to his and the class's delight.

It can backfire. A colleague was lecturing on human anatomy, when suddenly a side door opened, producing a belly dancer as a "demonstration" of the lecture material. During one exam I thought it would be nice to have some music in the background, only to get an uproar, demanding quietness. Such risks come with the fun.

What I am hoping for is that the students see in me a delightful sense of vulnerability. I tell the students that I made wine at home, and it tasted too sour. So, being a good chemist and knowing about acid-base reaction, I attempted to neutralize the sour acid taste with some base, only to get a soapy taste. The wine was used to clean the sink.

Hubert N. Alyea, the dean of chemistry lecturers, says "They pay me to have fun. I have fun all the time. I play. I do anything I want."

Some Fun Books

Berry, Martyn, H2O and All That, Heinemann Educational Books (1980)
Bloch, Arthur, Murphy's Law and Other Reasons Why Things Go Wrong, Price/Stern/Sloan Publishers, Inc., Los Angeles (1977)
Boschmann, Erwin, Yellow Pages, Science Enterprises, Inc., Box 88443, Indianapolis, IN 46208 (1988)
Bunch, Bryan, The Science Almanac, Anchor Books/Doubleday, New York (1984)
Chase, William D., Chase's Calendar of Annual Events, Apple Tree Press, Flint, Mich. (appears yearly)
Comenos, Cally and Ballenberg, Mary-Ann, Tons of Trivia, Scholastic Book Service, New York (1973)
Ertel, James, The Journal of Irreproducible Results, Selected Papers, J.I.R. Publishers, Inc., Chicago (1976)
Grun, Bernard, The Time Tables of History, A Touchstone Book, Simon and Schuster, New York (1982)
Hill, Morgan, The Student's Guide to Better Excuses, Ten Speed Press, Berkeley, Cal. (1979)
Harris, Sidney, What's so Funny about Science, (cartoons), William Kaufmann, Inc., Los Altos, Cal. (1977)
Harris, Sidney, All Ends Up, (cartoons), William Kaufmann, Inc., Los Altos, Cal. (1980)
Hauser, Josef, ed., Was Nicht in den Annalen Steht, Verlag Chemie, Weinheim/Bergstr. (1969)
McKenzie, E. C., Salted Peanuts, a Fun Filled Collection of 1800 Tantalizing Facts to Read, Relish, Remember, and Repeat, Signet Books (1976)
Peter, Lawrence J., The Peter Principle, Why things Always Go Wrong, Bantam Books (1969)
Peter, Lawrence J., The Peter Prescription, How to Make Things Right, Bantam Books (1972)
The Queensbury Group, The Book of Facts, Ballantine Books, New York (1978)
Vlasov, L. and Trifonov, D., 107 Stories about Chemistry, Mir Publishers (1977)

Delivery

"Given the recent invention of the printing press, why do professors continue to lecture so much?" With the advent of films, television, video, and computers, that long-ago uttered query might even be more appropriately asked today. Is there a legitimate need for live teachers? Consider the list of weaknesses of the lecture approach compiled by William Cashin: In lectures students are passive, their attention wanes, all are expected to learn at the same rate; lectures require an effective speaker, emphasize learning by listening; they lack in feedback, and are not well suited to higher levels of learning or for complex and abstract material. So why do we continue with lectures?

She walks slowly, then suddenly sprints with the large dog in tight control on a leash. Flashing eyes, shouting instructions, admonishing, repeating again and again, suddenly the dog learns that new behavior, which is immediately and profusely awarded with lavish praise and approval, all to the delight of the observant dog owners. The lesson moves smoothly without any loss of time. New challenges are set to master new commands. Her small body, yes her whole being, flows with the lesson. Total devotion and loss of self-consciousness are evidenced by beads of sweat on her forehead. Each of her actions reflects concern for learning, love for the subject, zest for the work. In just a matter of a quarter of an hour, the previously totally untrained dog is amazingly able to obey new commands. Both dog and dog owner have learned from a master teacher.

Try that on a computer. Good teachers in action model their profession. They give the student a chance to observe thinking, to see a mind at work when suddenly a wrong answer in the book is discovered, when a student poses a challenging question, or when the probing of a group is allowed to propose an answer.

It is through the lecture that we are able to add, delete, and reorganize new information; we can convey large amounts of it to a large audience. It is through lectures that we have high control over events with minimum threat to the student.

It is in the lecture that we combine all those things discussed in the previous chapters; the care, the preparation, the communication skillls, the enthusiasm, the positive attitude, the enjoyment, and focus them into a passionate one for the good of the subject and the students. We have our goals and objectives clearly in mind; we have a brief outline for the students to see; we understand the students' background; we speak clearly and with proper voice inflections, avoiding stereotyped behaviors like "ah, OK, you know"; we remember human limitations to retain information; we remember human limitations to retain information; we remember to be playfully redundant around major points; we establish two-way communication; we provide for change in routine, use visual aids, are enthusiastic, look at the audience, are not ashamed to present personal views. Here and there sprinkle a little humor, and summarize at the end.

To accomplish this takes years of practice. Lecturers may be Ph.D.s in their field, but many are in kindergarten in its presentation. It takes time to learn not to overlook the raised hand in the back of the room in favor of the obvious repeat hand up front; it takes time to realize that students tune in and out during the lecture and that careful repetition is not an insult but an aid; it takes time to learn to truly look at the audience and to converse with, rather than lecture at; it takes time to recognize the influence a teacher has, not just on the students, but far beyond into their circle of acquaintances. Some teachers, when given the chance, rather than one large section will teach several small sections, simply to acquire the desired experience to do it well.

Particularly helpful is Simonede's mnemonic technique known as the method of loci (places). In your mind's eye pick a route, say through your house, and attach a given idea to a given place (the foyer is the introduction). During the lecture simply retrace the route through the house. It is possible to handle sixty to seventy ideas in this manner. Memory advocate Billy Burden meets some fifty new persons just before his lecture, then during his presentation has them stand and then sit as he introduces them to the audience, both by first and last names.

There are three stages of development in the art of lecturing. The first stage is characterized by rigid adherence to notes, remaining fixed behind the lectern, with lack of eye contact.

It is often typified at meetings by those "reading a paper." Only information is provided. Interaction with the audience is absent.

Attainment of the second stage is evidenced by a sense of comfort with the material, usually acquired through repeated presentations. The lecturer is free to use some gestures, audiovisuals, demonstrations, analogies, but he remains behind the lectern; eye contact is quite evident but is shared with glances to the notes. While all efforts are devoted to the thorough transmission of material, it is still a one-way process.

The final stage melts the lecture, lecturer, and audience into one. The lecturer is free to walk about, and discussion is abundant. He skillfully steers student input and provides relevant information and insights. He truly thinks aloud in the presence of the class. He does not talk about economics, biology, or history, but instead he is an economist, a biologist, or an historian at work. More than that he is truly interested in the student as a person, his goals, his dreams, his fears.

When does one attain this level of achievement? How does one know that such a level has been attained? There is no test to indicate such attainment, but you will know when you are there. You will be there when you literally feel pregnant with excitement and can't wait to share it. It is a feeling of oneness with the class. It is complete absorption in the process; it is a therapeutic experience; it is a climax of euphoria like that reported by runners after the agony is overcome; it is an open discussion with yourself.

Johann Kepler was known as a notoriously bad teacher who bored his students with facts on astronomy. Kepler's sole interest was his research on the planets. He spent long hours checking his crude data, comparing it to what the Greeks said, attempting to reconcile it with theological persuasions of the times. Nothing seemed to fit as a model to predict the motions of the planets about the sun. Then it happened. During one of those boring lectures, he had an insight, a flash. Dropping his notes, he stared blankly into the class, then suddenly hurried to the blackboard, and while constantly talking, traced lines and drew diagrams of possible planetary motions. By connecting key points, he saw and shared the light–a law-obeying planetary motion. During those few minutes Kepler was thinking aloud in the presence of his class. Totally absorbed, the teacher knew the ripe idea had to be shared. Though often a dull teacher, this was a climactic moment, and every student saw the integrity of the process.

If we care, we prepare;
then are driven to share.

Here is a self-test on delivery to be used after lecture. Answer the following questions with a simple "yes" or "no."

___ Was I the first to arrive in class?
___ Was I free from notes at least half the time?
___ Did I move about freely?
___ Did I use students' names?
___ Did I radiate a positive, enthusiastic attitude?
___ Did the class mirror my feelings?
___ Were students free to interrupt me?
___ If need be, would students take issue with me?
___ Did I weave in appropriate humor?
___ Was I the last to leave?
___ Am I exhausted?

The more honest "yes" answers, the better.

Sample Lecture

When does a lecture actually begin? As far as the students are concerned it is at the prescribed time, say 8:00 am; however, for us as teachers, the lecture really begins much earlier. The actual delivery starts at about ten or fifteen minutes prior to 8:00 am.

For me the lecture begins as soon as I leave the previous lecture. I think about what I was not able to cover, what went well, and what did not. Immediately, I take the time to arrange all materials for the following lecture. For me this early time is very important, because my mind is still on the material; I am still keyed up and know exactly how and what I'll do differently.

Let's take a timed walk through a sample lecture.

6:15 a.m. Rise and get ready. During my shower, I review what the lecture topic is and some of its key features. I go over examples, illustrations, and demonstrations. Today we are talking about nuclear chemistry, a topic that does not easily lend itself to demonstrations, but I do have some good illustrative material.

7:00 a.m. After a good breakfast, I am ready to leave. In the car I turn the pad of quotes to Monday and find this interesting gem of wisdom by Bhagavad Gita:

> "Work done with anxiety about results
> is far inferior
> to work done without anxiety."

How appropriate for the work of teachers! As I drive I have a choice of inspirational or motivational tapes or listen to news items and dates in history. I choose the latter and find an interesting report on nuclear waste.

7:15 a.m. Arrive at the office, close the door, and begin to lay out all needed materials for the lecture session. These were, of course, prepared way ahead of time, but now is the time to review them in detail, though quickly. This triggers in my mind the needed details of facts and delivery. Then I set these aside and think, meditate, and brainstorm. "That news item on the radio–let's not forget it! Today would be a good time to remind the students of the help sessions. What about the chain reaction? How will that go over? Hard concept. It is really such an impressive number multiplication, how could that be brought across? I wonder if . . . I've got an idea!"

7:40 a.m It is time to gather the materials and leave for the classroom. I check my pocket change to make sure I have a penny.

7:45 a.m. In the class I see a few early birds. A quick nod greets them, and then the materials are laid out: books and notes on the lectern, lecture examples on the overhead projector table, and incidentals, demonstrations, and transparencies spread over the center table. The two overheads carry these displays:

Outline for November 15

Review

Nuclear Decay
- half life
- dating

Nuclear Reactions
- balancing

Chain Reactions
- fission/fusion
- reactors vs. bombs

Applications and Implications
- tracer studies
- waste storage

Nuclear Power:
Paradise, Perdition,
or Just Parboil?

Reprinted with permission of Macmillan Publishing Company from Chemistry for Changing Times by John Hill. Copyright c 1972, 1984(4/e) by Macmillan Publishing Company.

A few students come by to check some homework problems, and I have a minute to walk up to some others and chat for a bit. The room is now full.

7:59 a.m. Light controls are doublechecked and the microphone is put in place.

8:00 a.m. "It was on December 2, 1942, that a major event in the history of science took place beneath the stadium of Stagg Field at the University of Chicago. It was announced that afternoon at 3:25, using this coded telephone conversation:

Dr. Compton: 'The Italian navigator has landed in the New World.'
Dr. Conant: 'How were the natives?'
Dr. Compton: 'Very friendly.'

What did the speakers mean by the 'Italian navigator,' the 'New World,' the 'natives,' and 'friendly'? It is the purpose of our lecture today to decode this conversation.

8:02 a.m. "Good Morning! Did you hear on the news this morning about the government's proposal to build new nuclear waste sites? Thirty states are being considered as possible sites. Think about the implications. Do you want one in your state? We'll talk about this next time.

"The only announcement today concerns the special help session the staff is offering for you. We do invite you to make use of this.

"During the last lecture we introduced the topic of nuclear chemistry and discussed in some detail its history and development. We saw how Marie Curie processed a truckload of pitchblende to isolate a fraction of a gram of the essence of what we call radioactive material. We saw that there are three major types of radiation: the alpha, beta, and gamma rays; all have different mass, charge, and penetration properties. This transparency will help us recall the differences.

Outline for November 15

Review

Nuclear Decay
- half life
- dating

Nuclear Reactions
- balancing

Chain Reactions
- fission/fusion
- reactors vs. bombs

Applications and Implications
- tracer studies
- waste storage

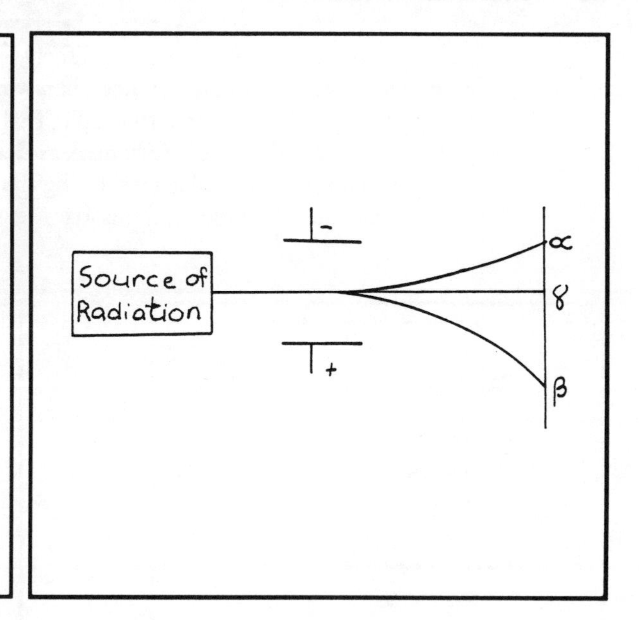

"We also introduced the different ways to measure radiation and got a feel for the awesome nuclear power: three million pounds of coal deliver as much energy as a single pound of uranium, do you remember?

"Today I would like to help us learn and understand three things: 1. Nuclear decay; 2. Nuclear reactions; and 3. Chain reactions.

'Would you like to know what will be on the next exam? I'll give you the answer right here. There will be several questions from each of these three topics."

8:10 a.m. "Nuclear decay. When a sample of radioactive material gives off radiation, we say that it 'decays,' meaning that it loses some of its properties and energy in the form of radiation. This decay is due to the fact that the nuclei of the atoms are decomposing, giving off one or several of the types of radiation we studied earlier. This then is a natural process. It happens by itself. Radioactive material is said to decompose spontaneously. It is also possible to induce decompositions. We will look into this later. As scientists, we are obviously interested in natural phenomena, and the decomposition is clearly one of these. How can we predict the decomposition? This has been one of the more frustrating and humbling experiences for scientists: not to be able to predict which atoms of a given radioactive sample will decompose next. However, we are able to predict the overall decomposition pattern for the process.

"It is much like the prediction by the maintenance department about the life of the lights in this room. Let's see, we have four florescent lights in each unit, and this ceiling looks like it has about six times ten, sixty units times four lights in each, there are about two hundred forty lights in this room. No one on the maintenance staff is able to predict when which light will go; however, from past experience, they are able to predict that about two lights per year will have to be replaced. So it is with nuclear decay.

"We can plot the decay by showing the number of available nuclei on the vertical scale and the time on the horizontal scale:

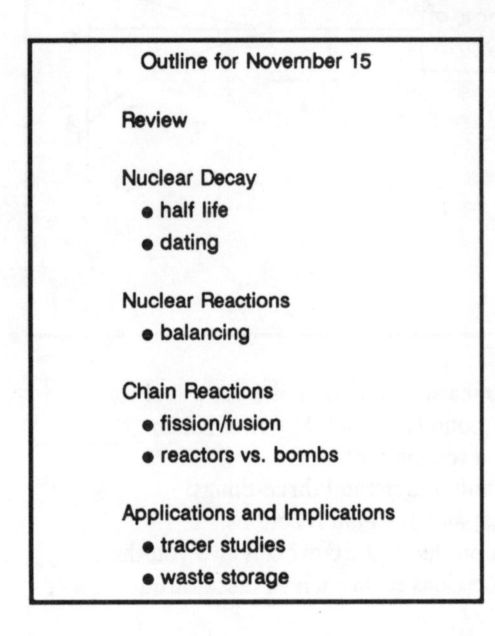

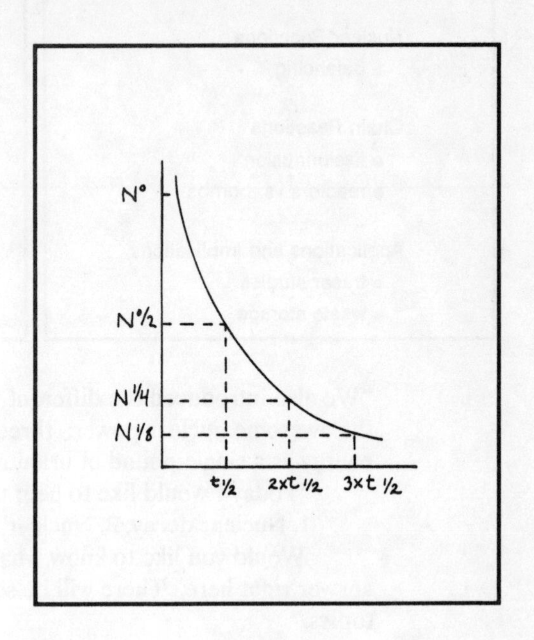

"We measure the time needed to lose half the nuclei (remember, we don't know which particular nuclei), and mark it. The amazing thing is that if we now measure the time it takes to lose half the remaining nuclei, it again takes the *same* amount of time as it did earlier. To lose half of the fourth left, it takes that same time and so on for the time to lose half of the eighth, the sixteenth, the thirtysecond, etc. That time we call half life and it is a characteristic of that particular radioactive material. No matter how much material is decaying, or what type or how much radiation is being given off, the half life stays the same.

Outline for November 15

Review

Nuclear Decay
- half life
- dating

Nuclear Reactions
- balancing

Chain Reactions
- fission/fusion
- reactors vs. bombs

Applications and Implications
- tracer studies
- waste storage

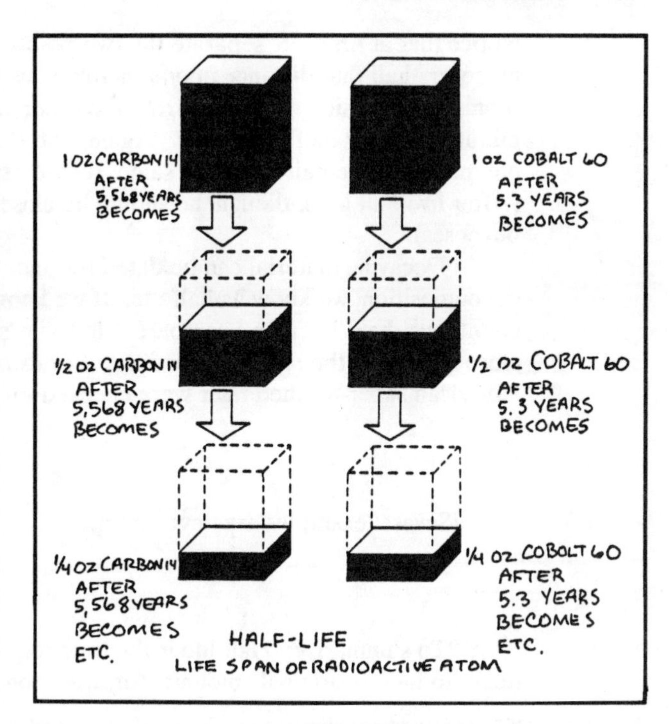

"This transparency illustrates the concept well. It takes 5568 years for an ounce of carbon-14 to decay down to half an ounce. Again, it takes 5568 years for the half to go down to a quarter ounce, for the quarter to an eighth, and so on. And the same thing applies to the cobalt-60 sample, except that its half life is 5.3 years.

"It is like the story about boy goes to see girl:

Outline for November 15

Review

Nuclear Decay
- half life
- dating

Nuclear Reactions
- balancing

Chain Reactions
- fission/fusion
- reactors vs. bombs

Applications and Implications
- tracer studies
- waste storage

Notice that at first 256' separate the two points of interest. Full of confidence, he covers half that distance in one minute leaving 128'. But because there seems to be no sign of interest from the other end, he takes the same time, one minute, to cover half of the 128'. Again, half the distance of 64' is covered in one minute. The half life is the same, regardless of the distance involved. (After five half lives, though, he should be close enough for all practical purposes).

"Decaying material can be dated for age. If we know the type of nuclear decomposition, we know its half life. If we know what its initial decomposition count must have been and compare it to today's count, we can get a fairly close handle on the age of the artifact. For example, the remains of the American saber-toothed tiger were checked for C-fourteen count . . . .

.
.
.

[Several examples are developed]

.
.
.

"To summarize: Half life is the time required for a radioactive sample to decay to half its original amount. Any questions?" [Pause]

8:24 a.m. "There is a story about American science students waiting at the Paris railway station when an elderly lady in plain dress came walking in and sat down, obviously exhausted.

'May I help you,' one of the students asked the woman.

'Yes, please, I need a glass of water.' In no time she was given the water. The student notified a medical student: 'I think the lady needs some help.'

'Nonsense,' he said, 'she is just a tired old peasant lady.' Her train arrived and the lady got up.

'Thank you for the water. What is your name?'

'I am Emilia Wood from Miami. What is your name?'

'Marie Curie,' said the lady as she entered the train.

'Marie Curie!' exclaimed the student, 'it is the one person I wanted to meet while in Europe!'"

8:25 a.m. "We will now take a look at balancing nuclear equations. As the name implies, changes take place in the nuclei, and that is where our attention will have to be. Enrico Fermi had noticed such changes as far back as 1934. The main thing to keep in mind is that we must be able to account for all nuclear particles. The total number of protons on the left side of the equation must equal the total number on the right. The same applies to the neutrons.

For example:

$$ {}^{6}_{3}\mathrm{Li} + {}^{1}_{0}\mathrm{n} \longrightarrow {}^{3}_{1}\mathrm{H} + {}^{4}_{2}\mathrm{He} $$

"Let's check our understanding on the spontaneous decomposition of uranium:

$$^{238}_{92}\mathrm{U} \longrightarrow {}^{234}_{90}\mathrm{Th} + ?$$

What is the missing species: beta, gamma, or alpha? [Pause]

"It reminds me of the professor who was concerned about the football players in the back of the room, who did not seem to grasp the material. So in a question like the one just posed he would ask:

(Very quietly) 'Beta?'
(Very quietly) 'Gamma?,' or
(Loud, and vigorously pointing) 'ALPHA?!!!'
Even the football players got the answer.

"Yes, the answer is alpha. Why? [Pause] Right, because the subscript for the remaining species must be 2 and its superscript 4, which pinpoints the alpha species. Good. Very good.

.

.

[More material]

.

.

"OK, the point we are trying to make is that to balance nuclear equations, all we have to do is keep straight the arithmetic for the subscripts and superscripts. Any questions?" [Pause]

8:34 a.m. 'Nuclear reactions can be fusion reaction, where several smaller nuclei are indeed fused together, or they may undergo fissioning, split apart. To illustrate the latter, let's assume that this represents a carbon nucleus composed of six protons, □ , and seven neutrons, ◆ .

Outline for November 15

Review

Nuclear Decay
- half life
- dating

Nuclear Reactions
- balancing

Chain Reactions
- fission/fusion
- reactors vs. bombs

Applications and Implications
- tracer studies
- waste storage

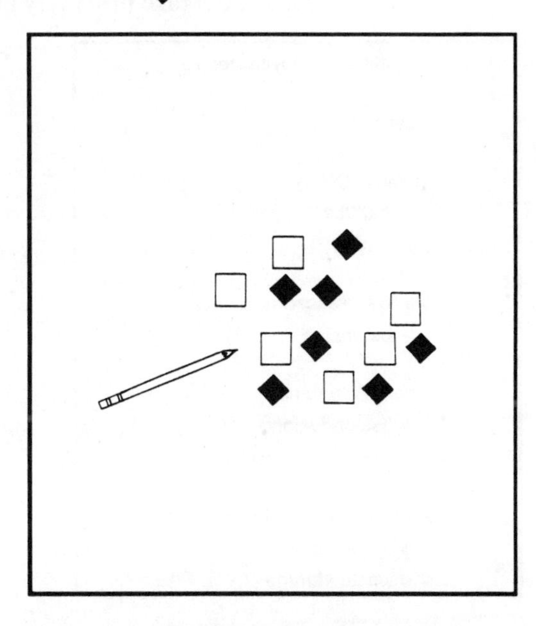

In this demonstration, a projectile, such as a stream of neutrons, may be represented by my pencil. If I shoot the pencil through the nucleus, a splitting takes place, which results in several smaller fragments.

Outline for November 15

Review

Nuclear Decay
- half life
- dating

Nuclear Reactions
- balancing

Chain Reactions
- fission/fusion
- reactors vs. bombs

Applications and Implications
- tracer studies
- waste storage

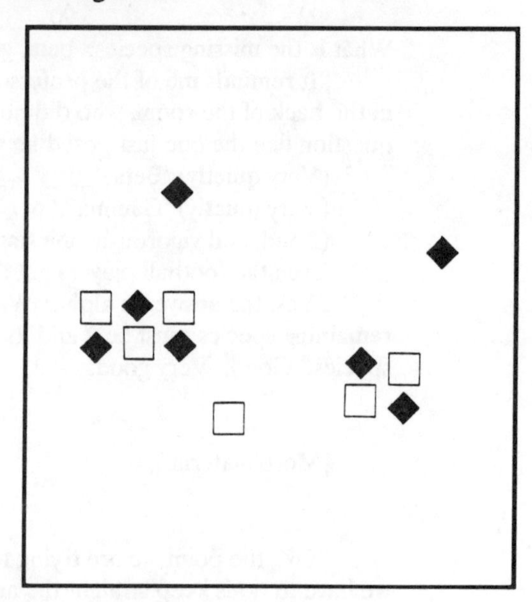

"Looking at the results, we find that the carbon nucleus has decomposed to form two neutrons, a proton, an alpha particle, and a lithium nucleus.

"The interesting fact is that the reaction was initiated by neutrons, but also produces neutrons. Is it not possible that these very neutrons could then go on and initiate reactions in other nuclei? Indeed that is the case! In fact a chain reaction can take place very quickly.

Outline for November 15

Review

Nuclear Decay
- half life
- dating

Nuclear Reactions
- balancing

Chain Reactions
- fission/fusion
- reactors vs. bombs

Applications and Implications
- tracer studies
- waste storage

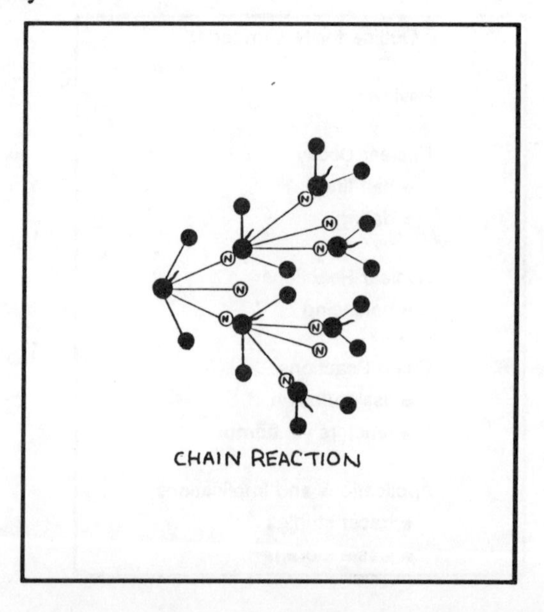

"It really does not take long at all for the process to multiply itself very quickly. For example, here I have a penny. I'll give it to Ron here in the front row. Ron, if you would take out a penny of your own, so that you now have two, and give each to a different person sitting behind you. Each of you that receives a penny, please add one of your own and pass both to two different people behind you, and so on until we reach the last row.

"Uncontrolled nuclear chain reactions are nuclear bombs, whereas controlled chain reactions are reactors. The uncertainty of not knowing which way the reaction would go filled the pioneers of nuclear reactions, like Fermi, with a sense of fear and healthy respect. Fortunately, however, the reaction was controllable ('the natives were friendly').

.
.
.

[More material]

.
.
.

"To review: unless reaction products are controlled, chain reactions are quite likely."

8:47 a.m. "Would you pass all the pennies arriving in the last row to your right and give them to Jane. Please count them.

"Before you close your books, let's review: We learned that half life is a good measure of the nuclear decay process; that nuclear equations can be balanced easily by watching superscripts and subscripts; and that nuclear reactions can easily result in chain reaction.

"Jane, how many pennies?"

"528"

"One penny yielded 528 via a chain reaction! Truly amazing! Are you all impressed? Jane would take those pennies some evening when you go to the shopping center and put them into the water fountain. From there they will go to some charity here in town.

"Next time we will consider the Applications and Implications. How does a nuclear power plant work? What input do we have in decisions as to where nuclear wastes go? Please don't miss the session. Thank you for coming."

8:50 a.m. "You are dismissed."

Conclusion

Observe students studying on computer terminals. It is possible to walk into a room full of students sitting in front of terminals and be totally ignored by the students. They are absorbed in the process of learning. Can we do this with the process of teaching? Is my teaching so absorbing that a stranger could walk into the class and be essentially ignored? It is a worthy goal to strive toward.

We come close to the goal when we are able to catalyze the "aha" experience in students. Such wonder and excitement! Of the hundreds of persons I interviewed concerning their perception of a good teacher, an eleven-year-old girl's response speaks for them all: "A good teacher is one who is not mean, and explains things."

WHAT YOU CAN DO . . .

1. Smile.
2. Practice delivery aloud just to yourself and the mirror.
3. Use three main points.
4. Emphasize key points, and repeat them at least once.
5. Provide a mental break every fifteen minutes.
6. Wait two to three seconds after asking a question.
7. Study your taped delivery.

Further Reading

Norman Vincent Peale, Power of the Plus Factor, Fleming H. Revell Co. 1987
Norman Vincent Peale, The Power of Positive Thinking, Prentice Hall, Inc. 1952
Napoleon Hill and W. Clement Stone, Success Through a Positive Mental Attitude, Prentice Hall, Inc. 1960

SOME CONNECTING THOUGHTS

In this first part we have considered the care for the student, the preparation of the subject, and the delivery by the teacher. How do these three foci interplay? Obviously in many different ways, but a desirable relationship is shown below.

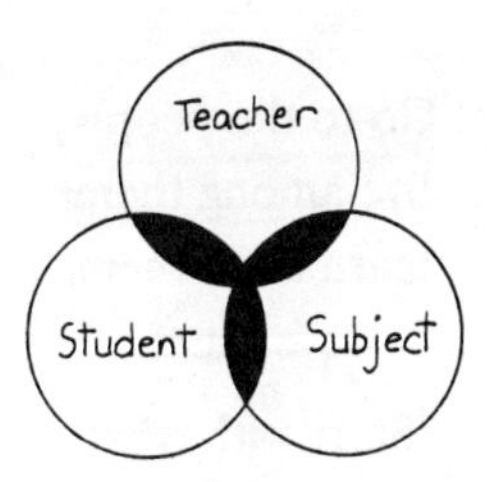

It is in the willingness to sacrifice short-term center stage that we will gain long-term rewards. The glory of teaching comes much after the act of teaching. The less of you, the teacher, is projected, the more the subject has the spotlight. The axiom is "forget about yourself!" A Chinese proverb says "What is most needed for teaching is a humble mind.'

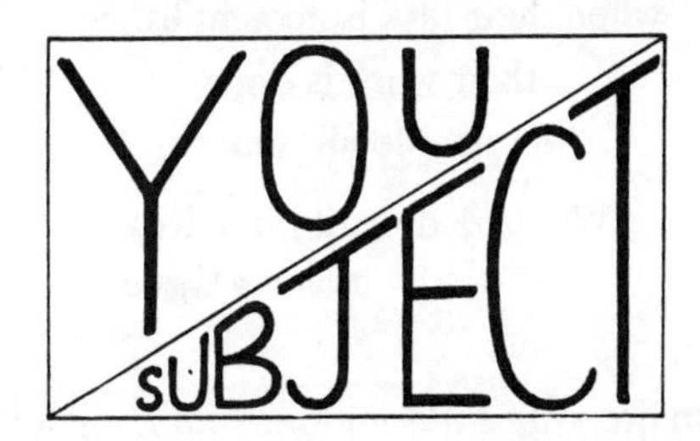

The less of you shows, the more the subject is center staged.

Ancient wisdom tells us that teaching is an art, not a science. Therefore, it is not possible to give a set of rules, which when followed will produce good teaching. There is no one formula of success in teaching. Rather, as an art, it calls for the coming together of many ingredients, none of which, by itself, assures good teaching, but taken as a whole adds up to success. For one teacher, one set of ingredients works best; for another it may be a different combination. The types and amounts of ingredients are different from teacher to teacher. Nevertheless, there are some things that can be said about all good teaching.

When a teacher presents the topic in such a vivid manner that all attention is drawn to the topic . . .

when there are no distracting, self-centered comments . . .
when there is no self-glorification . . .
when all attention to the person melts away in favor of focus on the topic . . .
when there is no false humility begging for adoration . . .
when the subject is made so clear that learning is obvious and automatic . . .
when the subject is offered to the students and placed high on a pedestal . . .

when the teacher fades into the background like music in a film . . .
when the students fail to notice the teacher but see the subject . . .
when the teaching is both conscious and subconscious . . .
when the teacher makes himself obsolete . . .
when such a set of circumstances is brought about, THEN HONOR HAS BEEN DONE TO GOOD TEACHING!

Go to the people,
live among them,
learn from them,
love them.

Start with what
they know,
build on what
they have.

But of the best leaders,
when their task is accomplished,
their work is done,
the people all remark,

"We have done it ourselves."

Chinese Wisdom

Though I was a science major with little understanding or feeling for other fields, it was a professor from another field whom I consider my best teacher. Honora Becker and I had little in common: she was approaching retirement, I was a sophomore; she taught English literature, I was still learning how to speak English; she taught appreciating, I liked solving; she could feel poetry, I only saw a printed page. Yet, I consider the late Honora Becker my best teacher.

Honora Becker

There you stand,
A blessed assembly of knowledge, experience, wisdom and dignity;
In simple, yet neat decor
You stand erect and in control;
Without a hint of pride or arrogance
You command respect for who you are;
I'm drawn by the power of your person
Not to you, but to the poetry you read;
As I look at you and listen, I suddenly see beyond you and–
Behold! I do indeed feel

the rolling hills,
the life abundant,
the tears and the joy.

As my spine tingles with sensation
I realize a poem has spoken to me, and
You, my teacher, you have touched my soul,
You are forever.

Erwin Boschmann

PART II

POINTS TO PONDER

What the Research Says

Be Creative

Chapter 4
What the Research Says

Let not many of you become teachers, for you know that we who teach shall be judged with greater strictness.

James 3:1

What a perceptive admonition! To teach calls for that extra responsibility, both for the teaching process and the renewing of ourselves. It behooves us as teachers to know what the best teaching methods are. This means we need to know something about the research on teaching and learning–it is our duty to keep abreast. We may be naturally good teachers, but we cannot rely solely on our intuition.

Antigone Sophocles put it this way: "The ideal condition would be, I admit, that men should be right by instinct. But since we are likely to go astray, the reasonable thing is to learn from those who can teach."

And so this chapter is devoted to a few research findings. No pretense is made to be complete or even to be balanced in the presentation of facts. At times opposing views or findings will be evident. The bibliography at the end of the chapter lists many sources for the findings.

Research facts may not tell us what to do when a tearful student bursts into the office, but they do provide generalizations pointing in an overall direction, which I have always found very helpful.

Body and Mind

It is estimated that one fourth of all children under the age of ten possess near photographic memory. Like an unused muscle, this recall ability is lost by adolescence due to lack of use.

For the majority of persons, mental capacity is at its peak on Wednesday mornings at about 10:00 am.

There is a theory of biorhythm which advocates that we ought to chart our natural cycles. For most persons the *physical* cycle, which correlates well-being and fatigue, is twenty-three days. The *emotional* cycle, which determines moods, sensitivity, and creativity, takes twenty-eight days. The *intellectual* cycle, which relates to mental activity, memory and decision making, is the longest at thirty-three days.

–Thommen

Thinking efficiency, such as in organization of thoughts, and mental outputs, as performance on multiple choice tests, are heightened after vigorous exercise.

–Cacioppe

A person's pupils tend to dilate when interested, but they contract when hearing something of dislike.

—Hall

Choline, found in egg yoke, meat and fish, aids the brain in the production of acetylcholine, which improves memory.

–Wurtman

Mental activity requires more sleep than physical labor.

–Taylor

The left brain is	The right brain is
masculine	feminine
active	passive
logical	intuitive
mathematical	artistic
analytical	creative

–Taylor

Learning takes place using all senses, but with very different efficiencies.

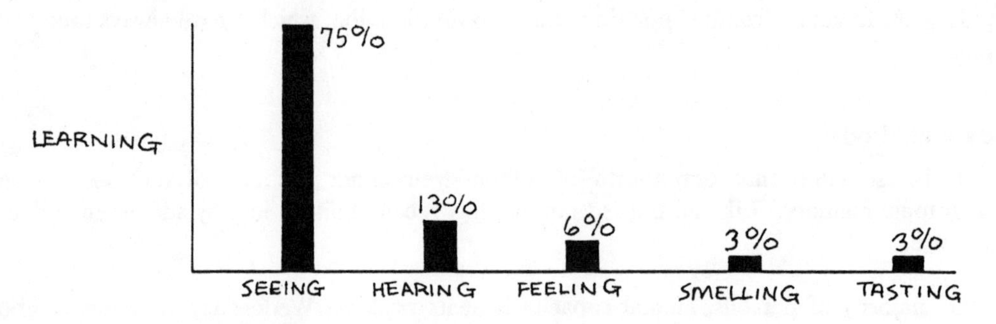

Best learning is attained through repeated involvement using all senses.

–Taylor

Mental Development

Probably no individual has ever lived whose full potential for happy intellectual interest and growth has been achieved.

–Hunt

Intellectual development may be described in four stages:

1. Sensory-motor (birth–2 years)
2. Pre-operational (2–9 years): language development

3. Concrete operational (9–15 years ?): needs reference to familiar objects and properties.
4. Formal operational: can reason, abstract, and carry independent thought.

–Piaget

A widely used classification system for the cognitive domain has the following hierarchy

1. Knowledge: recall of facts
2. Comprehension: ability to translate, use equations in problems
3. Application: concept application, problem solving when equation is not given.
4. Analysis: distinguish relevant from irrelevant facts.
5. Synthesis: assemblage into new forms, plan design.
6. Evaluation: judging the value of observations.

The last three are usually concerned with college teaching.

–Bloom

Good instructional objectives contain three elements:

- the behavior to be demonstrated,
- the conditions for performance, and
- the performance criteria.

–Mager

The cumulative learning model suggests a hierarchy of learning development:

1. Signal learning: terminology
2. Chain learning: sequence responses
3. Multiple discrimination: ability to distinguish
4. Concept formation: generalization
5. Principle formation: ability to relate concepts

Signal learning is the lowest level and principle formation requires familiarity with all the levels.

–Gagne

Only 25% of college freshmen can function at the formal operational level and a full 50% are able to function only at the concrete operational level. Education can lead to improvement in formal thinking.

–McKinnon and Renner

Students can learn to function at the formal operational level if given extensive experience with concrete props which model the abstract concept.

–Herron

Only 58% of college students and 47% of high school students have an abstract concept of volume.

–Elkinel

Learning occurs from the near to the far; from what is close to personal experience to what is farther removed.

–Herron

As people get older, they become more heterogeneous.

–Hodgkinson

Studying and Learning

Student self-concept is a key ingredient in achievement.

–Purkey

The more meaningful the association, the better the learning:

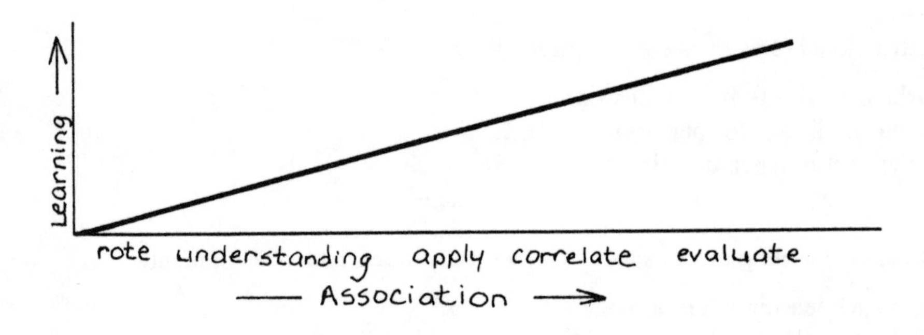

–Taylor

Most learning takes place outside the classroom.

Sixty percent of college students spend eight or more hours weekly studying.

–Mc Cormack

It takes about two hours of studying per week for every credit hour taken in order to earn an average grade.

SAT scores have been declining for the last twenty years.

–Associated Press

Statistics

Visual capacity, including musical and rhyming patterns, is far more efficient than verbal memory capacity. 85% of what we comprehend and remember is learned through the eyes, 11% through the ears and 3-4% through taste, touch and smell.

–Montgomery

The average person remembers only 10% of everything that he reads. However, one can dramatically increase the learning process to 45% by reading and hearing, and to 85% by actually doing.

–Haroldsen

The average student remembers 40% of the material for up to 15 minutes after lecture, and 20% is retained for 30 minutes.

–Hodgkinson

The amount a person learns is related to social class, race, sex (women are verbal, men are quantitative), urban/rural setting, region (SE has lower IQ than NE), birth order (oldest knows more), family size, infant nutrition, amount of activity shared with parents, TV (scores are increased for youngsters, but decreased for teens) and age (slight decrease for ages 30-50).

–Hodgkinson

Age, sex, politics or religion of either student or instructor have no bearing on student learning, whereas student study, teacher experience, and class attendance do.

–McGee

Students with class attendance of 79% or less earn a grade in the low "C" range; those who attendance is 90% or better score above a "B" average.

–Walsh

Twenty minutes of pre-guessing prior to a one-hour class produces 1.75 times as much learning.

–Taylor

The Learning Environment

Learning is the responsibility of each person. The teacher is the enabler as lecturer (to give information), as discussion leader (to guide exchange of views), or as practitioner (to be a model). Learning is a combination of experience and conceptualization and is at its best when free and open relationships exist in the group and members can analyze and receive response.

–Hertzler

In math and science learning the learners construct understanding, and understanding something is to know relationships, and all learning depends on prior knowledge.

–Resnick

True learning means to gather, then apply facts:

Gather facts				*Apply facts*
Study		Know		Learn
"What?"	⟶	"How?"	⟶	"Because"

Consider the example of smoking. A person gathers facts on what the effects of smoking are. The facts lead the person to know how smoking affects the health. Learning has taken place when the person stops smoking.

There are four personality types with opposite learning preferences:

	vs.	
1. Extrovert	vs.	Introvert
• likes group learning		• works alone
• does trial and error		• likes lectures
2. Sensing	vs.	Intuition
• likes direct experience		• constructs concept before application
• likes audio visuals		• prefers open-ended instruction
3. Thinking	vs.	Feeling
• learns independently		• needs harmony
• prefers logic		• likes democratic atmosphere
4. Judging	vs.	Perceiving
• needs order		• likes autonomy
• likes goals		• dislikes organization

–Myers-Briggs

In learning the packaging of the material is less important than what goes inside the package.

–Herron

Activities that assist students in placing information into some meaningful context lead to more learning and greater retention.

–Herron

Things that are taught are usually learned better than things that aren't.

–Herron

Practice is important in learning only if the learner sees results and gets feedback.

–McKeachie

Learning is more efficient when frequent, unambiguous feedback is given.

–Herron

Learning Tips

The secret to outstanding success is drive and determination, not natural talent.

–Bloom

Environment serves as a memory cue. Students can recall material easily if they are tested in the room in which it was originally learned, or if they visualize the room before taking the exam. The technique is most helpful for essay exams, but is virtually useless for multiple choice exams.

–Smith

Things that dissatisfy students (teaching style, temperature, noise) are not the opposites of those that satisfy (satisfaction of insight, of accomplishment).

–Davies

To be helpful, notetaking has to be individualized.

–Davies

The practice to develop principles rather than a pattern is more important than repetition alone.

–Wolfle

Students using an algorithm solve class problems better than those who are taught the principles. However, the latter do better when the problems are varied out-of-class situations.

–Mayer

Simple repetition has little effect on retention, however, review of ideas in a meaningful context does enhance memory.

–Herron

Difficulties of performance are reduced through repetitions of performance:

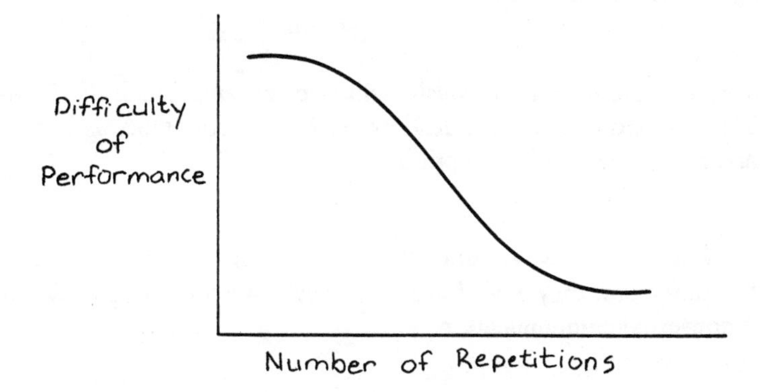

Teaching

The Statistics

The average faculty member in the humanities and social sciences has 1.5 publications in his first five years at the institution compared to 2.3 for the faculty member in the natural sciences. During their 15th to 20th year the publication total is 1.6 for faculty in all divisions. Thereafter the totals decline rapidly.

–Centra

55% of meaning is conveyed through body language; 38% through tone of voice and 7% through actual words.

Pauses between teacher's questions and student replies average 1.25 seconds, while the time lapse between student replies and subsequent teacher input is only 0.55 seconds. Student comments will nearly double if a three second pause is allowed prior to teacher input.

–Swift

Americans fear public speaking more than they fear heights, bugs or death.

–The Book of Lists

Teacher Characteristics

Twenty-one studies on the qualities of effective teaching include these ten most frequently named characteristics:

- communication skills
- favorable attitude toward students
- knowledge of subject
- good organization
- enthusiasm
- fairness
- willingness to experiment
- flexibility
- encouragement of students to think for themselves
- interesting lecturer–good speaker.

–Centra

Distinguished teachers are enthusiastic, businesslike, clear and precise. They initiate, seek clarification, explain, respond to student questions, introduce spontaneous humor, use gestures (looking at students) and allow free interruption.

–Ebro

Top teachers display inventiveness, spontaneity, perceptiveness, high aims, persistence, confidence and intuitive judgment; they work hard, have high expectations, use classroom time efficiently and rely on nonverbal communication.

–Rubin

The best student teachers are not the ones who score highest on standardized tests or have the top grade point averages, but rather those with self-assured, outgoing personalities.

–Weddle

Students, faculty and alumni all agree that of 60 teacher behaviors. most important are being well prepared and exhibiting interest. Least important are being neatly dressed or having irritating personal mannerisms.

–Centra

The Teaching Process

Most teachers tend to teach as they were taught.

The form of instruction makes no difference in the amount of student learning.

–Dubin and Taveggia

Most teacher input in the classroom is relatively unrelated to student out-take. Students teach themselves.

–McGee

Books convey information most efficiently, but lectures are more effective. Discussions are most effective in integrating ideas.

–McKeachie

Objectives are helpful to students as much as they are to the instructor. Objectives should state what the student should be able to do, the conditions for performance, and the criteria used for evaluation.

–Davies, et al.

Research is not convincing whether learning objectives help the student learn, however, students do need to know what is expected of them.

–Herron

There are four interrelated teaching/learning variables: the course content, the teaching approach, the student characteristics as learners, and the learning outcomes.

–Knefelkamp

There are four levels of teaching:

1. Intentional disinviting
2. Unintentional disinviting
3. Unintentional inviting
4. Intentional inviting

–Purkey

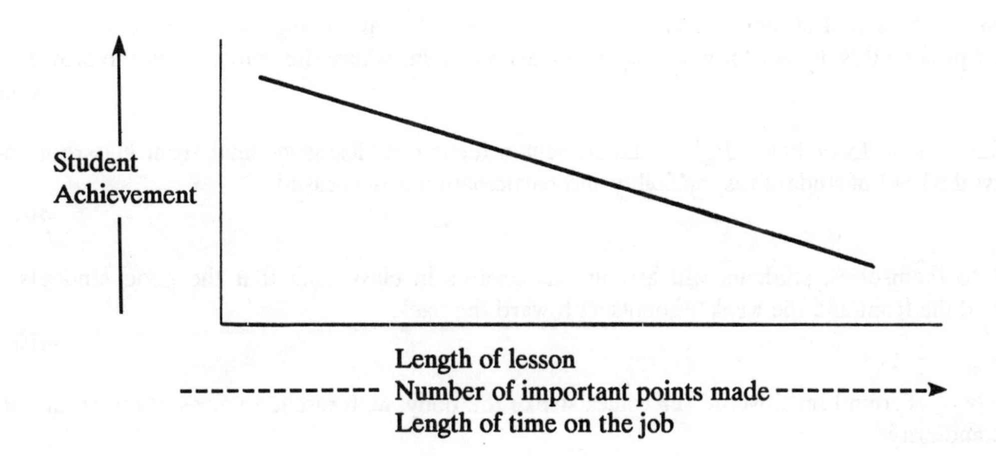

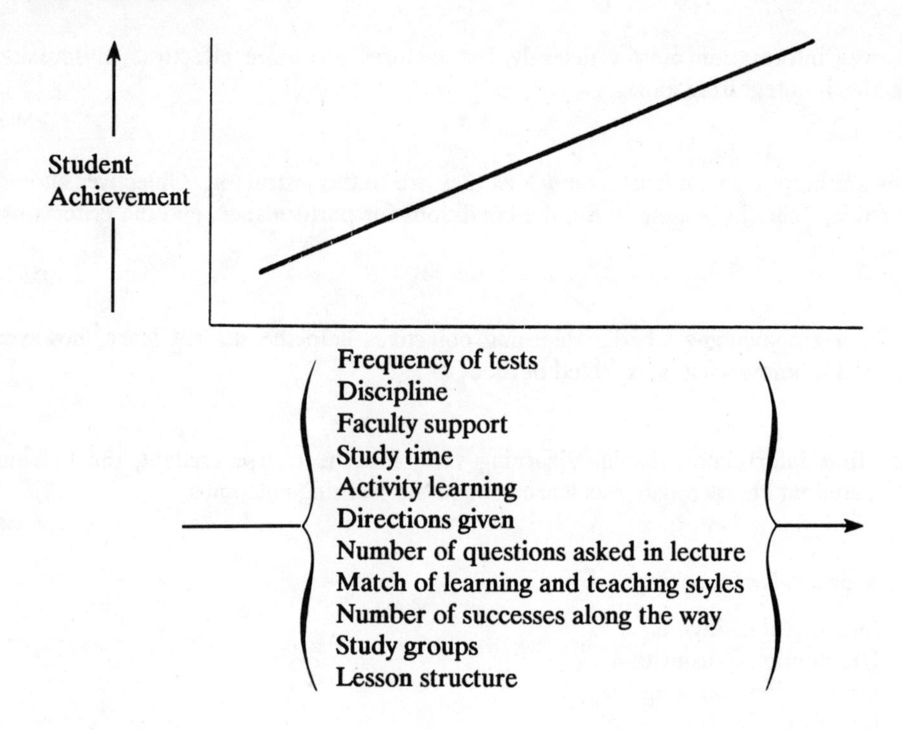

Tips for Teaching

Most teachers and students prefer sitting in a semicircular arrangement facing the teacher. Least preferred is the cluster grouping, or an arrangement where the teacher is in the crowd.

–Feitler

Sitting in row 15 or beyond gives the student a feeling of disengagement from classroom activity; the level of student responsibility and participation is decreased.

–Herron

Left to themselves, students will arrange themselves in class such that the good students sit toward the front and the weak students sit toward the back.

–Herron

The body is sound sensitive: lower voices stroke the body; high pitched voices often irritate and lack authority.

–Darnoff

An appropriate speaking rate is about 170 words/minute. A faster rate becomes impersonal.

–Darnoff

A nervous, squeaky voice can be overcome by reading aloud angry poetry just before giving the talk. Shaky knees can be overcome by brisk walking and light exercises.

–Darnoff

Women speakers have special trouble with negative body language since traditionally feminine behavior often conveys insecurity. Try to stand firmly on both feet.

–Darnoff

Eye contact held for less than three seconds simply acknowledges the presence of another person. However, if contact is maintained for more than three seconds it says "I am interested in you."

–Fast

After five minutes of lecture stop for two minutes allowing student to compare notes. Research shows this technique to help in learning.

–Herron

It is a proven fact that students are better able to retain something that has been reinforced through the use of audio visual aids. Such aids provide one-on-one attention to each student, show things, events and phenomena not possible to see otherwise.

–Davies

Program instruction is at least as effective as teaching the same content by an experienced teacher, and it takes as little as two thirds the time for average students to cover the same ground.

–Beard

The use of concrete props, such as physical models, to grasp abstract concepts can double test performance.

–Talley

A teacher's question should be followed by a three second waiting period allowing class response. By waiting, all class members are given a chance to think.

–Project TEACH

After a point, adding information does little more than cause confusion and decreases what is actually learned.

–Katz

Students are aided in problem solving when the instructor habitually "thinks aloud" as he is solving problems.

–Whimbey

The least effective strategy for teaching students to solve problems is working examples for the learners.

–Katona

Expository presentations are best for difficult materials, while discovery learning is preferable when relationships are more transparent.

–Herron

Two closely related ideas are easily confused if taught simultaneously. However, when one is already well known, the other is quickly learned by contrasting the new with the old.

–Herron

It is best to teach the idea first, and name it afterwards.

–Arons

The best way to organize information after it is understood is not always the best way to organize it for teaching.

–Herron

Questions interspersed in the text are very effective in guiding instruction.

–Rothkopf and Frase

Verbal analogies are of little help to the student who still operates on the concrete operational level.

–Herron

Sharing incidents from one's own life–if on target–will help the bright students.

–Feldhusen

When teachers have positive views of student's abilities, students are likely to respond in positive ways.

–Purkey

Learning cannot be observed directly, but only from the type of behavior a student exhibits. Behavior is controlled by its consequences. Behavior can be changed (best by immediate action) through positive or negative reinforcement and by extinction (preferable approach) or punishment or discouragement.

–Skinner

No learning takes place during the last five minutes of class. Inject an anecdote.

–Eble

Faculty Development–Self-Improvement

While teaching does not seem to make much difference to student outcome, teachers do.

–McGee

At 40% of all institutions, very few faculty have ever been involved in development activities.

–Centra

A survey using a random sample of 4,300 faculty members from 158 institutions showed these statistics:

29% have never published an article;
59% have never written or edited a book or monograph;

60% have never published more than four articles;
60% have never received research funding.

–Centra

A major problem with high school chemistry is the [lack of] preparation of teachers, rather than the text they use.

–Herron

Teachers with highest self evaluations make the largest adjustments as a result of student ratings.

–Centra

A "teacher helping teacher" approach shows significant effectiveness in faculty development.

–Hoyt

Motivating

Given a choice, people avoid unpleasant experiences and are attracted to pleasant ones.

–Herron

Errors erode motivation, but performance leads to effort.

–Davies

Member risk taking is a function of the extent to which a member feels secure within the group; feelings of security are a function of the extent to which the member perceives him/her self as having power.

–Cartwright

The average human machine does not wear out–it rusts out.

–Hodgkinson

Children stop doing puzzles if rewards are given.

–McKeachie

In a required course, at least 5% of the students dislike the teacher–no matter what is done.

–Jegen

People who don't want to learn usually don't; people who do want to learn, may.

–Herron

People learn more when they are interested. And people are more interested if the environment is pleasant and things make sense.

–Herron

Fear of failure is a major reason that students do not take elective science courses.

–Lawrence and Sprung

Students who fear failure, improve in performance when they are helped to attribute failure to lack of effort rather than lack of ability.

–Heckhausen

When placed in a stimulating environment with enthusiastic people, some who think they don't want to learn change their minds.

–Herron

Students perform at highest levels under teachers with enthusiasm.

It is relatively easy to teach teachers to be enthusiastic.

–Collins

There is a significant increase in teacher enthusiasm as a result of enthusiasm minicourses.

–Collins

Written teacher comments on student assignments have profound positive influence on students.

–Feldhusen

Asking questions of students stimulates more interest than simply presenting facts.

–Berlyne

Losers . . .

- let it happen
- step on flowers in search of weeds
- always have excuses
- identify with problems
- say "It's not my fault"
- see a problem for every answer
- are down on life and high on drugs
- fix the blame
- see the thunderstorm and icy streets
- say "Why don't they do something"
- are failure conscious
- do it to others and split
- say "It might be possible, but it's too difficult"

Winners . . .

- make it happen
- pull up weeds while enjoying the fragrance of the flowers
- always have an idea
- identify with solutions
- say "Let me help you"
- see an answer for every problem
- are down on drugs and high on life
- fix the situation
- see rainbows and ice skates
- say "This is what I'm going to do"
- are success conscious
- do it for others
- say "It might be difficult, but it's always possible"

–Waitley

Testing

It has been shown that objective and multiple choice questions separate equally well between good and poor students. The only difference is that the average may be higher for multiple choice tests.

The longer a multiple choice or true/false option, the likelier that it is the correct option.

When in doubt, students will usually pick the middle option ("c" or "3") on a multiple choice examination.

Students who change their first answer on a multiple choice examination, will usually go from a right to a wrong answer.

The best review for a test is not to go over the material, but rather to do problems and take practice tests.

–Feldhusen

Evaluating

Most teachers tend to give themselves better ratings than their students do.

–Centra

Colleagues rate each other very kindly (94% are judged as excellent or good). Peer evaluations are not reliable and may be helpful only for instructional suggestions.

–Centra

Instructors who rate themselves more favorably than their students are more likely to improve their teaching performance as a result of student rating feedback than those who rate themselves less favorably than their students.

–Levinson & Menges

Fewer than 15% of students rate instructors as below average. This gives many faculty an inflated view of their teaching.

–Centra

First and last day course evaluations correlate very highly (0.6-0.7).

–Feldhusen

Student evaluations of a course are essentially the same whether taken immediately after a course or years later.

–Feldhusen

Students and alumni agree substantially on faculty evaluation.

–Centra

Nationwide classroom teaching is the major criteria used for evaluating total faculty performance at the post-secondary level.

–Centra

Systematic student ratings are of prime importance for evaluating teaching performance.

–Centra

Nearly 70% of a national sample of faculty agree that "faculty promotions should be based in part on formal student evaluations of their teaching."

–Centra

Ratings from five or more courses in which some 15 students responded will result in a "dependable" assessment of teaching effectiveness.

–Centra

There is essentially no relationship between student rating of teacher effectiveness and student GPA, sex, college year, academic ability and age. However, class size, subject matter, type of course requirement and expected grade do affect the ratings.

–Centra

There is no significant difference in student ratings according to the teacher's rank and sex. However, there is a positive relationship between student ratings and faculty teaching load and research productivity.

–Centra

Evaluation of faculty must go hand in hand with student evaluation.

–McKeachie

The following is the order of emphasis used by students in teacher ratings:

1. caring about students;
2. skills in communication;
3. knowledge of subject.

Students are capable of considerable objectivity in course and instructor evaluation.

–Crittenden

Student ratings of teacher effectiveness are slightly higher in the humanities than in the social and natural sciences.

–Centra

Students give slightly higher ratings in their major or elective courses than in required courses.

–Centra

Students may give their instructors lower ratings if their actual grades are lower than those they had expected.

–Centra

Students in classes of less than 15 rate their instructor most highly. Students in classes of 35-100 students give their instructors the lowest ratings.

–Centra

Higher ratings are given by students who learn more.

–Centra

Many studies indicate great improvement in end-of-term student evaluations if mid-term evaluations are run.

–Centra

Student evaluations of instructors correlate very highly with student performance and are valid indicators of instruction.

–Frey

If students think their values are congruent with those of the professor, they will rate him highly.

–Feldhusen

Some Publications on Teaching

Bloom, B. S., Taxonomy of Educational Objectives: The Cognitive Domain, David McKay (1956)
Centra, John A., Determining Faculty Effectiveness, Jossey-Bass Publishers (1979)
Davies, Ivor, Instructional Technique, McGraw-Hill (1981)
Eble, Kenneth E., Professors as Teachers, Jossey-Bass Publishers (1973)
Eble, Kenneth E., The Aims of College Teaching, Jossey-Bass Publishers (1983)
Ericksen, Stanford C., The Essence of Good Teaching, Jossey-Bass Publishers (1984)
Feldhusen, J. F., The Three-stage Model of Course Design, Educational Technology Publications (1980)
Fink, L. Dee, The First Year of College Teaching, Jossey-Bass Publishers (1984)
Fuhrmann, Barbara S. and Grasha, Anthony F., A Practical Handbook for College Teachers, Little, Brown and Company (1983)
Gagne, R. M., The Condition of Learning, 2nd ed., Holt, Rinehart and Winston (1970)
Gross, Francis L., Jr., Passages in Teaching, Philosophical Library (1982)
Herron, J. Dudley, "Piaget in the Classroom," J. Chem. Educ., 55, 165 (1978)
Highet, Gilbert, The Art of Teaching, Vintage Books (1950)
Hodgkinson, Harold L., All One System: Demographics of Education-Kindergarten through Graduate School, Washington, D.C., Institute for Educational Leadership (1985)
Hoover, Kenneth H., College Teaching Today, Allyn and Bacon, Inc. (1980)
Levinson, Daniel J., The Seasons of a Man's Life, Alfred A. Knopf (1978)
Levinson, Judith L. and Menges, Robert J., Improving College Teaching: A Critical Review of Research, Northwestern University (1979)
Lowman, Joseph, Mastering the Techniques of Teaching, Jossey-Bass Publishers (1984)
Mager, R. F., Preparing Instructional Objectives, Pitman Learning, Inc. (1984)
McKeachie, Wilbert J., Teaching Tips, a Guidebook for the Beginning College Teacher, D. C. Heath and Company (1978)
Morris, William H., ed., Effective College Teaching, American Council on Education (1970)
Myers, Isabel Briggs, Gifts Differing, Palo Alto: Consulting Psychologists Press (1980)
Peck, M. Scott, The Road Less Traveled, Simon & Schuster (1978)
Piaget, J., "Development and Learning," J. Res. Sci. Teach., 2(3): 176-186 (1964)
Piaget, J. and Inhelder, B., The Psychology of the Child, Basic Books, New York (1969)
Purkey, William W., Inviting School Success, Wadsworth Publishing Co. (1978)
Schwartz, David J., The Magic of Thinking Big, Simon & Schuster (1981)
Scott, John Anthony, Teaching for a Change, Bantam Books (1972)
Sheehy, Gail, Passages, Predictable Crises of Adult Life, Bantam Books (1981)
Skinner, B. F., "The Science of Learning and the Art of Teaching," Harvard Educational Review, 24, 86-97 (1954)
Taylor, T. E., Unlimited Learning, Information Unlimited, Box 361, Bryan, TX 77802 (1983)
VanTil, William, The Making of a Modern Educator, Bobbs-Merrill Company, Inc. (1961)
Waitley, Denis, Seeds of Greatness, The Ten Best-kept Secrets of Total Success, Fleming H. Revell Company (1983)
White, Emerson, E. The Art of Teaching, American Book Co. (1901)

Chapter 5
Be Creative

To know is nothing at all; to imagine is everything.
Anatole France

Creativity is to the mind what exercise is to the body. Our brain cells are the muscles of the mind. I cannot perform great physical feats without proper exercise. This is true of the mind. Without practice it dulls. One of the most complete and well-rounded exercises for the mind is to engage it in creative work.

There is evidence that creative work, research, is required for good teaching, and that teaching improves research. In other words, the two are synergistically related; one feeds the other. Dr. Lillis, dean of the School of Business at the University of Colorado, has studied the role of research and teaching and found "a very high correlation between those who are high-quality researchers and those who are high–quality teachers." Creativity and teaching are checks and balances to each other; creativity challenges the use of new ideas, whereas teaching controls narrow specialization. Teaching forces one to go back to basics, whereas creativity explores new horizons.

How does one become creative? One of the best ways is to stay mentally very busy. Students often experience their best academic performance during the busiest semesters. If ideas are the architects of the mind, then the mind should be put in high gear and always kept busy. Amazingly, ideas are produced even after we go to sleep. The subconscious processes whatever it is fed in the hours before retiring. During one particularly busy two-day period, I found myself involved in staff meetings, end-of-semester grading, preparation for an international trip, listening to the problems of several students, preparing several hundred small potted plants to be handed out to each of my students, and talking to some students who just wanted to visit. In the midst of all of this, I was notified that some paperwork needed to be done for an additional visa for the trip. This required several hours of unexpected time. During the night an idea struck as to how to show my appreciation to the staff who had helped so valiantly during the semester and especially during the hectic last days. So I quickly organized a luncheon. I have found that extra efforts will be returned in ever so much more abundant ways.

One can stay mentally busy when less active. This may mean reading, doing puzzles, doodling, or drinking coffee. My list of "Symphony Thoughts" is often a long, sometimes useful, listing of ideas that come to mind while enjoying good music. The hours at a concert are an excellent time to explore multiple options to a problem. It is a good time to make courageous resolutions to get out of a rut and broaden the panoramic view. Pen, paper, and datebook are always with me.

I like to be in the company of stimulating friends who widen or even explode my horizons. Asking and listening allows for more learning than does talking. Contacts with such friends make it apparent that anything the human mind can conceive, man can achieve.

Meetings, conferences, and workshops not only allow me to acquire new knowledge or confirm information, but they also are wonderful opportunities to gather seeds for the mind. Letting the mind wonder and wander freely often will lead to most surprising results. Jotting these ideas down, testing them against the criticism of others, trying them, refining them, will eventually lead to implementation.

> **TO DISCOVER YOUR OWN CREATIVITY**
>
> 1. Trust your instincts and intuition.
> 2. Recognize that there is more mental power available to you than you are currently using.
> 3. What you are is more the result of environment than genetics.
> 4. Rational thinking can kill good ideas. Free the mind to wander.
> 5. Know your "inner rhythms" to find the best times when your mental processes are at their peak.
>
> –Ned Herrmann
> WHOLE BRAIN CORP.
>
> USA TODAY, October 29, 1985

Albert Einstein once said that "the value of an education is not the learning of many facts, but the training of the mind to think something that cannot be learned from textbooks." Certainly, if that is the road for our students–it behooves us to lead by example. Not only is it our God-given right to be creative, but as teachers it is our responsibility as well.

As a chemist I have had the opportunity to lead research groups in the discovery of dozens of new chemicals and the analysis of their properties. These are published in professional books and journals. Here, however, are presented some of the creations particularly applicable to educators.

Readiness Profile

Just as a speaker inquires ahead of time about his audience, so a teacher wants to know about his class. One of the first questions a teacher has about a new class concerns the preparedness of the students. Are they ready for this class? What will permit them to succeed, what might cause failure? How must I, the teacher, adjust to meet the student's level?

Previous performance is often checked and used as a guide to predict future performance. Grades and reports from previous work and comments from previous teachers are possible guides. Because algebra and mathematics are so basic to all science courses, we have often used performance in these fields as indicative of likely success in, say, chemistry. However, often we found this, by itself, to be an unreliable indicator. Many personal variables are as important as mental dexterity.

Counseling thousands of students has made it clear that mathematical thinking ability is but one facet of student life that will measure performance. After much thought and inquiry, it became clear that there really are four areas contributing to success or failure in a student's performance.

The first of these is the student's educational background. Proper previous training is a must for many courses. The rigor of studying mathematics or foreign languages trains the mind to be flexible.

A second area is that of the student's personal affairs. If the home life is in disarray, there just is not much of a chance for successful studies. The number of hours on a job, the habits of entertainment, family obligations–all influence studies.

The next indicator is self-motivation. One's outlook on life, attitude, extent of self-discipline, and perceived reason for studying–all say something about how one will approach studying.

Finally, the maturity of the thinking level is important. If the student continues to operate strictly on the concrete level and is virtually unable to reason in abstract terms, there very likely will be upcoming problems.

Given the above truths, I have developed a set of forty questions, ten in each of the four areas, to gauge the readiness of my students. Table 5.1 gives the currently used items. The Educational Background is measured in questions 1, 2, 3, 13, 14, 21, 22, 29, 33, and 37. Personal Affairs are tested in questions 4, 7, 10, 15, 18, 23, 26, 30, 34, and 38; whereas the level of Motivation is looked for in questions 5, 8, 11, 16, 19, 24, 27, 31, 35, and 40. Finally, an attempt is made to understand the student's Thinking Level through questions 6, 9, 12, 17, 20, 25, 28, 32, 36, and 39.

The students are given this questionnaire soon after the second week of the term, with the announcement that "this is not a test or quiz, but rather a counseling tool meant to help us help you." The answer sheet is simple and easy, providing plenty of space for scratch work. Twenty minutes working time is allowed.

Four sets of keys are prepared, one for each of the areas being tested. Some questions may have numerous acceptable answers, others may have only one true or acceptable answer. Thus, question 2 we find acceptable for our course if b, c, d, or e are checked; however, in question 37 only b is true. The key for one of the areas is laid over the Answer Sheet (see Figure 5.1); the number of acceptable answers out of ten possible is counted; and the result drawn as an arrow on the appropriate gauge, as shown in Figure 5.2. The overall readiness is simply a composite of the four areas.

While this tool is an interesting and powerful predictor of grade, it should be used strictly as a counseling tool. It can be considered valid only at the time it was taken. It may remain valid if nothing in the student's life changes, and it becomes invalid as soon as something does change.

A quick glance at the Readiness Profile tells me where I can make suggestions to the student without having to ask forty questions. If the Educational Background gauge shows a low reading, I may suggest reviews, or other coursework; if Personal Affairs is low, I may suggest reducing the hours on the job or the course load, or I may not be able to change much, but at least I can be understanding; if Motivation is low, I have a challenge on my hands; and finally if the Thinking Level is low it may mean that the student operates on the concrete and must be helped through examples, graphs, and diagrams.

Table 5.1 C 101 readiness profile.

This questionnaire is meant to help us help you. It is therfore important that you answer all questions in complete honesty. Don't try to "psych out" the answers. All results will be held in strictest confidence.

- **Be sure you answer *all* question.**
- **Pick only *one* answer to each question.**
- **Answer by *filling* in the circles on the separate ANSWER SHEET.**

1. How much math did you take in high school?

   a none
   b. 1 class
   c. 2 classes
   d. 3 classes
   e. 4 or more classes

2. How much college math have you taken or are you now taking?

   a. none
   b. 1 class
   c. 2 classes
   d. 3 classes
   e. 4 or more classes

3. On the average your math grades generally were about

   a. does not apply–never taken
   b. C or less
   c. B
   d. A

4. About how many hours per week do you spend on the job?

   a. I have no job
   b. 14 hrs. or less
   c. 15 to 19 hrs.
   d. 20 to 24 hrs.
   e. 25 or more hrs.

5. On a scale of *a* to *e* define your general attitude:

depressed	positive
unsure	confident
dragging	eager

   a b c d e

6. Think of a ball of clay with a certain volume. The ball is now rolled into a sausage shape. The volume of the sausage shape is

   a. the larger
   b. the smaller
   c. the same
   d. depends on the length

7. When do you usually study?

   a. early morning
   b. between classes
   c. after work
   d. evenings
   e. weekends

8. Which statement do you agree with most? Life is . . .

   a. a series of obstacles
   b. a lot of work
   c. a big challenge
   d. an exciting venture

9. You are in the grocerey store to buy Pork and Beans. Brand A offers a 32-oz can for 89¢, while brand B offers three 15-oz cans for $1.29. Which is the cheaper buy?

   a. brand A
   b. brand B
   c. both cost the same

Table 5.1 Continued

10. As far as your college work is concerned, do you receive support and encouragement from home?

    a. yes b. no

11. On a scale of *a* to *e* define your level of self–discipline.

no self–discipline			very self–disciplined	
a	b	c	d	e

12. Insert the missing number in the sequence: 2 5 8 11 __?__

    a. 12 c 14
    b. 13 d. 15

13. Of the subjects chemistry, physics, astronomy, and geology, how many semesters total have you taken (include high school and college)?

    a. none c. 2
    b. 1 d. 3
    e. 4 or more

14. Your average grade in the above subjects usually was about

    a. does not apply–never taken
    b. C or less
    c. B
    d. A

15. Are you responsible for children or other members of your household?

    a. yes b. no

16. In the last year or so, how many books have you read whch are not related to class work?

    a. none d. 4 to 5
    b. one e. 6 or more
    c. 2 to 3

17. Insert the number missing from the brackets:

347	(418)	489
643	( )	721

    a. 650 c. 702
    b. 682 d. 714

18. Where do you study most of the time

    a. table in my room
    b. on the bed
    c. dining room or kitchen
    d. library

19. While studying, most of my time is devoted to

    a. reviewing notes
    b. outlining
    c. reading
    d. rewriting
    e. doing problems

20. Consider the following four animals and four names: cat, dog, goat, horse; Angel, Beauty, King, Rover. Which name goes with which animal? You know that
    –King is smaller than dog or Rover
    –horse is younger that Angel
    –Beauty is oldest and is good friend of dog.
    Match the correct animal with its name.

    a. the goat's name is Beauty
    b. the dog's name is Rover
    c. the horse's name is King
    d. the cat's name is Angel

Table 5.1 Continued

21. How many semesters of foreign languages have you taken (include high school and college)?

    a. none
    b. 1
    c 2
    d. 3
    e. 4 or more

22. Your average grade generally received in foreign languages was about

    a. does not apply–never taken
    b. C or less
    c. B
    d. A

23. Do you have to work in order to be able to go to school?

    a. yes
    b. no

24. Think about your study pattern and answer one of the following.
    I study . . .

    a. some
    b. whenever there is time
    c. a lot before exams
    d. on a set schedule

25. Enterprise: tripe, peer, rite, rent, print, pair, rips.
    Which is the odd-man-out?

    a. tripe
    b. rite
    c. print
    d. pair

26. Think about your leisure time. About how much time per week is devoted to socializing, dating, TV, movies, play, etc.?

    a. 4 hrs. or less
    b. 5-6 hours
    c. 7-9 hours
    d. 10-12 hours
    e. 13 or more hours

27. Why are you in college? (Choose one):

    a. parent encouragement
    b. employer encouragement
    c. need credits for a degree
    d. I want to

28. Which does not belong:

    New York, London, Paris, Tokyo

    a. New York
    b. London
    c. Paris
    d. Tokyo

29. How much studying did you do in high school?

    a. less than 5 hrs./week
    b. 5-9 hrs./week
    c. 10-14 hrs./week
    d. 15 or more hrs./week

30. On a scale of *a* to *e* describe your relationship with those with whom you live.

    stressful — happy
    anxious — harmonious
    impossible — peaceful

    a b c d e

31. Do you have definite, detailed goals which are checked periodically?

    a. yes
    b. no

32. A 250-g rock is crushed and treated to remove all the iron. After all the iron is taken out the rock residue weighs 200 grams. What is the percent of iron?

    a. 12.5%
    b. 20.0%
    c. 25.0%
    d. 80.0%

Table 5.1 Continued

33. Your GPA (based on 4.0 = perfect) is closest to

    a. 2
    b. 2.5
    c. 3
    d. 3.5
    e. 4

34. How many credit hours are you taking?

    a. less than 6
    b. 6–11
    c. 12–15
    d. 16 or more

35. What are your true feelings about taking chemistry?

    a. would never take it if I didn't have to
    b. would prefer taking something else
    c. it may be tough going, but I'm ready to make a go of it
    d. it is a challenging adventure
    e. I chose to take it

36. It is possible to predict temperature by adding 40 to the number of chirps the snowy tree cricket produces in 15 seconds. What is the temperature, if a chirp count was 120 per minute?

    a. 30
    b. 55
    c. 70
    d. 80

37. Given: 3 - x = 5, what is x?

    a. -3
    b. -2
    c. 0
    d. 3
    e. 5

38. In your opinion, do you eat,drink, smoke, or sleep too much?

    a. yes
    b. no

39. A box contains 18 donuts. At first sampling a third of them is eaten. An hour later, a third of the remainder is eaten. How many donuts are left?

    a. 4
    b. 6
    c. 8
    d. 12

Fill in the weekly schedude below using the week just past for a guide. It may be difficult to put down exact activities for all slots because schedules are at times unpredictable. But try to pick an average response and fill in all blanks:

TIME	MONDAY	TUESDAY	WEDNESDAY	THURSDAY	FRIDAY	SATURDAY	SUNDAY
6-7am							
7-8							
5-9							
9-10							
[illegible]							
[illegible]							
[illegible]							
[illegible]							
[illegible]							
[illegible]							
[illegible]							
[illegible]							
[illegible]							
[illegible]							
[illegible]							

Table 5.1 Continued

40. Based on the above schedule, what is your study time for chemistry?

    a. up to 5 hours per week
    b. 6 to 10 hours
    c. 11 to 14 hours
    d. 15 hours or more

Your Name ______________________

Name ______________

ANSWER SHEET Section ______________

	a	*b*	*c*	*d*	*e*		*a*	*b*	*c*	*d*	*e*		*a*	*b*	*c*	*d*	*e*		*a*	*b*	*c*	*d*	*e*
1.	0	0	0	0	0	11.	0	0	0	0	0	21.	0	0	0	0	0	31.	0	0	0	0	0
2.	0	0	0	0	0	12.	0	0	0	0	0	22.	0	0	0	0	0	32.	0	0	0	0	0
3.	0	0	0	0	0	13.	0	0	0	0	0	23.	0	0	0	0	0	33.	0	0	0	0	0
4.	0	0	0	0	0	14.	0	0	0	0	0	24.	0	0	0	0	0	34.	0	0	0	0	0
5.	0	0	0	0	0	15.	0	0	0	0	0	25.	0	0	0	0	0	35.	0	0	0	0	0
6.	0	0	0	0	0	16.	0	0	0	0	0	26.	0	0	0	0	0	36.	0	0	0	0	0
7.	0	0	0	0	0	17.	0	0	0	0	0	27.	0	0	0	0	0	37.	0	0	0	0	0
8.	0	0	0	0	0	18.	0	0	0	0	0	28.	0	0	0	0	0	38.	0	0	0	0	0
9.	0	0	0	0	0	19.	0	0	0	0	0	29.	0	0	0	0	0	39.	0	0	0	0	0
10.	0	0	0	0	0	20.	0	0	0	0	0	30.	0	0	0	0	0	40.	0	0	0	0	0

Scratch Work Here

Figure 5.1 Readiness profile answer sheet.

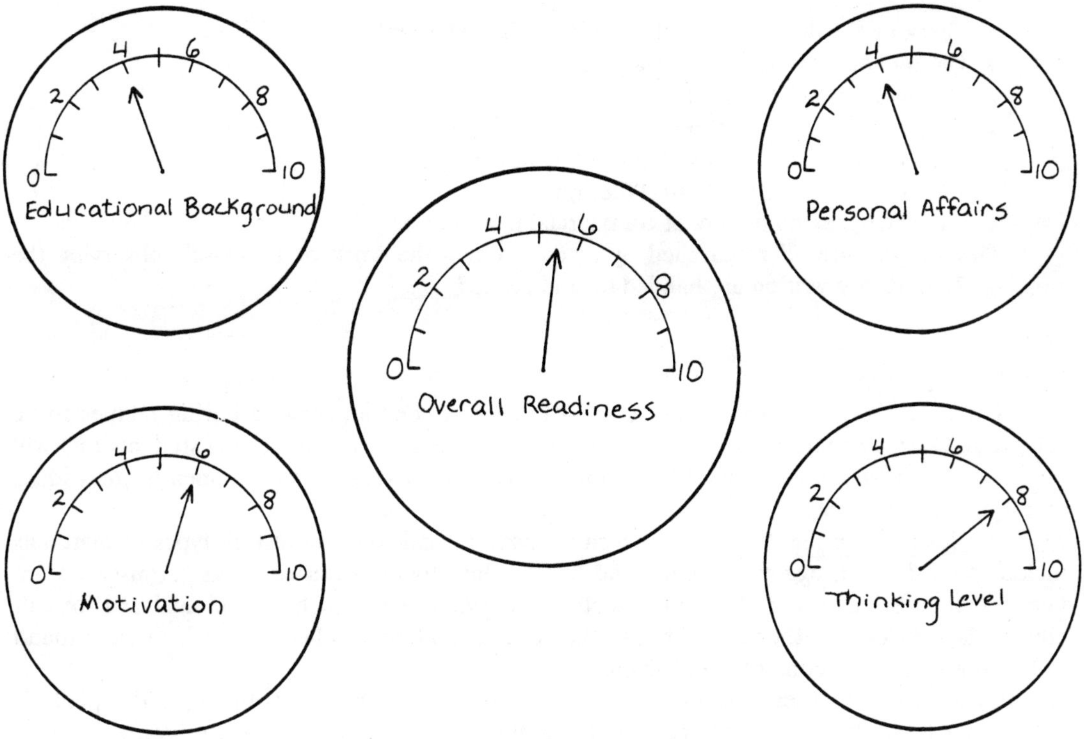

Figure 5.2 Readiness profile gauges.

Speed-Chem

Some students come to a course with excellent background training, good study skills, high level of intelligence, motivation and self-discipline. Some of these students will find the normal class pace much too slow and would prefer an intensive, but shorter, period of study. Speed-Chem allows this to be possible.

If qualified, students are invited to sign up for the program. The requirements include a self-designed plan of studies, a weekly session with me to check progress, and maintaining a high grade in the course. All work is precisely the same as for the rest of the class, except that it is performed at a faster pace. Speed-Chem students are good candidates for peer tutors.

Experiences Unlimited

Just as there are students who prefer a faster pace, so there are students who prefer exploring the unknown by working semi-independently. Students enrolled in this option are given special topics in lieu of regularly scheduled assignments. The work is handled as independent study or, at times, even borders on research experiences. Typical are the substitution of a laboratory experiment for a special study, or a paper in lieu of an exam. The following is a list of some topics explored by students in the past.

- Checking the degree to which clothing is fire retardant.
- The role of radioactive material in cancer treatment.
- The functioning of a dialysis machine.
- Design and operation of batteries.
- Analysis of ink solvents used in printing newspaper.
- The use of gas laws in physical therapy.
- A typical research project at commercial laboratories.

These topics are all researched by actually doing the work or by closely observing the process. Reports are written up, handed in, and graded.

New Experiments

Laboratory experiments can be fun and instructive, or they may be boring recipes to be followed. Over the years it has been my attempt to create experiments for my students that will be relevant, fun, and instructive. To do so means constantly keeping an eye open for new ideas and listening to students.

For instance, in the experiment which analyzes for calcium, we test all types of materials including hard water, egg shells, milk, and bone. One student even received permission from her mother to bring in one of her baby teeth to be ground up, dissolved, and analyzed for calcium. The results were then compared to the calcium content in adult teeth, which were found to have lower calcium content than baby teeth.

Of considerable interest is atmospheric pollution. One factor contributing to this plight is sulfur in coal. So, an experiment analyzing for sulfur in different coals is quite relevant.

Similarly, the tar content in cigarettes is easily measured and a health lesson hopefully learned.

When studying osmosis, everyday experiences are brought in. Thus, the students learn why carrots stay fresh in water, but go limp in dry environments; why raisins grow a lump when placed in water, but not when placed in sugar water; why blood cells shrink in salt water, but swell and burst in natural water. The function of naturally occurring semipermeable membranes is explained via osmosis of the carefully exposed skin of an egg and the marvelous mimicking that takes place through the use of synthetic semipermeable membranes.

In similar fashion, many other studies are carried out, such as chloride analysis in waters, phosphates in detergents, caffeine in tea, cholesterol in gallstones, and lactose in powdered milk. Special studies include the decomposition of household peroxide, which depends on temperature, catalysts (such as proteins in blood), and concentration, the making of soap, aspirin, and perfumes, all done by understanding the chemistries involved. We even attempt to understand why some flowers and leaves change color, by using them as indicators in acid/base reactions.

All these efforts have but one goal: to capture the student's interest and imagination by tying into an existing experience and exploiting the natural curiosity of the human mind. I keep a small "black box" on my desk as a reminder to avoid what is often called "black box experiments," where the student simply follows a written procedure, gets good results, and may finish the work without really knowing what went on. It is my purpose to train students who can think, not technicians who can insert a sample into an instrument ("black box") for analysis and get good results without understanding the chemistry.

Demonstrations

These are quick experiments done for the students by the instructor. Demonstrations are very powerful teaching tools, useful in any field (for instance, role playing in nonscience fields). Certainly they are entertaining, but they are much more than that. They graphically illustrate a principle; they provide a change of pace, giving the mind a break from lecture; they reduce an abstract idea into a concrete example; but most importantly, they allow me to not just talk about chemistry, but to be a practicing chemist.

As with the development of experiments, here too I must be on the lookout at all times. Glancing through journals and books often will spark an idea; lecturing and desperately wishing for a demonstration may force the mind to search; or watching life on the street may provide the right catalyst.

When adding an acid to a base, it is found that at first the acidity changes very little, then suddenly, as the neutral point is approached, it changes dramatically fast and repeats the same in reverse for the acid side. That is an abstract concept, and I searched for a proper demonstration for a long time, when suddenly, while driving down a street, I saw a rotating store sign. As it was turning, the lettering was visible for a relatively long time, but when the end began pointing toward me, the lettering very quickly disappeared, and suddenly the advertising on the opposite side appeared. The idea clicked; the demonstration was developed, used in my class, and later published in a professional journal.

How does one show to a large class that the mixing of two chemicals produces heat or coldness? Again, some ideas struck and demonstrations were developed: iodine is observed subliming from a hot test-tube surface, and a cork freezes instantly to a beaker.

How does one teach students that it is much more efficient to clean out glassware (or pots and pans for that matter) with several small portions of water, rather than one larger portion? After solving the mathematics involved, a simple demonstration was developed which we use every term to teach students to be both more efficient and frugal with expensive solvents such as distilled water. All ideas have been refereed by peers and are published.

When consulting in developing countries, I find institutions constantly faced with the lack of funds and supplies for even basic teaching equipment. Resourcefulness is indeed a virtue, and for teachers in such settings the need becomes the mother of invention. In Indonesia we were able to develop a very simple apparatus to allow the students to observe the change in gas volume as the pressure changes, something which prior to this time had only been studied on the blackboard. At a university in Lima, Peru, there was some interest in a gas chromatograph, an instrument costing thousands of dollars. We were able to construct one for the few dollars, using an old oven, some copper tubing, a few fittings, and an existing detector device.

Formula Slide Rule

Beginning students in chemistry must learn the formulas for many molecules. To aid in the process, we developed a device which has the capability of giving both names and formulas for 1,643 inorganic chemicals, as well as those for many organic chemicals.

Yellow Sheets

Throughout my teaching career I have collected anecdotes, cartoons, stories, jokes, definitions, books, and devices, which in some fun and humorous way, illustrate science and the life of scientists. These are used during lectures as quick breaks to relieve the mind for a minute to cement a point through an interesting anecdote. My students know that when a yellow sheet appears, a short rest is coming. The entire collection is published separately.

Set-a-Goal Plate

Figure 1.7 shows the design of a license plate which was created as a tangible motivational item to be given to students as a special award.

The above are some examples of efforts on behalf of my students. There are many, many others which are specific to the courses I teach, such as analogies, tape/slide series, transparencies, films, computer programs (which take about one hundred working hours to produce one usable hour of lesson), a periodic table with actual samples of many elements, a periodic table made from styrofoam balls showing relative sizes, and many original handouts. I find that the student's positive responses to good teaching devices is the best fuel to energize my creativity.

What follows are some ideas particularly helpful to me as a teacher and some which hopefully are helpful to the wider community of colleagues.

Day vs. Night Students: Relative Performance*

We had noticed for some time that students in day classes may show performance differences as compared to night students. While we had no proof, we suspected that the night students outperformed the day students. With the opportunity of a large sampling and carefully controlled parameters, we undertook to investigate whether there is indeed a pedagogically significant difference in performance between day and night students.

Study Design

We chose to investigate a freshman course which I taught for three successive semesters for a day and a night section with a combined enrollment approaching one thousand students. The parameters were well controlled. Both day and night sections were taught by the same professor using precisely the same course objectives, classroom methods, and course materials. The homework assignments, the laboratory experiments, and the final examination were exactly alike. Two sets of similar tests were prepared and then randomly assigned to the day and night sections. The same set of teaching assistants was used for both sections. Although the total weekly lecture time was the same, the day sections met for three fifty-minute lectures per week, whereas the night students met twice each week for a seventy-five minute lecture and a ten-minute break.

Findings

Table 5.2 and the bar graph in Figure 5.3 give the data for our findings. Because there were more day students than night students, all averages reported are weighted averages. The

*This study was conducted with the assistance of Starla J. Glick.

		Number of Students	Average Age	Percent Male	Percent Female	Class Standing	Percent Allied Health	Percent Undecided Major	Percent With-drawals	Final Grade
Fall '81	Day	290	22.53	30	70	1.62	61 *	13 *	24	1.76
	Night	112	26.88	32	68	2.60	37 #	24 #	23	2.57
Spring '82	Day	158	22.56	34	66	1.85	43	22	20	1.82
	Night	70	30.03	53	47	2.74	20	27	31	2.25
Spring '83	Day	199	22.71	38	62	1.77	36	25	18	2.18
	Night	66	26.05	33	67	1.97	44	28	15	2.60
Overall	Day	647	22.59	33	67	1.72	48	20	21	1.90
	Night	248	27.55	38	62	2.47	33	26	23	2.49

* Based on 225 students

Based on 70 students

Table 5.2 Student data for day enrollees and night enrollees.

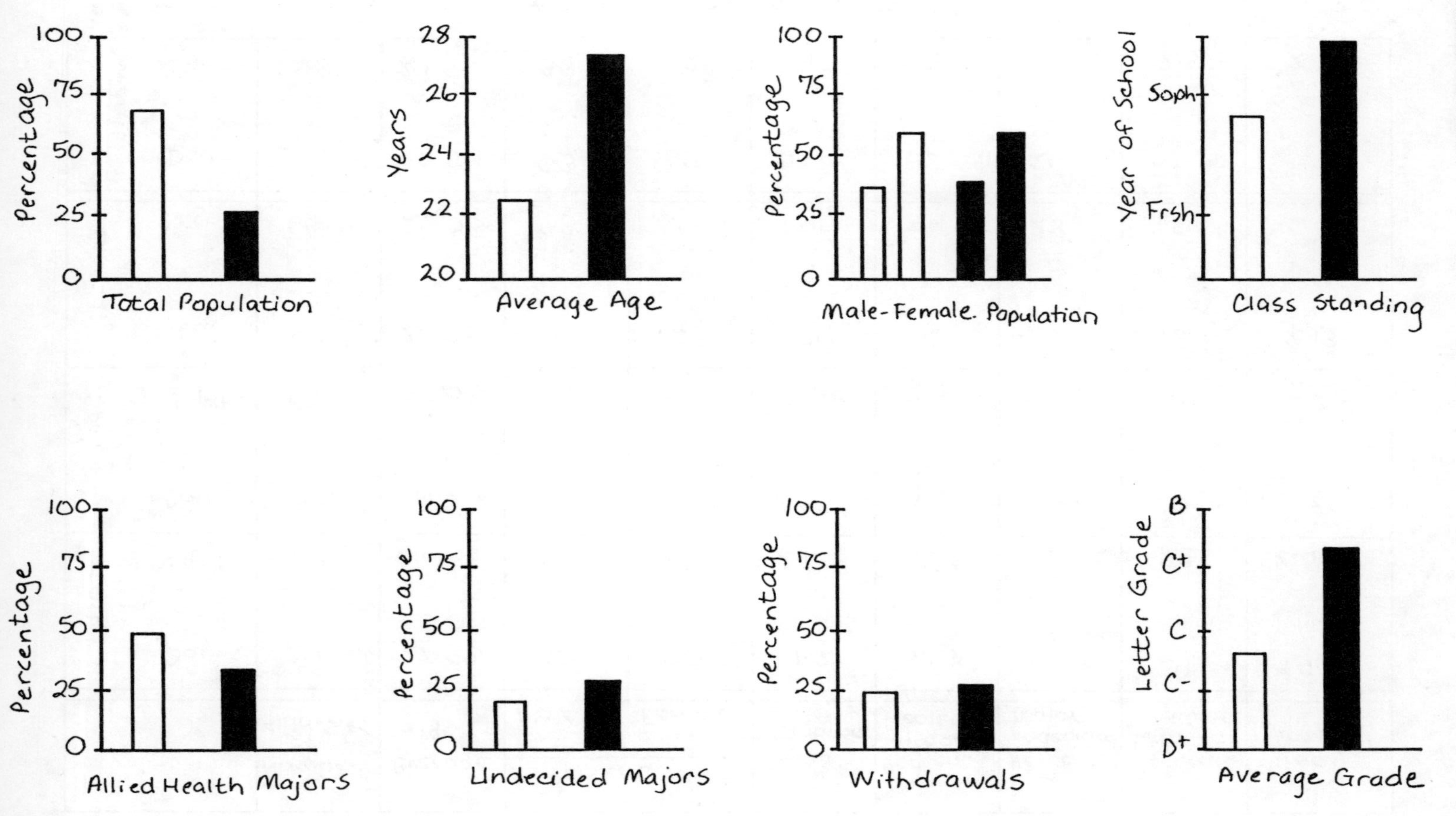

Figure 5.3 Student data for day *vs* night enrolles.

largest observed difference is the age; the night students are, on the average, about five years older than the day students. In both the day and the night sections, the female population is somewhat higher than the male population, likely reflecting the fact that the course is generally taken by students majoring in allied health fields. The night students are almost halfway through their sophomore year, whereas the day students are about two thirds into their freshman year.

Almost half of the day students are in allied health fields, but only a third of the night students claim this as their area. The night students show slightly more indecisiveness about a declared major, and also tend to withdraw from the class more frequently than their day counterparts. Lastly, the average final grade for the night student is between "B-" and "C+," while the day student average performance is just below "C."

Interpretation

It is clear from this study that the older night students outperform the younger day students. It has been shown that, in general, adult students do as well or better than their adolescent counterparts. Knox reports that mental capacity and performance, learning ability and social performance when plotted against age, show a dramatic rise to an age level in the late 20s, whereafter these functions either remain level or fall off slightly. Our data support this.

Much can be speculated about the reason older students outperform the younger ones. First, it is clear that the older students in our study are at the very peak of Knox's performance curves. Most probably a higher average age would have shown a somewhat lower performance. Along with the night student's more advanced biological maturity comes a maturing in seriousness, motivation, firmness of purpose, goal setting, and an acquired regimentation. A second factor is the feeling of a new experience. Night students come to class with a certain extra amount of excitement, in part because they have chosen the class for a definite purpose, and in part because this may be one of few classes taken in recent times. Day students have been in school all their lives and have become somewhat passive. Thirdly, there seems to be a selection factor which works in favor of the night students. For the majority of the day students, school is a way of life. The night students, on the other hand, are self-selected from a large community and are, therefore, highly motivated. Research by Cross supports the notion that young students have a subject-centered orientation to most learning, while adults tend to have a problem-centered orientation. Perhaps the adults wish to advance at their place of employment or address a particular need in their lives. While they know that education is the solution, the precise area of study is not necessarily clear. This may account for the larger number of the night students who are uncertain about their major. Finally, the night students do have more outside responsibility. They usually take a night course because they do have a full-time job and a family. They are "out in the world," are self-supporting, while their daytime counterparts live relatively sheltered lives as dependents. Generally, it appears then that night students send themselves, while day students are sent by their parents.

Tuesday Luncheons

Whether it is the carpenter, the lawyer, or the teacher, everyone wants to be good in his/her chosen field. Each has learned his skill in some formal or informal setting, but most college and university teachers have a unique problem in that they have never been taught how to teach. No education courses, no certificates, no practice teaching, only a possible stint as a teaching assistant in graduate school may have provided some experience. So it should be particularly important for these teachers to take every opportunity to learn, even if it is just learning from each other. I find college and university teachers surprisingly resistant to visiting each other's classes but have found informal get-togethers among them quite successful.

Tuesday luncheons provided such an experience. Our entire department agreed to meet on Tuesdays over lunch and have a brief presentation by a member, followed by an open discussion. One member of the group spoke on his most successful approach to class preparation; another spoke on teaching the very large classes; yet another spoke on teaching the very small (seminar type) classes; someone else devoted a discussion period to grading the research student. Still other topics included educational research, how to write a textbook, or how to teach a particularly difficult topic.

It is generally agreed that student evaluation of teaching, while very important, should be coupled with peer evaluation in order to be a complete assessment of someone's teaching. However, while student evaluation is fairly well established, peer evaluation has yet to come into equally wide usage. The lack of implementation is, in part, due to a feeling of invasion of privacy or even a sense of threat. Informal topical gatherings as described here provide the best chance for knowing each other's teaching methods.

Grade vs. the Time an Exam Is Handed In

We often wondered if the student who hands in an exam early in the period is a predictably better or poorer student than the one who hands the exam in late in the period. Over a period of several years, we carefully monitored the handing-in pattern of students in large classes (200+), and found that there seems to be no good indicator. Figure 5.4 shows typical results for one examination. If there is any pattern at all, it may be the very slightly lower average for those students handing the exam in early as compared to those who hand it in later, a slight rise peaking at about two thirds of the time period, followed by another drop. But overall, the curve is close to flat, indicating that all types of students hand in the exam throughout the period.

This tells us that some good students work quickly and with self-confidence, while other good students take the available time to review their work. Average and poor students fall into the same pattern; some give up early, others agonize for a long time.

Computer Grade Book

My students are given many, many chances to prove themselves: six exams, a final exam, twelve experiments, twelve quizzes, and fourteen homework sets. In addition, I allow the lowest exam, experiment, and quiz scores to be dropped. In a class of 250 students, this means some 12,500 entries into the gradebook for one semester–not only a huge task, but also one that can easily result in errors. Since the advent of personal computers and the introduction of spreadsheet programs, the task has been made much more pleasant.

The class is divided into laboratory sections of about thirty students each. Each section is placed on a separate disk with periodic backups for safety. On the spreadsheet the students' names are alphabetized in the first vertical column (see Figure 5.5), while the horizontal rows give the titles of each entry: Homework 1, 2, 3 . . .; Exam 1, 2, . . . etc. At the end of each of

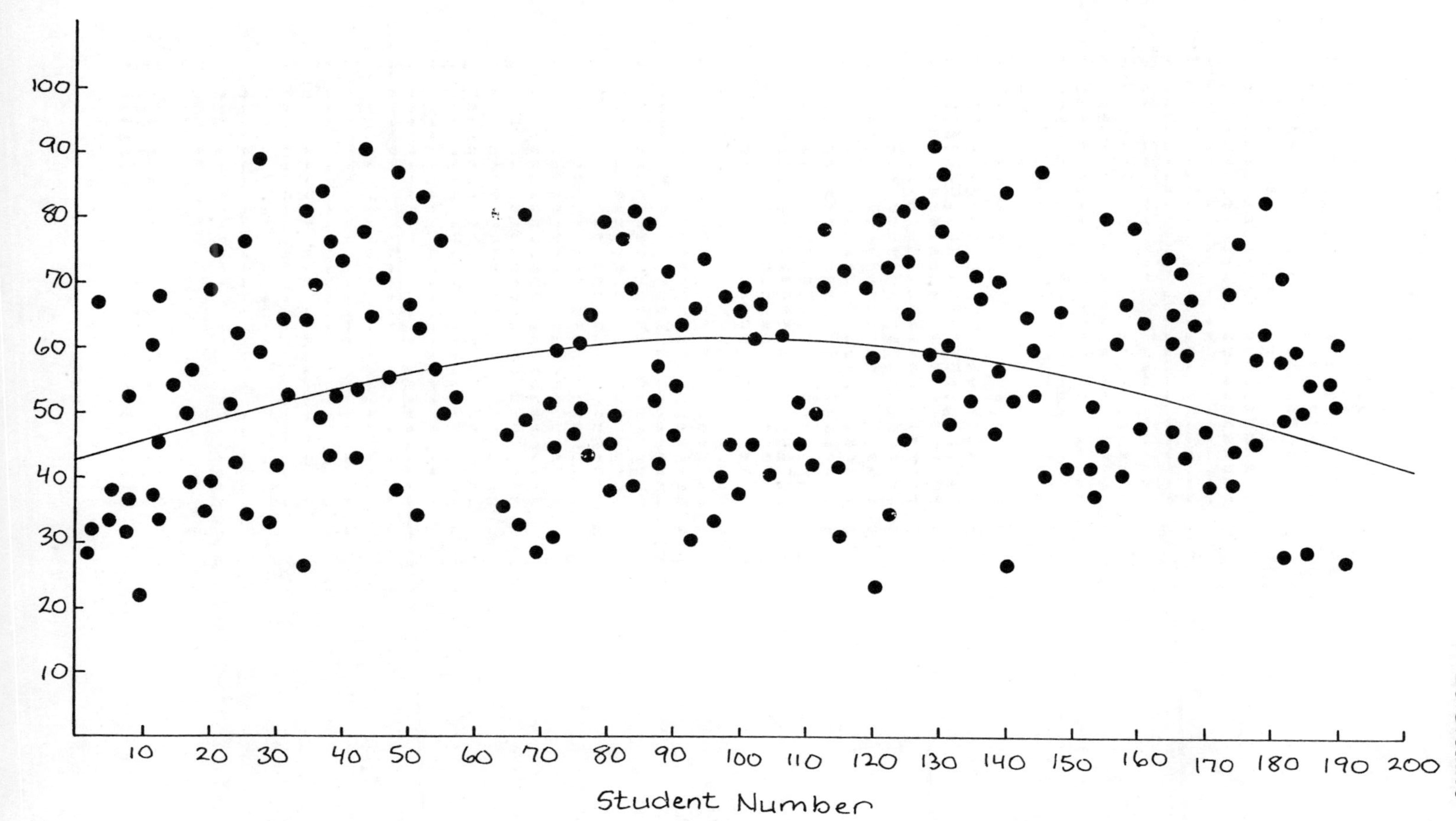

Figure 5.4 Test scores *vs* the order in which tests were handed in.

C101 FALL '86

A646/7 Marie - Friday

HOMEWORK

STUDENTS	SEP8	15	22	29	OCT6	13	20	27	NOV3	10	17	24	DEC1	8	15	TOT
POSSIBLE:	0	1	2	3	4	5	6	7	8	9	10	11	12	13	14	105
Barnhart	0	1	2	3	3	5	6	7	6	9	8	10	11	12	12	95
Beaman	0	1	2	3	3	4	4	6	7	7	7	9	11	11	10	85
Bedwell	0	1		2	2			5		3	8	8	9	3	5	46
Beidelman	0	1	2	3	4	5	6	5	8	9	9	10	9	11	10	92
Beiswanger	0				2											2
Cardwell	0	1	1	3	3	5	6	3	6	5	9	10	8	9	12	81
Carlton	0	1	1	2	4	5	6	6	8	6	7	9	10	5	10	80
Flynn	0		1	3	3		6	7	6	9	9	10	9	8	12	83
Gibson	0	1	1	2	3	5	4	4	4	3	8	8		4		47
Hall					3			7		6	5	8	10		10	49
Hillebrand	0	1	1	3	3	5	5	7		7	8	10	9	6	11	76
Howard	0	1	1	3	3	5	3	4	3	8	7	7	7	5	7	64
Hunt	0	1	1	3		4	5	7	3	8	7	9	9	11	12	80
Jessie	0	1	2	2	4	4	5	7	3	9	8	10	10	9	10	84
Jones		1	1	2	3	5	6	6	4	6	8	10	8	7	10	77
Kidwell	0	1	1	3	3	5	5	6	4	5	9	4		7	10	63
Litten	0	1	2	3	4	5	6	7	8	8	10	11	12	10	12	99
Luria	0	1	2	3	3	3	6	5	5	7	8	10	7	5	12	77
Mankus	0	1	2	3	4	5	6	7	7	7	8	9	12	9	12	92
Marchetti	0	1	1	3	3	5	6	7	8	5	10	8	10	8	10	85
O'Riley	0	1	1	2	3	5	6	7	6	9	10	8	11	8	10	87
Phillips	0	1	2	3	4	5	6	7	8	8	10	10	12	10	12	98
Quinley		1	2		4	5	6			3	10	10	11	8		60
Rodriguez	0	1	2	3	3	5	4	6	5	8	10	10	10	9	13	89
Roembke	0	1	1	3	3	4	6	7	8	9	10	9	10	11	12	94
Sell		1	2						5		8					16
Sterrett	0	1	1	3	4	5	6	7	7	8	9	11	12	9	10	93
Walden	0	1	2	3	3	5	6	7	7	9	9	10	10	9	11	92
Weidman	0	1	2	3	3	5	6	7	5	9	10	11	8	8	10	88
AVERAGES	0	1	1.5	2.8	3.2	4.8	5.5	6.2	5.9	7.0	8.5	9.2	9.8	8.2	11.	75.

LABS

STUDENTS	MEAS	OCC	OBS	SBI	TRE	AVO	PRO	SOL	KIN	ION	ACI	TOT	T-LO
POSSIBLE:	20	20	20	20	20	20	20	20	20	20	20	220	200
Barnhart	20	19	16	17	20	19	18	19	20	18	16	202	186
Beaman	12	19	20	19	20	20	18	19	20	18	16	201	189
Bedwell	17	15	13	8	18	10	8		14			103	103
Beidelman	20	17	18	16	20	19	19	19	17	18	18	201	185
Beiswanger	19	17	19	12	18		18	19	17	18	18	175	175
Cardwell	13	16	17	17	17	19	10	18	17	17	14	175	165
Carlton	17	17	19	19	16	19	16	17	14	15	19	188	174
Flynn	18	20		18	20	19	16	19	18	18	18	184	184
Gibson	16	16	15	14	20	17	14	16	18	14		160	160
Hall	16	18	16	15	20	18	17	20	18	18		176	176
Hillebrand	17	14	9			17	13	16	15			101	101
Howard	16	20	17	18	20	19	18	15	17	16	14	190	176
Hunt	17	18	18	18	18	19	17	19	19	15	18	196	181
Jessie	18	18	19	18	18	18	17	20	19	18	15	198	183
Jones	14	20	16	18	17	19	17	18	15	14	14	182	168
Kidwell	9	16	13	17	16	17	9	17	15	17	17	163	154
Litten	19	17	20	19	19	19	18	19	16	19	20	205	189
Luria	16	14	19	16	19	19	14	18	16	16	18	185	171
Mankus	18	19	18	16	18	19	17	19	18	19	14	195	181
Marchetti	17	16	17	19	20	19	18	17	15	19		177	177
O'Riley	15	17	19	16	20	18	15	18	17	15	15	185	170
Phillips	20	20	20	18	18	18	19	19	18	19	19	208	190
Quinley	16	20	17	19	20	19		18	17	15		161	161
Rodriguez	16	19	19	19	20	19	18	18	18	17	15	198	183
Roembke	17	20	18	18	20	19	18	19	18	19	17	203	186
Sell	13	13	5	10	17	18	15		16	11	8	126	126
Sterrett	17	18	17	18	18	19	18	16	19	18	16	194	178
Walden	18	19	18	20	20	18	17	17	19	19	16	201	185
Weidman	17	16	19	20	17	19	15		15	15	16	169	169
AVERAGES	16.	18.	17.	17.	19.	18.	16.	18.r		17.	16.	179	170

EXAMS / QUIZZES

STUDENTS	EXAMS I	II	III	IV	V	VI	TOT	T-LO	QUIZZES I	II	III	IV	V	VI	VII	VIII	IX	X	XI	TOT	T-LO	SUB TOT	FIN	GRAN TOT	COR TOT	% GRAD	PRED GRA
POSSIBLE:	100	100	100	100	100	100	600	500	10	10	10	10	10	10	10	10	10	10	10	110	100	905	100	1E3	T+56		
Barnhart	97	91	84	83	86	68	509	441	10	8	10	10	10	11	8	7	4	6	8	92	88	810	75	885	941	94	
Beaman	90	72	85	71	94	71	483	412	9	8	7	10	10	12	10	8	6	9	7	96	90	776	80	856	912	91	
Bedwell	52	46	50	34	64	32	278	246		6	4	5	5	5	10	5		5	5	50	50	445	40	485	541	54	
Beidelman	74	70	66	78	58	68	414	356	10	4	9	5	9	9	10	7	4	6	6	79	75	708	77	785	841	84	
Beiswanger	84	80		78	61	62	365	365		10	10	7	10		10	5	1	7	8	68	68	610	75	685	741	74	
Cardwell	65	57	80	58	61	68	389	332	8	7	6	8	9	7	10	6	5	7	8	81	76	654	60	714	770	77	
Carlton	81	67	68	66	53		335	335	8	8	7	9	5		10	9		7	7	70	70	659	57	716	772	77	
Flynn	84	80	80	85	81	65	475	410	7	4	8	10	9	11	10	7	8	10	8	92	88	765	68	833	889	88	
Gibson	58	76	55	66	75	65	395	340		4	4		5	3	10	5	2		3	36	36	583	77	660	716	71	
Hall	77	76	75	83	72	76	459	387		4	6		9	9	9	3		5	2	47	47	659	28	687	743	74	
Hillebrand	81	67	82	73	67	74	444	377	10	7	3	9	10	9	10	6	5	8	7	84	81	635	77	712	768	76	
Howard	81	67	75	59	58	56	396	340	8	7	10	10	9	11	10	4	6	8	6	89	85	665	67	732	788	78	
Hunt	71	50	77	63	44	44	349	305	6	5	3	8	9	6	8	4	3	4	4	60	57	623	47	670	726	72	
Jessie	97	83	91	68	75	79	493	425	10	7	4	10	9	10	10	7	8	8	10	93	89	781	83	864	920	92	
Jones	65	63	70	51	78	56	383	332	8	5	10	10	9	9	10	5	6	3	4	79	76	653	55	708	764	76	
Kidwell	35	43	59	63	36	50	286	251	7	4	5	5	10	4	8	3	3	6	4	59	56	524	47	571	627	62	
Litten	71	70	73	80	69	79	442	373	10	8	7	10		11	11	7	9	7	8	88	88	749	60	809	865	86	
Luria	65	70	68	66	67	38	374	336	7	9	7	5	6	9	8	7	5	9	8	80	75	659	58	717	773	77	
Mankus	87	93	75	73	75	74	477	404	10	9	10	8	9	12	10	7	6	7	4	92	88	765	87	852	908	90	
Marchetti	71	54	66	49	75	59	374	325	8	4	7	7	10	7	10	5	5	9	6	78	74	661	62	723	779	78	
O'Riley	68	63	86	56	58	76	407	351	9	7	9	10	10	8	10	6	6	7	8	90	84	692	60	752	808	80	
Phillips	94	89	87	93	94	76	533	457	10	9	10	10	10	10	10	7	8	10	8	102	95	840	85	925	981	98	
Quinley	77	74	82	75	72	71	451	380	7	7	9	7	9		9		4	8		60	60	661	62	723	779	78	
Rodriguez	77	83	70	49	42	71	392	350	8	9	10	10	5	4	10	8	3	3	8	78	75	697	52	749	805	80	
Roembke	84	76	65	71	78	76	450	385	9	5	8	10	9	9	10	5	8	8	8	89	84	749	55	804	860	86	
Sell	71	65	34	41	83	56	350	316	6	2	1	5		8	10	7		9	2	50	50	508	45	553	609	61	
Sterrett	81	87	89	78	78	71	484	413	9	7	10	10	7	11	10	7	7	10	8	96	89	773	75	848	904	90	
Walden	71	74	77	71	78	74	445	374	9	9	9	7	10	10	10	9	5	6	7	91	86	737	70	807	863	86	
Weidman	74	76	82	68	75	38	413	375	7	10	8	10	10	7	11	6	7	7	7	90	84	716	70	786	842	84	
AVERAGES	75.	71.	73.	67.	69.	64.	415	362	8.4	6.7	7.3	8.3	8.6	8.5	9.7	6.1	5.4	7.1	6.4	78.	75.	681	64.	745	801	80.	

COUNT: 29

Figure 5.5 Computer print-out of student records.

those segments a column is allowed for the "Total" and one for the "Total–Lowest Score." At the far right after all entries have been made, a column is made for the "Grand Total" and one for "Percentage." One row is set aside to indicate the total number of points possible for that work. Each row and column is provided with the appropriate formula, and the body of the spreadsheet is then set aside for entries of student work. At the end of the list of students, a row is set aside for vertical averages.

This method provides for totally accurate arithmetic; it allows for routine updates and quick corrections, for instant review of a student's standing, of average performance of the section in any one portion of the work, or the overall average performance. A printout allows for easy posting, instant survey of missing work or trends in student performance. Truly an amazing work saver!

Writing Better Multiple-choice Questions

Multiple-choice examinations are both a fact of life and, for many settings, a necessity. High enrollment classes, availability of computers, objective scoring, fast and accurate results, and the detailed statistics available make multiple-choice examinations attractive. The attractiveness is strengthened by the fact that, while there are pros and cons, there is no pedagogical difference between a multiple-choice and an essay examination. Furthermore, because of faster student response time, the multiple-choice examination allows for wide sampling of many topics. Here, then, are some guidelines that are worth keeping in mind when writing multiple-choice questions.

Layout

- Options should be labeled in the same manner as they are on the scoring sheet. Thus, if the latter uses a., b., c., and d., the same should be used on the examination.
- A test is easier to read if two columns are used per page, rather than writing across the entire page. The lines are shorter and the eye is not so easily confused. Newspapers use this approach.
- The same applies to the layout for the options. If very short answers (numbers) are given, it is better to use the setup:

  a. c.
  b. d.

  rather than the setup

  a. b. c. d.
- Attention should also be paid to the layout of the scoring sheet: are the question numbers written vertically or horizontally? Perhaps the above setup should be:

  a. b.
  c. d.
- Be sure that correct options are randomly distributed.

Content

- Distribute the questions so as to cover all stages of mental development (Bloom's taxonomy): recall and recognition, comprehension and interpretation, application and convergence, and induction and deduction.
- Write questions in topical order.
- Each test item should contain only one central idea.
- Guarantee, within reason, only one correct answer.
- There should be no superfluous information given.
- Avoid a question where the answer depends on the correct answer to the previous question.
- Avoid dating the question (i.e., In a recent article . . .)
- Avoid unintentional clues to the correct answer (i.e., use of "always," "never,").
- Avoid the use of double negatives (. . ."not incorrect . . .").
- Make sure that the stem and each option read as a complete and correct sentence.
- It is usually best if the question (both stem and alternative) are kept short.
- Questions should require less than a minute to respond. Student patience declines as the allowed time per question approaches a minute.
- At times it may be best to repeat a part of the stem with each alternative to clarify and emphasize the idea.
- Avoid "none of the above." If there is the slightest misinterpretation of an option, the student can (rightfully) mark "none of the above."
- The use of "all of the above" or "a. and b., but not c." is acceptable if used routinely and not just on questions where it does apply.
- Use four, rather than five alternatives. Modern testing agencies now use four alternatives because the discrimination provided is essentially the same. If, however, you like to use five alternatives, do so consistently.
- Numerical answers should be given in sequential order from smallest to largest or vice versa. Where appropriate, others should be listed alphabetically.
- All options must be plausible. There is no purpose in giving answers such as

  a. 5.4   c. 7.0
  b. 6.9   d. 100

  where option d. does not compare reasonably with the rest.
- Avoid true/false or yes/no type of questions in multiple-choice settings.
- Avoid grading: #right–1/4 # wrong. In checking with several university research centers, as well as the Educational Testing Service in Princeton, N.J., the consensus seems to be that the hoped for intent of avoiding guessing is not achieved at all. In fact, the use of penalties has been judged pedagogically unsound.

It is always a good idea to be aware of student testmanship. For some students, when in doubt means checking "c," because it may be statistically favored. It has also been found that some test writers will unconsciously make the correct answer the longest answer. This is done with the intention of being precise and complete.

Quintile Analysis

Quintile Analysis is a tool designed to quickly assess the quality of multiple-choice test items. To do this, the students taking a test are divided into performance groups, which are then plotted against the percentage of correct student responses within each group. In other words, the student's test scores are ranked from highest to lowest and the scores divided into five separate performance groups called quintiles. The first quintile includes the scores above the 80th percentile, the second quintile includes those students scoring between the 60th and the 80th percentile, and so on.

After the quintiles have been established, the percentage of students in the first quintile responding correctly to an item is found and plotted. The same is done for the percentage of students from the second quintile giving the correct response, and so on for each quintile. This is repeated for each question on the test. Figure 5-6 shows a typical plot.

The basis for analysis is the position and the slope of the "line" going through the points of the plot.

1. Discrimination is a common check for the soundness of a question. A line going from 25% correct response for the bottom quintile to 100% response for the top quintile would show maximum discrimination.

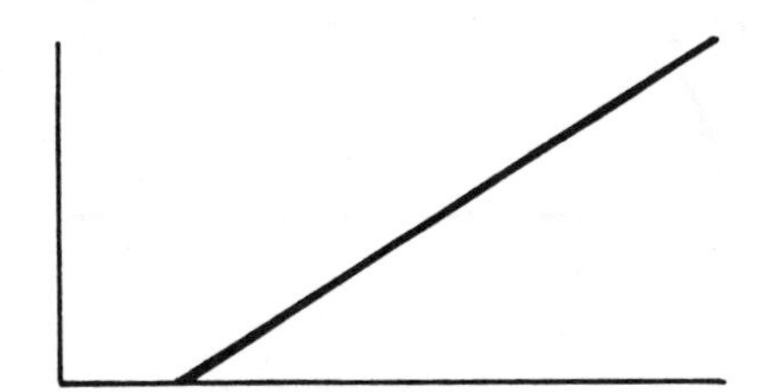

2. Mastery of a topic can be measured by the steepness of the line toward the 100% response point. The steeper the line, the more equal the mastery by all students, and the farther this steep line is to the right, the better the mastery.

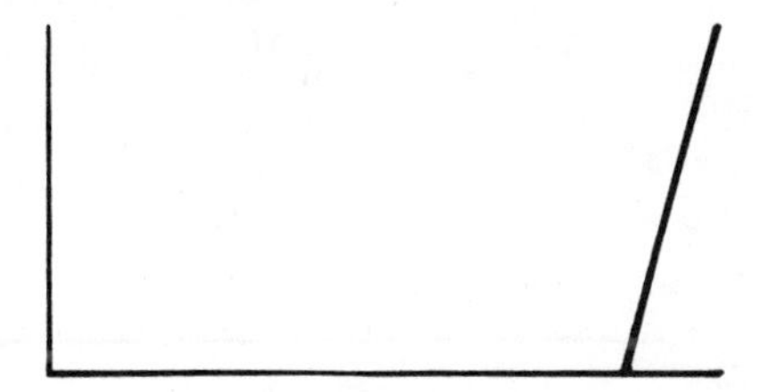

3. Difficulty of a question is also measured by two factors. First, the position of the base of the line. The more it moves to the left, the more difficult the item. Second, difficulty is measured by the slope of the line. The steeper the slope, the more difficult the item.

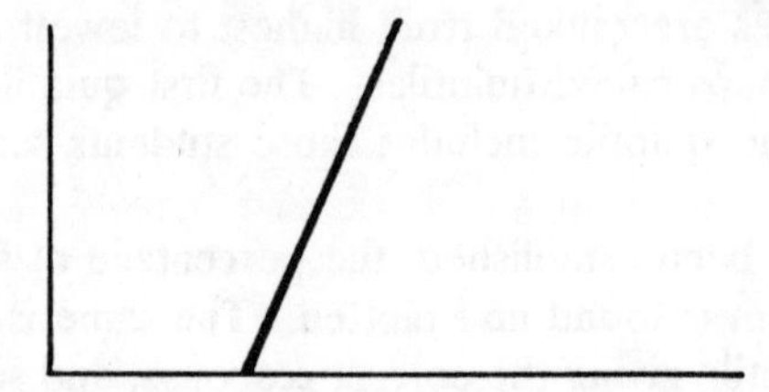

4. Derailer questions are those which mislead students. These would show a very steep slope starting below the 25% response (chance) level. If the slope should be negative (leaning to the left), the misleading is more severe for the top students than for the poor students.

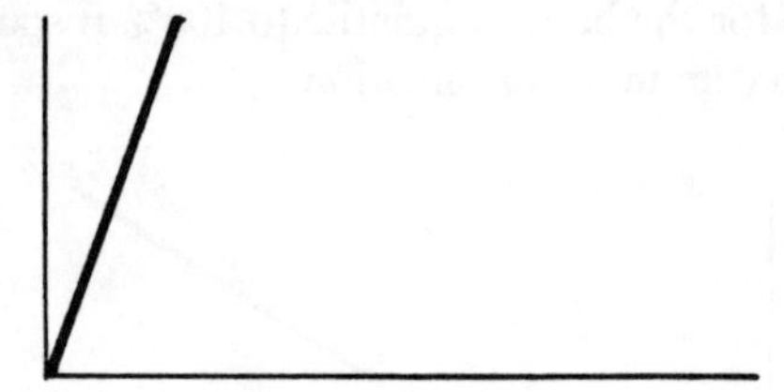

We use the quintile analysis on each and every examination given. Each question is carefully analyzed and, if need be, corrected for future use. Student concern about a question can

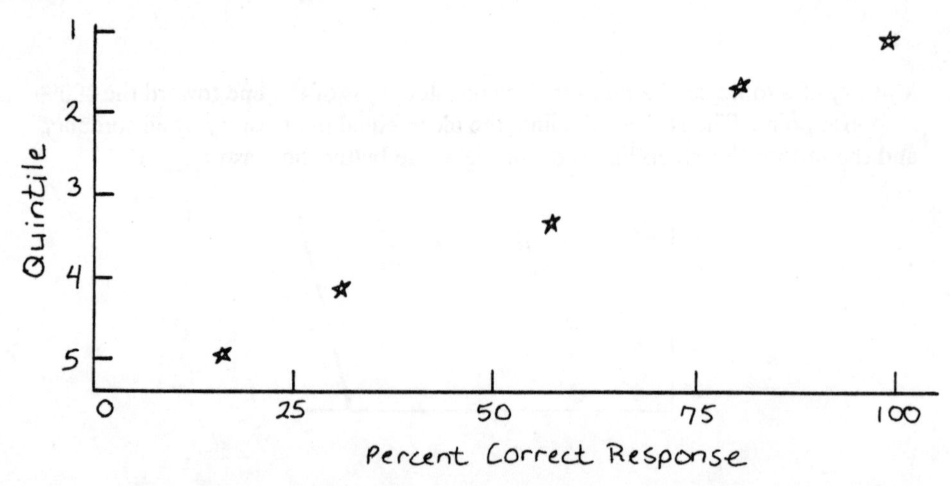

Figure 5.6 Plot of student quintiles *vs* percent correct response.

be checked quickly against the quintile plot. We have been able, through this method, to rewrite items, which when tested against new student groups, have then proven to be sound questions.

Team Teaching: Adjusting for Different Grading Patterns

There are many settings where several instructors have input on the final grade for a student. While the individual styles must be respected, the student's right to uniform grading is obvious.

Let us consider a class in which the final grade depends on many different portions which may be graded by different instructors. While these different portions can be term papers, quizzes, field trips, homework, etc., let's illustrate the approach using the portions from my experience:

5 Exams	500 points
Final Exam	100 points
Quizzes	100 points
Homework	100 points
Experiments	200 points

The exams are the same for everyone, are given simultaneously to the entire class, and are computer scored. The quizzes, on the other hand, are written, administered, and scored individually by each assistant for his section of perhaps thirty students. The homework (HW) and experiments, while the same for all sections, are also scored by the teaching assistants. Therefore, only the exams are truly uniform for all students, while the quizzes, experiments, and homework are subject to different grading styles.

In an attempt to overcome any differences in scoring, we use two approaches. First, during weekly staff meetings we discuss grading habits, use of partial credit, average grades for quizzes, homework, and experiments. This provides an overall perspective and helps to minimize scoring differences.

Second, we use a formula, first suggested by Raymond N. Keller of the University of Colorado, which takes the overall class performances as reference points. The Correction Factor is defined as:

$$\left(\begin{matrix}\text{Section Average}\\ \text{on all}\\ \text{Exams}\end{matrix} - \begin{matrix}\text{Class Average}\\ \text{on all}\\ \text{Exams}\end{matrix}\right) - \left(\begin{matrix}\text{Section Average}\\ \text{for}\\ \text{HW + Quiz + Exp}\end{matrix} - \begin{matrix}\text{Class Average}\\ \text{for all}\\ \text{HW + Quiz + Exp}\end{matrix}\right) =$$

$$\textbf{Difference A} \quad - \quad \textbf{Difference B}$$

Correction Factors are computed at the end of the term on the basis of all scores except the final exam. The formula uses performance on exams as an equalizer, a point for comparison. It assumes that if, for instance, a given section's exam average is above that for the entire class average, that section's HW + Quiz + Exp average should also be proportionately above that of the entire class. The following typical results are for a class with eight sections, with 24 to 35 students per section.

From the two Average columns in Table 5-3 the weighted Class Average on all exams is computed as 328, and that for the HW+Quiz+Exp is found to be 312. These values then allow the computation of the values for the Differences and the Correction Factors columns.

Section #4 has an exam average of 322, which is six points below the class average of 328 points. One would, therefore, expect this sections's HW+Quiz+Exp performance to also be six points below the class average of 312. In this one case this happens to be so, and the correction factor is zero.

Section #2 exam average is nine points above the class average (337 *vs.* 328), yet the teaching assistant graded strictly enough to cause the section to fall eight points below the class average for HW+Quiz+Exp (304 *vs.* 312). Therefore, 17 points should be added to each student's score in that section.

In section #7 the reverse holds: the section shows an exam performance of two points below the class average (326 *vs.* 328), yet the HW+Quiz+Exp scoring was 11 points above the 312 average (323 *vs.* 312). Therefore, 13 points are subtracted from each student's score in that section.

Table 5.3. Score data used to compute correction factors.

Section	Sect Avg on all Eams	Difference A	Sect Avg on HW+Quiz+Exp	Difference B	Corr Factor: A - B
1	320	-8	297	-15	7
2	337	9	304	-8	17
3	310	-18	306	-6	-12
4	322	-6	306	-6	0
5	358	30	333	21	9
6	336	8	319	7	1
7	326	-2	323	11	-13
8	319	-9	314	2	-11

When the differences A and B have the same sign, the section's standing relative to both class averages is the same, either above or below, and corrections are likely to be small. If A and B have opposite signs, corrections are likely to be larger.

Our corrections in recent years have never been more than 25 or 30 points out of 1000. The more communication there is among the staff during the term, the lower the correction will be. It is important to inform the students early in the term that "corrections will be made to adjust for different scoring patterns." But it is not useful (in fact it is a nightmare) to try to explain the formula used. If correction factors are published, it is psychologically wise to make the lowest negative factor a zero and adjust all others to positive numbers.

It should be noted that if a very good (or very poor) student finds himself in a very poor (or very good) section, he may be unduly penalized (or helped). Such a case must be considered on an individual basis.

The formula does not demand detailed statistical analysis, yet provides a very useful way to solve an often nagging problem of different scoring patterns.

As we think about new and creative ways to help the students and improve the efficiency of the things we do, it naturally follows that we will then also think about ways to help and encourage others to do likewise. Serving others gives ultimate satisfaction.

Lecture Exchange

While attending a concert given by our local symphony orchestra, a guest conductor was on the program, since the resident conductor was, in turn, guest conducting elsewhere. My thoughts about how this might be applied to the teaching field eventually led to Lecture Exchange, a nationwide program permitting faculty to be one-time guest lecturers. Tremendous benefit may be derived from lecturing elsewhere, and observing someone else lecturing on familiar topics. To implement the program, the idea was checked with key people in the profession, support was received, and proper announcements were distributed at national and regional meetings, as well as through direct mailings. Respondents from thirty-two states were listed alphabetically, giving lecture topics and special needs (audiovisual). The end of the booklet carried cross-references and a topical index. Made available to participants and others interested, the booklet and its program are self-run.

Figure 5.7 Reduced facsimile of lecture exchange booklet cover.

Symposia

One of the best ways to serve the local community is through campus or city-wide symposia. These may be of interest to just one discipline or have much wider appeal. It is interesting that funding always becomes available when good ideas are put forth. Here are a few examples.

As a way to thank and acknowledge the contribution of a retiring faculty member, I organized one such symposium, which had both general and professional interest. The community became involved through an evening banquet for friends and colleagues, and the mayor declared an "F. J. Welcher Day" for the city and personally congratulated the honoree. For the scientific day-long meeting, professional friends were invited from across the country to share their latest research.

While on sabbatical leave, I noticed another university paying special tribute to A. Einstein. The seed of an idea eventually grew into a week-long Einstein festival on my home campus involving many departments. The science departments held special displays on Einstein's contributions; the audiovisual department ran daily films; the publications department developed announcements including a beautiful, most sought-after poster for the event; the speech and drama department hosted a professional actor who presented a one-man show, "Einstein the Man"; and the local media honored the event with copious coverage.

There are many worthwhile workshops available which can be of great benefit to a school community. One such workshop on chemical demonstrations was organized in conjunction with the local section of the chemical society. Made available for any local college or high school teacher, the day-long affair featured the master lecturer Prof. Hubert Alyea, providing everyone with new ideas, materials prepared during the session, and a detailed book of suggestions was taken home. During the evening a public lecture was given to a standing-room-only audience.

For years I have attended professional meetings where educators speak about their teaching experience. During a time of reading and reflecting made possible by a Lilly Endowment fellowship, I explored the idea of inviting the nation's top chemical educators to our campus for a conference, not to talk about teaching, but to actually teach students. The lectures were to be given to scheduled undergraduate classes, on the topic due for that day, a topic which the regular professor would not repeat, and which the students would be held responsible for. All this would be done in the presence of conference participants.

Sixty persons from throughout the Midwest assembled to watch five top educators lecture, and later discuss their presentations. The event was judged novel and successful.

Science Enterprises, Inc.

Over the years we developed many interesting experiments which we distributed to our students for laboratory use. In an effort to improve the print quality of the collection, we searched for a publisher, but realized that the price would be prohibitive. After much checking and doublechecking, I started a corporation, obtained a bank loan, and published a professional book, *CHEMISTRY IN ACTION–Novel and Classical Approaches*. Students were able to use it at a much reduced cost. The manual was also used by a good number of other institutions across the nation and eventually was published by McGraw-Hill.

Always Search

Perhaps the best suggestion to keep creatively alive is to always search for ideas. Stimulation comes from scanning the literature, through correspondence, conferences, TV programs, talks with colleagues, etc. I do this constantly to update and add to the programs and projects discussed in this chapter. In addition, many other little things are put to good use.

Some years ago I received a note in the mail written on scratch paper. The back of the paper had an idea I use nearly every semester in my class to make the point that mine is a class where high premium is given to the thinking process. The problem stated simply: a student is given eight coins, one of which is counterfeit, and known to be slightly heavier than the others. The student is permitted only two weighings on a balance. How will he determine which is the bad coin?

At a conference someone used an example of a town which is served by two hospitals. In the larger hospital about 45 babies are born each day, and in the smaller one about 15 babies are born each day. The exact percentage of boys to girls varies from day to day. Over a period of a year, which hospital is most likely to record more days on which over sixty percent of the babies born are boys? What a lesson in statistics!

A teaching assistant discussed with me the idea of receiving teaching credit for his experience as an assistant. This was pursued with our education department and may eventually lead to a new opportunity for science teaching assistants.

A book on the beautiful Escher drawings came to my attention and provoked the possibility of using these to teach symmetry in chemistry.

The television special on The Search for Excellence gave me the idea of creating a class council. I have used a randomly chosen group of students from my class to serve as the "eyes and ears" of the class as a whole. They are the ones charged with the responsibility of letting me know what is wrong, what needs improvement, and what works well. They are the ones to whom students can pass ideas, suggestions, and complaints for possible action by me.

My filing cabinet has a section of folders for continuous collection. One of these folders holds ideas for analogies and stories to illustrate concepts and principles. Another folder collects suggestions for possible demonstrations, and one for "openers," the thought stimulators used during the first few minutes of class. Other folders collect colorful pictures for slides, drawings for transparencies, cartoons for inclusion on exams, and so on. Talks and workshops have special folders; one gathers references for a future talk on "Chemistry in the Bible," another assembles ideas for workshop exercises. Always search!

WHAT YOU CAN DO . . . .

1. Take time out at least once a week to browse in the professional literature.
2. Attend a conference at least twice a year.
3. Participate in workshops whenever possible.
4. Fill the mind with worthy challenges, especially before going to bed.
5. When an idea strikes, write it down and commit yourself to implementation. To encourage action, make yourself accountable by announcing your plan.
6. Engage your mind in doing hard tasks.
7. When in a passive role (taking in a concert, traveling, driving, etc.) allow the mind to free flow. Pursue the unconventional.
8. Be risky–take on a challenge!
9. By all means, seek chances to participate in brainstorming sessions, especially where no ideas are judged "wrong."
10. Speak up at meetings.
11. Affirm within yourself that creativity can be learned.
12. Remember, the best way to improve your own lot is to improve that of others.

Further Reading

Cross, K. Patricia, Adults as Learners, Jossey-Bass Publishers, San Francisco, 1981, p. 189.

Gaudet, Frederic J. and Martin, A. Herbert, "Some Factors Contributing to the Relative Success of Day and Evening Law School Students," Journal of Educational Research; 40:187-95; November, 1946.

Kidd, J. R., How Adults Learn, Second Edition, Association Press, New York, 1973, pp. 33-4.

Knox, Alan B., Adult Development and Learning, First Edition, Jossey-Bass, Inc., Publishers, San Francisco, 1977, pp. 414-9.

Schultz, Raymond E. and Ulmer, R. Curtis, "How Do Day and Evening Students Compare?" Junior College Journal; 37:34-6; September, 1966.

von Oech, Roger, A Kick In The Seat Of The Pants, Harper & Row, Publishers, New York, 1986.

PART III

IDEAS YOU CAN USE

Teach How to Study
Use of Gadgetry
Effective Administration
Office Time Savers
Evaluate and Improve

Chapter 6
Teach How to Study

They know enough who know how to learn.
Henry Adams

It has been said that most important is not what we teach, nor even how we teach, but what the students learn. That, of course, is the ultimate goal. It is for this reason, then, that we devote an entire chapter to teaching students how to study. This service is one of the ten teaching tools.

For a good many years I have devoted some class time giving my best on the subject of how to study. At first this was a fifteen-minute portion of the lecture and soon developed into a full class session. I now take the entire class period, not because I have so much material, but because of the overwhelming positive student response. Never yet has a student suggested that the time away from chemistry is wasted time, but many, many have brought compliments and even asked for more. Students have tape recorded the lecture and passed it along to fellow students and to family members. I have printed the lecture as a booklet and passed it out to all those who asked for it. It is written in letter form, "Dear Chris," whose introduction reads as follows:

Dear Chris:

I am writing this letter to help you. Circumstances have brought us together for a semester; you are here to learn, and I am here to help. If you take my suggestions seriously, I know that you will benefit immensely.

Very likely you feel anxiety about this course. You may have heard that chemistry is a difficult subject; perhaps your high school experience with the subject was not good. You may wonder whether your math background is sufficient. You are certainly also anxious because you know that you must divide your time among many demands–other courses, employment, family obligations. You may even wonder whether you really know how to study at all for college courses.

It is also quite understandable that you may be somewhat upset because it is not clear to you why you need chemistry. (After all, you've heard your aunt say many times that in all her twenty years of nursing she has never yet used chemistry!) You may be angry because you wish you had learned enough in high school to test out of this course.

Perhaps you also carry a heavy burden at home: a family problem, a major mishap, a tragedy, an impossible roommate, an unfortunate marriage; any of these will influence your academic performance. Perhaps you just need a dose of motivation.

This letter attempts to speak to all of these aspects of our lives. I hope you read it in its entirety. It is somewhat long, but if you let it speak to you, you will find that it has tremendous power to help you. What is this power? Somewhere in the reading of this letter you will get a glimpse of what I mean. You may not see it for some time, or you may sense it in the next few paragraphs, but a powerful answer will come. When it comes you will know it, because it will feel right. You will then naturally begin to study the right way. When that insight comes, take a moment to celebrate!

While the "how to study" session occasionally refers to chemistry, it truly is applicable to all disciplines. What follows is a presentation as though given to a class.

Today I want to take time to talk about the art of studying. We don't naturally know how to study. We have to learn how to study. There are many things that we can do wrong and consequently waste a lot of time and energy without accomplishing much. It is for this reason that we can all benefit from learning from each other about the successful methods we have found on "how to study."

I have been a student for many years. I continue being a student. There are some definite steps which I have found helpful, and I would like to share these with you. I have developed these steps based on my own experience of being a student and also based on watching and counseling thousands of students.

You may say "Yeah, its easy for you to talk, you're the prof, and we're the students who have to study." Not so. I practice what I preach. After developing the steps I am about to share with you, I decided to test them out. I enrolled in a course on a subject totally foreign to chemistry and proceeded to study, using my own recipe. The course was not an easy one. It was rigorous and demanding with a nationally standardized final examination. I am happy to tell you that I did very well in the course, because the "how to study" steps worked for me, as I know they can work for you.

Basic Requirements

Among basic human needs, studying does not really rank very high. First and foremost are the needs that ensure human survival: food, shelter, and protection. However, once these basic needs are met, less vital needs and interests may be pursued. Studying is truly a less-than-vital need. It is a privilege not enjoyed by many in other countries, where students often sit in cold rooms, late at night, studying by candlelight. Fortunately, in this country it is a fairly common privilege. Nevertheless, for many people even in this country, survival cannot be managed unless study competes with work or family obligations. Here, then, are some of the basic requirements needed to make possible the best conditions for learning.

Priorities

We all set priorities every day. When I decide to go shopping now and to study later, I have set priorities. When I get up in the morning just in time for class, and must eat breakfast later, I have set priorities. When I get a daytime job and study at night, I have set priorities. Of course the ideal situation would be to take care of survival needs so that study time could be arranged as desired, but the ideal is not always possible. So if you must spend some hours each week at a job, you must adjust your study accordingly. There is simply no way that you can be excellent both as a full-time employee and as a full-time student. Study and work cannot both be your first priority, for living two lives at the same time simply does not work! Decide on your priority. It may have to be work for now. But for the sake of your own peace of mind, decide! So I may urge you to take only half a course load if you must work part-time. Half-

time study will prolong the period of academic training, but the quality of your study will pay off. Keep your long-range goals in focus. True, you need money for sandwiches, but the time spent earning money does not really pay if, in the process, grades suffer. Money is replaceable; grades stick. Is it worth the agony, the time, and the money to go through a frustrating semester, trying to study on the job and not really doing well at work or at school? Caught with the requirement of a full-time course load to keep your loan, you may find yourself unable to achieve the good grades that you must show in order to keep that loan or to reach your goal. It may be that by taking only one course per semester and attaining admission to your professional program a few semesters late is really a wise decision.

When is it easier to study for ten credit hours as opposed to nine credit hours? The answer is when two courses add up to ten credits and three courses add up to nine credits. It takes a certain amount of energy just to tool up for each course. Taking more courses means more requirements, more papers; more study time is needed, even though the total number of hours may not be as high as when you take only a few courses.

But perhaps your decision among priorities is different. You may have the problem of too much time on your hands or too many distractions. The great temptations for many is to waste time. It is not uncommon for some of my students to be severe TV addicts, scheduling their courses around the noon soap operas. To see how firmly your priorities are established, check how often something comes up during the week that makes you change your priorities. Change is bound to come occasionally, but it should be the exception, not a habit.

The point of all this advice is that I want you to be sure you know where your true (not hoped-for) priorities lie. State these to yourself; write them down; tell them to someone who will hold you accountable. If studying cannot come in at the top of the list, that is fine; but then I don't want you to feel guilty or stupid for not earning a good grade. Low grades usually indicate simply that a student is unable to devote sufficient time to study.

> So, put your best efforts
> into what is most important!

Prerequisites

Successful learning assumes several prerequisites. One is good health. Your health largely determines how well you can function in school. Don't abuse your body! More on this later.

Basic verbal and mathematical aptitudes are two more prerequisites needed before you can expect to be successful. For twenty years SAT scores have shown a general national decline in both of these skills. A student recently puzzled over a problem involving the phrase "yield of a reaction." She could not solve it, simply because to her the only meaning of "yield" was "stop, look, and go," as in traffic laws. Another student, who had just been recognized for his high achievement in chemistry, also suffered from some verbal inaptitude. He had missed a question because he thought the word "modest" meant "large, majestic." Verbal facility is necessary!

But the prerequisite most important to chemistry is a certain level of mathematical aptitude. Most students who do have difficulty in chemistry do so because of their inadequate mathematical background. There are many ways in which you can brush up on these basic tools: by taking refresher courses, using a computer teaching aid, auditing courses, studying on your own, etc.

And finally there is yet another prerequisite that you must possess: the willingness to work very hard without many initial rewards. It is a fact of life that, whenever you go into a new field, before you can expect any kind of success at all, you will have to have acquired a minimum amount of basic information. Learning this basic material is not easy; and not only that, but it is a lonesome experience, for no one is going to praise you for it until you have reached a certain stage of accomplishment. Say that you want to compete in a roller skating event that takes place on the tenth floor of a building. All the competitors, judges, and spectators have assembled there, but your initial requirement is to walk up to the tenth floor, step by step, on roller skates. This is a frustrating experience; no one encourages you as you climb, or praises you when you do make it to the fifth floor, to the ninth floor, or even to the tenth floor. All you have earned on arrival at the tenth floor is the right to compete for the praises with which spectators greet success in competition.

Similarly in studying, a certain amount of knowledge must be acquired before there will be even the possibility of your succeeding. In chemistry this may mean purchasing the chemistry text and a box of Kleenexes. But success will come. Once you have mastered the basic information, success will come quickly and often.

> So, prerequisites assumed include reasonably good health, satisfactory verbal and math abilities, and the willingness to work hard, without at first being rewarded for your work.

Positive Attitude

Schools are the only business where the customer never wants to get his money's worth. You pay tuition, yet if I dismiss class early, you will probably like it. In school you don't get paid for your work; you pay to work. The tuition that you pay does, of course, not pay for a grade you may want; it does not even pay for the right to study (many successful people are self-taught). All that tuition buys is the right to an official statement assessing the quality of your work. You will have to want to study.

I hope you don't ever find yourself doing something that is not fun; even hard work should be fun. You buy tickets to a concert, expecting to have fun. You've worked hard for that money, and you wish to enjoy it. The same applies here; you don't want to spend all that tuition money and not have fun. But how in the world can one have fun studying? Perhaps "fun" is not the right word. "Reward" may be a better one. It is a reward that comes from within; it is a lasting wholesome, and uplifting feeling.

When you come to class well prepared and can therefore anticipate the professor's thoughts as he goes along in the lecture, you feel a tremendous sense of satisfaction, a reward. Your mind works on the same wavelength as the professor's; two minds have met. Your feeling of accomplishment is your reward for having worked long and hard on a problem. When you can feel in your bones that the answer to a problem you worked so hard on is right, it usually turns out to be right. You are rewarded in lecture when you work with or even ahead of the professor, rather than expecting to be fed and entertained.

Nancy, a student who was in this course some years ago, took the first exam in a class of about three hundred students and received an "F", not only that, but it was the lowest "F." Fortunately, she had the courage to come to see me in the office. What a pitiful sight she was: depressed, physically stooped, crying, helpless, and showing an aimless attitude. All she could say was that she needed a good grade. Because she was in no shape to talk, I asked her to return the next day. When Nancy came back, she seemed a different person; her eyes were aglow, her hair groomed, her posture upright, her voice firm and confident. But most important was what these appearances signaled: her positive attitude! She gave me a piece of paper asking me to read and file it. It read simply "I, Nancy, will receive an above average grade on Exam II." Signed: "Nancy." She left the office without further ado and performed according to her newfound confidence. What happened to Nancy? Something; somehow she changed her attitude. She was a delight to watch. Always interested in the right way to think about a problem, she devoted much time and study to chemistry. To her it was not a chore but a pleasure, and time seemed to fly as she worked. In class she was delightfully responsive. When an insight came to her, her face lit up as brightly as a two-hundred-watt bulb. Nancy was having fun; she was feeling rewarded. I cannot take the credit for her changed attitude. Nancy wanted to change.

There are many ways to develop an eager, positive attitude. Just as you can train yourself in a dance, so it is with attitude; both require training. On a gloomy day it helps to smile; it's catchy, and the act soon becomes reality. Attitude responds to whatever you feed on. If you read a good book or talk with someone whose goals are hitched to the stars, you feel good and confident. But with equal certainty comes a tired and drained feeling if you listen to gloomy news or read a cheap book.

Occasional depression is a fact of life for most persons. The difference is that successful people know that 98% of all our worries never come about; they know that perfectionism and unreasonable goals are demoralizing; and they know how to steer out of depression, or to seek professional help when necessary. Physical activity is one surefire way to combat depression. The box gives additional suggestions.

HOW TO BEAT THE BLUES

1. Identify what's bothering you. Depression is caused not so much by what we eat and do, as by what we think.
2. Exercise. It is a first antidote.
3. Change your daily routine. Go somewhere for a change of scenery.
4. Engross yourself in a new project.
5. Follow a meditation program.
6. Talk about your feelings with someone close.

–J. Walters, USA TODAY

Say you have enrolled in a more advanced class, found it too difficult, and have been advised to take a lower level class first. What is your attitude in class? Do you feel demoted, are you boastful ("I've had all that stuff!"), super confident, reluctant to do that menial homework? Soon such attitude snowballs, and your performance suffers. Show some humility and dig in.

What do you do when a hard decision must be made? Do you procrastinate, or do you instill in yourself confidence that you can decide and stick to your resolve? It feels good to set a deadline and make a decision; it gives peace. I often see students who realize (admit!) late in the semester that things are not going well. I feel impatient with such students who arrive at this death-bed repentance. The agony of indecision must have gnawed at them mercilessly for weeks; yet they have put off building a positive view of their work.

Be good to yourself! Groom yourself well: your appearance reflects your soul. No one likes to be around people whose appearance is repulsive. Listen to good invigorating, though not deafening, music. Read good books such as *The Power of Positive Thinking*, the *Psalms* and

Proverbs, and books by Dale Carnegie. Remember the gigo principle: garbage in, garbage out. You watch a trashy movie, and you feel like trash; you listen to wild music, eat junk food, and you feel like wild junk. But good books enoble the thoughts, wholesome food invigorates the body, and a well-groomed appearance instills confidence. You say that you cannot afford the time for such things. I say you cannot afford not to do it! Get up one half hour earlier just for this important purpose. Furthermore, get someone who can give you encouragement and useful criticism. A friend, a family member, a teacher, anyone you can see regularly, anyone you can tell about your failures and successes, anyone who understands both, lifts you with his comments, and encourages you with his attitude. Such a person is heavenly gold.

Learn the rules of life and abide by them. Move with, not against the natural flow of life. Obey words of wisdom, be creative, and do hard things. Love yourself so that you feel good with and about yourself. Develop a good self-image. Ask yourself: "Would I like to be a friend of mine?" Be true to those around you. Just think: of all the eons of years gone by, and of all those still to come, NOW is the time in which you have been placed on this particular planet, with these particular people about you. Life is an exciting adventure, to be had but once. Make the most of it.

So, nurture an eager, positive attitude.

Discipline

It has been said that there are three kinds of people: those who make things happen, those who watch things happen, and those who wonder what happened. People who make things happen do so because they have plans and goals and have the discipline to implement them. In other words, something is wrong when you must study much more the night before an exam than you do on any other night. Discipline is like democracy; there is a lot of freedom

within self-imposed restrictions. It is not so much the IQ that counts, as it is the "I will." Plan your work and then work your plan.

Set your own deadlines. After all, unless you set them, someone or something else will. Why not show up at your job ten minutes early, instead of coming to work at eight sharp, when the boss says you must be there? Arriving early, you set your schedule; the boss doesn't. Why not fix your own deadline for completing your income tax return, instead of delaying until the date set by the IRS? Why not draft your own timetable to master a given block of material, instead of letting your teacher's exam date determine your actions?

Start by setting goals. Say your goal is to be a good nurse. This goal dictates many requirements; you must care for and like to work with people, you must master knowledge in several fields, one of which is chemistry. So to enter the School of Nursing, one requirement is to do well in chemistry. To do well in chemistry, you must do well on exams, and to do well on these you must undergo certain training. The training required on exams is not so much reading the text as it is doing problems and interpreting results. You must train to do these problems within the imposed limits: fifty minutes, closed book, etc. You know you can't get this training by doing problems the night before the exam, any more than you can practice just the day before a ten-mile run. You train by running for many months, adding an extra block each day. In the study for chemistry you train by doing, say, twenty new problems every day. Of course this will automatically restrict other activities, but the practice moves you closer to your goal. To set and reach goals, many people make lists, using a format something as shown in Figure 6.1.

You may choose to decide on a grade you will earn even before the course begins. Chisel it in stone, and tell the world. Ask your teacher what you will have to do to earn that grade.

Studying is likely the most demanding activity you undertake this semester. So set aside the best hours of the day to study. Most people are most alert in the mornings.

That you can easily stay up late at night does not mean that your mental capacities are at their best late at night. Make yourself a schedule as shown in Figure 6.2, blocking in the best times for study. Stick to a routine. There is energy wasted by changing routines. That is why assembly lines are so efficient. Do the hardest work when you are most alert, and alternate subjects at least every two hours, with five-minute breaks in between to rest body and mind. You don't want your brain (or your seat) to go flat.

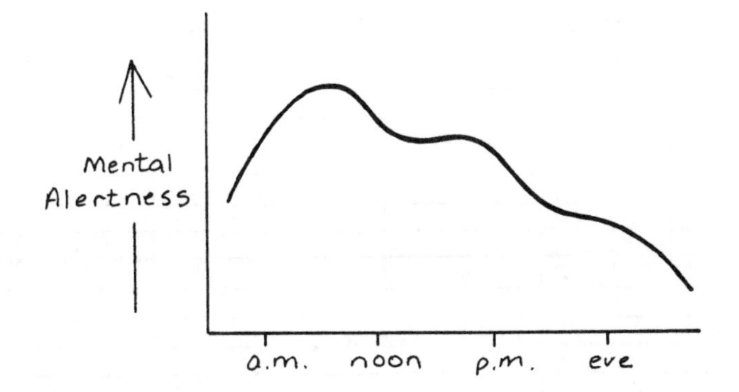

In your mind rate these three persons as successes or failures:

> He wanted to be president of his college class but was the first to be eliminated.
> He flunked the entrance exam to military school not once, but three times.
> His record was 2 and 7; he won 2 out of 9 elections.

You judge: the persons were John F. Kennedy, Winston Churchill, and Abraham Lincoln. If they had one thing in common it must be discipline. It is much more fun to accomplish something through self-discipline than through imposed discipline. (Remember your piano lessons, when your mother *made* you practice?) The key, then, is to work consistently, attacking small blocks of material at a time. Ben Franklin said "little strokes fell great oaks."

So, set a reasonable goal,
Then pursue it doggedly.

PLANNING

AREA OF INTEREST	PERIOD: WEEK ● MONTH YEAR ▲ DECADE |	DATE
PROJECT		COMPLETED
1.		
2.		
3.		
4.		
5.		
6.		
7.		
8.		
9.		

Figure 6.1 A simple planning guide.

TIME	MONDAY	TUESDAY	WEDNESDAY	THURSDAY	FRIDAY	SATURDAY	SUNDAY
6-7am							
7-8							
5-9							
9-10							
[illegible]							
12-[illegible]							
[illegible]							
[illegible]							
[illegible]							
[illegible]							
[illegible]							
[illegible]							
[illegible]							
[illegible]							
[illegible]							

Figure 6.2 A weekly schedule.

Personal Affairs

Happy is the person whose relationships with other people bring peace. Often relationships don't bring peace, and severe tensions affect mental well-being and, with it, ability to work at school. Follow the teachings in the book of Romans; be at peace with everyone, just as much as possible. To whatever extent you can do so, set straight your relationships with others. Straightening may just mean talking with family members about your purpose in going to college, or asking them to trade household chores with you while you study. Sometimes family members do not easily understand a student's need to devote long hours of study in addition to attending classes. It may be best to just schedule study at school right along with class hours, so that the two become a part of a routine for all concerned.

To bring peace may mean confronting someone or apologizing to someone. It may mean facing a superior about a mistake you have made. It may mean simply taking a bit of time to talk with your spouse, or child, or parent, or brother. Remember, you get respect by giving it away.

So, be at peace with others.

Your Body

Our hospitals are full of people who have abused their bodies. Though they may be relatively young in age, their bodies have deteriorated with excess food, drink, drugs, work, or smoking. Eat, drink, and work regularly but moderately, and you will live longer. To eat three good meals a day is much wiser than to snack constantly. And please, don't smoke, please! Overwhelming evidence suggests that smoking reduces alertness and shortens life.

If you have been involved in any kind of competitive sport, you remember the coach stressing sleep as preparation for physical competition.. You need even more sleep for mental competition. When you stay up all night before an exam "to study," it is almost guaranteed that you cannot do well. After all, the mind, which is part of your body, has been forced to run for hours on end without proper rest. "Mens sana in corpore sano" was a Roman saying: "Healthy mind in healthy body."

Know your body. Find out how it functions best. To what diet does it best respond? What schedule is best for you? Have you found that a routine is better than changing patterns of living? Does coffee affect you adversely?

Does lunch on the run upset your stomach? Do you not feel better about yourself when you are clean, carefully dressed, and wisely groomed? Adopt a consistent pattern of living, coupled with a real physical exercise program, and watch your mental alertness grow.

> "Good for the body is the work of the body, good for the soul, the work of the soul, and good for either, the work of the other."
>
> —Henry David Thoreau

Place of Study

Where should you study? The answer is simple; whenever possible in the same place. Just as your body adjusts to routine diet and exercise, so it also adapts to routine surroundings for study. When you sit down at a familiar desk, books beside you, light falling at the same angle, the room smelling familiar, the fan's accustomed sound about you, and the chair's good feel beneath you, then the entire environment calls on your body to do but one thing: concentrate in study. But remember, you can't study in your room at home if you lie on the bed, an arm bent, a leg going to sleep, pencil pushing through the scratch paper into the bedcover, your radio going loudly, inviting pictures of your loved ones all around you, the phone, the TV, the fridge, and the cookie jar all nearby, your dog begging to be walked, your siblings whispering "Quiet, she's studying," and the Avon lady ringing the door bell. You cannot study in such an

environment! True, the mind works best when just a bit tense and challenged (as it might be in a slightly cool room); but not when the tension is irresistible temptation. So, unless no temptations are possible in your home, I suggest that you use a school or neighborhood library for study. These really are usually very quiet, comfortable, and inviting places for study. Best of all, whatever may happen in these surroundings, it really does not call for your involvement. When the phone rings, it's not for you; when someone walks by, they are not needing your attention. Find an isolated spot, and try to use it day after day. I believe that one hour of good study in the library is worth two hours of half-study managed at home or three hours of sneaked-in study on the job.

Also stick with fixed seating in class. An interesting study has shown that, if left to themselves, students will seat themselves in such a manner that on the average the better students sit toward the front of the room, while the poorer ones prefer the back. This is especially true in larger classes, where group dynamics past row 15 seem to develop a different atmosphere. To become disengaged from what happens in front of the class is much easier when you are sitting in seat number 505, way in the back of the room, than if you are sitting in the front.

So, develop a routine and fix on a regular site for study.

Studying

We have seen that requirements essential to healthy mental exercise are: setting priorities, determining to keep reasonably healthy, understanding the value of verbal and mathematical abilities, willingness to work hard, positive self-discipline, peace with others, and a quiet place to study. It is only after these basic requirements are met that we are ready to consider studying itself.

We study in order to learn, and the purpose of learning is first, to acquire a body of knowledge and second, to become so familiar with that knowledge that it can be applied to a useful purpose. We learn at different rates; some material we forget very quickly, other information we retain longer.

Retention depends somewhat on the individual mind but primarily on the kind of material to be studied. On the average, it is easier to retain concepts and principles than, say, prose or unconnected bits of information. Fortunately, as a college student you are usually expected to learn by thinking about concepts and principles, rather than through memory alone. Sheer memorizing and other purely technical skills belong to the vocational-technical schools. And it is because you are in college, rather than a technical school, that the question "Why do I have to take chemistry for nursing?" is not really an appropriate one. Certainly facts learned in

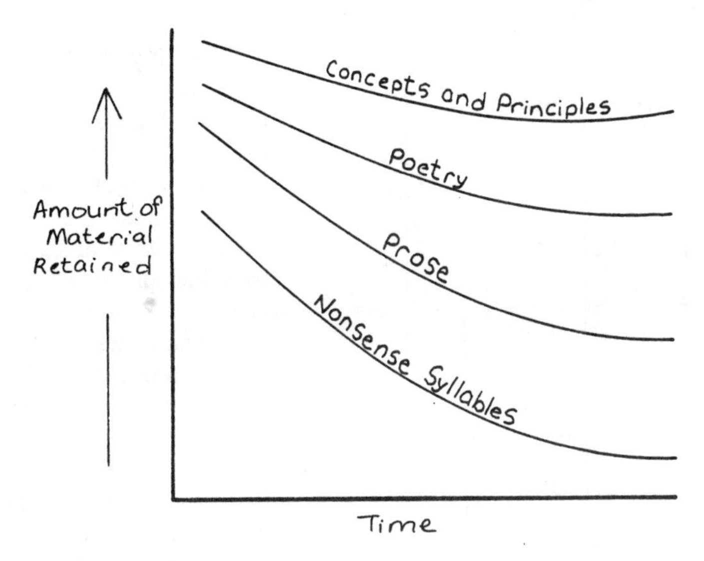

chemistry may not apply directly to work as a nurse. However, the School of Nursing finds it necessary that its students shall have been exposed to the rigor of scientific thought. Science courses in general are excellent vehicles for helping students learn to think. In your nursing career you may never be called on to prepare 0.35 M saline solution (because they are generally purchased ready made), but the understanding of the preparation process is very important. It is important to know what concentration means, what the concentration of salts in body fluids is, and what the causes might be of higher or lower concentrations.

How Much to Study

The time you spend studying depends on you: on your goal for mastery, on your practice in the art of studying, on your ability to satisfy all or most of the prerequisites, on your motivation. Chemistry students who are very weak in math may find that they really need to study as though they were taking two courses, chemistry and math. In high school most of the day is spent in classes, with much of the homework being done in school. In college the reverse is true; relatively little time is spent in classes, but a lot is spent studying outside of class. The general guidelines laid down by many college counselors suggest that, to obtain an average grade, a student must spend two to three hours a week in study for every credit hour taken. Thus a five-credit-hour course will require ten to fifteen hours of study per week in order for the average student to come out with an average grade. An unusually gifted student may spend correspondingly less time; but one with a weak background, poor study experience, one who has been out of school for some time, or who has difficulty learning, will find it necessary to study more. The diagram suggests a relationship between study hours and grades. Look at it carefully. It has been found to be a powerful tool for predicting; given the number of hours devoted to a subject, a grade can be anticipated, and conversely, given a grade, the number of hours a student likely spends on the subject is fairly predictable. This stands to reason, because every achievement in life calls for exercise, and more exercise brings higher achievements. When we think of someone being "lucky," it is well to remember that luck lies at the intersection of preparation and opportunity.

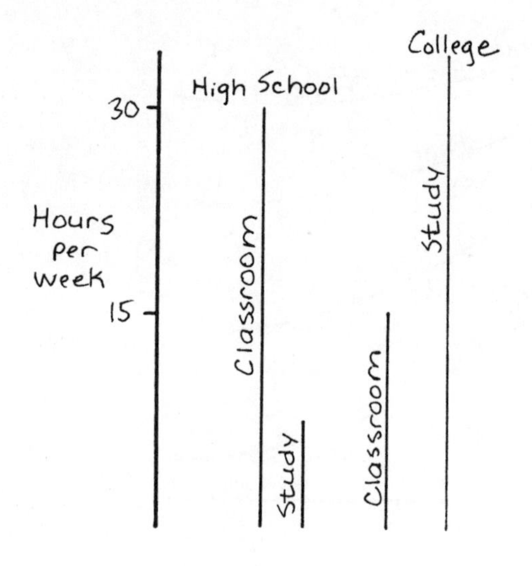

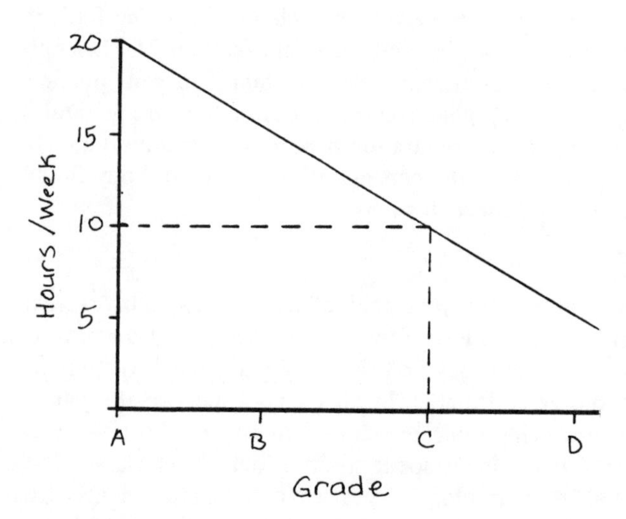

Each year children are born with the minds that hold the potential of a genius. Unless that potential is realized in disciplined training, such children cannot develop into productive geniuses and stay just average. Edison said "Genius is ten percent inspiration and ninety percent perspiration."

There are some quick self-tests on the amount of time you take to study. Look at your textbooks. Clean, unruffled books are often unused books. How long does it take you to find a particular item in a text? Preparation results in familiarity.

If you don't put time into study, no matter what your reason (work, family, illness, lack of motivation), you can't expect a good grade. If you have a job, you know it requires a certain amount of time input for pay output. The same applies to studies; you cannot leave before the work is done, else your payback will be reduced. Decide on the grade you want, then be prepared to spend the time necessary to earn that grade. It really is that simple.

> So, there is no such thing as a free lunch.

When to Study

The best answer to this question is to study consistently! A consistent routine is what will result in success. When we talked about discipline, we mentioned a schedule for the week's activities. Decide what are your own limitations, the importance of school work in your list of priorities, and your personal obligations. Now taking these into account, prepare a schedule allowing for proper study time for each course.

You may want to begin with twenty-four hours for a day or 168 hours for a week. Subtract the hours you need for sleeping, eating, getting ready, travel, and any other fixed obligations. This leaves a block of hours to be distributed among your priorities. If your top priority is work, subtract the needed hours; if study is next in line, build in those hours; and so on down the line. In this manner a fairly detailed budget of your time is established. As you determine the hours needed for each activity, you also assign the times to the proper slots throughout the day. By this means you are designing a timetable that is workable for you. Post the schedule or take it with you to remind you, and STICK TO IT!

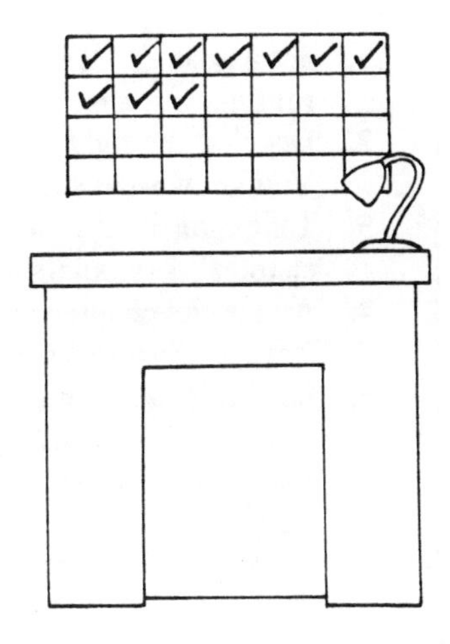

There is something special about an organized person. Such a person feels and imparts confidence and finds that life goes smoothly. I often wonder if a person who drops courses is really well organized. Dropping courses just does not reflect an orderly will.

Remember: to study daily or every other day is much more efficient than an occasional all-day study marathon. Consider the two learning curves below.

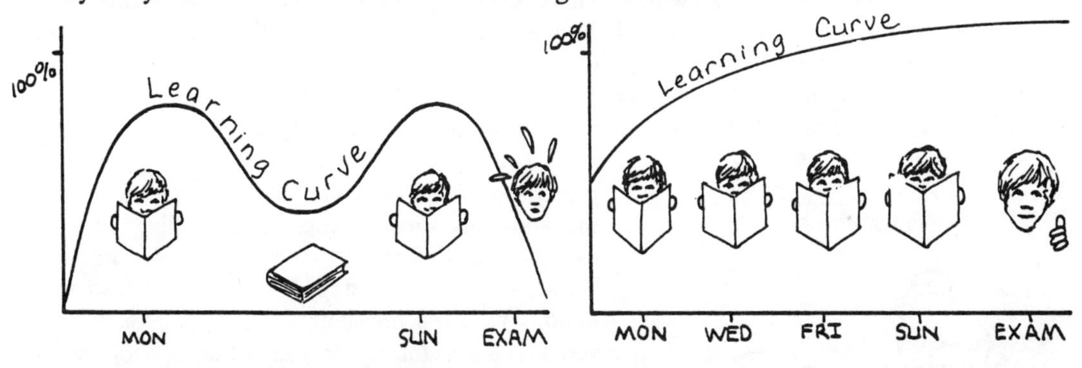

There are other ways to use the power of repetition. The best time to begin the study process is immediately after the class session. Thoughts are still fresh, notes are easy to clean up, and it is the best time to make associations. (Therefore, try not to schedule courses back to back; it has been shown that you will have to study more). Furthermore, it is a good idea to review just before going to sleep. Sleep is a separator of the important from the trivial; it is a dumping mechanism. The last thoughts at night settle onto the subconscious mind, which of course continues to work and process throughout the sleeping period.

Studying is somewhat like the first grader learning to read. At first he reads haltingly, slowly, stopping to decipher words, occasionally asking about the sounds of a word. The first time through, he probably does not even know what the story is about, for he is too busy just sounding out the words. Unless he repeats and repeats and repeats, he does not learn to comprehend as he reads. Unless you repeat and repeat and repeat, things that you hear or read cannot sink in deep enough to become a part of you.

So, study consistently.

SEVEN KEYS TO BETTER LEARNING

1. Set a goal. Why are you in school? When will that report be in? Determine a study routine. Promise yourself a reward. Share your goals with the teacher.
2. Develop the right frame of mind through proper physical and emotional environments. You know what's good and right.
3. Take a bird's-eye view of the immediate task at hand. Write down what you think the chapter's key points might be.
4. Attack the chapter in small segments. Don't leave a section until it is understood.
5. Review. Surprise yourself by stopping at unexpected times to force a review.
6. Be sure you are in control when studying. Don't allow the book, the time, or peers to dictate. But get help when needed.
7. Test yourself by simulating real life situations: exams, interviews, job situations, case studies.

How to Study

Although we have emphasized the importance of enough study time, there is no more important aspect than to use the time wisely. There are many materials available which talk about how to study. One authority suggests it is best to study by using the following steps: Survey, Read, Recite, Write, Review, and Question. Another author suggests a similar sequence of steps: Preview, Question, Read, State, and Test. Essentially the methods are the same, and the steps of each sequence fall into two distinct categories, the intake and the output.

The intake–Intake is that portion of the study process in which you acquire information. From the above mentioned steps, those falling into this category are Survey, Read, Review, Preview. These, then, are the steps by which you feed your mind. You, the consumer, occupy a passive role; you are a spectator. In the actual school setting this takes place as you hear a lecture, as you read, as you listen to tapes, as you watch a film, or as you listen to a tutor. (I am usually reluctant to recommend tutors, since many of them tend to lecture.) The intake process is absolutely essential. It is the time when you absorb basic facts, when you learn how and where to find information. However, for most fields of study, intake is the lesser important study, requiring perhaps a third of your study time.

The output–About two thirds of the study time should be devoted to output, for it requires you to *act* on the information obtained during intake. Here you take the active role; you produce, you give, you do. In other words, output trains you to do what exams, and ultimately what the real world, ask you to do: to show how you can apply the principles and facts. Output takes place when you take notes, outline, solve problems, finish exercises, write reports and papers, take quizzes and exams, teach another student, study intensively with a partner, consult with the teacher, or work with a computer-aided instruction tool. To Recite, Write, Question, State, and Test are steps all falling into the category of output.

The smoker who knows that smoking is dangerous but does not stop smoking has not gone past the intake (literally!) step.

I love to read success stories. I read about people who win the Boston Marathon, about their training, their agonies, their failures, how they keep on training, their victories, about changes success brings to their lives, etc. But as long as I just *read* and don't *train*, I cannot expect to be a success in running. The same logic applies to studying. Just because you understand what the teacher says does not mean that you can do it. Watching someone lead does not make you a leader. You have to do and fail, and do and fail, and do and do and do until it is right.

All study requires both intake and output. Fields such as literature, history, art, and music appreciation likely call for a great deal of intake; whereas mastery of science demands greater output.

You can usually tell the type of study a student is engaged in by the way he or she sits. A student with an easygoing posture, sitting deep in a soft chair, feet propped up, casually leafing through the book–such a student is probably a consumer spending time on intake. But a student sitting on the edge of a hard chair leaning heavily over the paper on his table, completely oblivious of the surroundings as he crosschecks book against notes, against scratch paper, as he underlines, uses the calculator, and essentially loses track of time–that student is a producer deeply engaged in output.

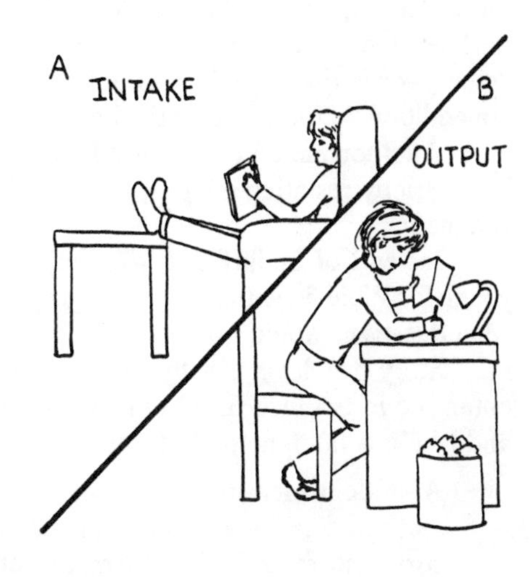

I often hear students make statements like: "The questions on the test are so different from those in the text," or "I read the chapter three times, and I still failed the quiz," or "If I have a formula to work with I can do the calculation." Usually this translates into an admission to the fact that most of their study time was spent on the intake, rather than output, method.

> So, study by getting, but then give, give, give!

Some helpful steps–Each student develops his own method of successful study. But all studies do involve some common steps, which include note taking, outlining, problem solving, self-testing and consultation.

Note taking--The table below gives a summary of advice.

NOTES ON NOTE TAKING

1. Write down the questions asked by the professors. These usually lead to key points of the lecture.
2. Write entire phrases–not long sentences, nor just words.
3. Write only on the right side of the notebook. Leave the left side for later additions and corrections.
4. Go over your notes very soon after class.
5. Use different color pens for content, illustrations, references, etc.
6. Use separate notebooks for separate topics.
7. Use a ring binder notebook for easy inserts.

Outlining–The simplest method for outlining is probably underlining, but it is also the most cumbersome method to do correctly, since it is hard to know what and how much to underline. Underlining 50% of the page or underlining whole sentences is not helpful. Look for "clue" words that signal an important thought on the horizon. Such words may be "because," "in addition," "therefore," "the best," "also," "in spite of," "on the other hand."

Another method often used successfully is the production of an altogether separate outline. Briefly restating the gist, the main ideas of each section, the outliner makes a personalized summary.

Instead of underlining you may find it helpful to outline in your mind by simply asking yourself "What is it that this paragraph is saying?" "If I were to write a test on this section, what questions would I ask?"

Story problems usually cause the most difficulty, because the thoughts and principles are entangled in both words and numbers. In such cases outlining, using a combination of drawings and labels, is often helpful. Consider this problem:

> A student measures 100 g of water into a calorimeter and finds that its temperature is 23.1°C. She then drops into the water 39.0 g of a hot metal of unknown specific heat, stirs, and records the maximum temperature as 29.6°C. If the temperature of the metal was initially 98.2°C, calculate its specific heat. The specific heat of water is 1.0 cal/g deg.

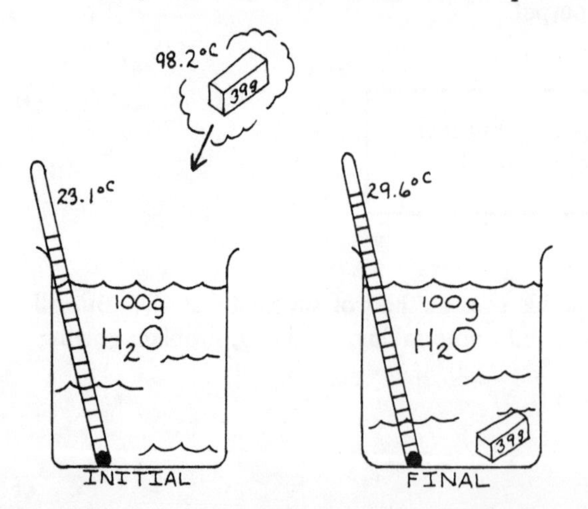

This problem rests on a lot of information, which, when sorted out, might look something like the figure on the left.

The advantage of this approach lies in "seeing" what is happening. Most of us learn better when we can consider the concrete, before moving to the abstract.

I hear and I forget,
I see and I remember,
But I do and I understand.

Put in a different way, we retain about 10% of what we hear, 20% of what we see, 30% of what we hear *and* see, and 50% of what we do.

Problem Working–There really is no substitute for the working out of problems. The best way to study a chapter is to get a general overview of the entire chapter by looking at its headings, illustrations, and bold prints. Next read a single section, stopping to do each example or illustration by covering up the answer. Review the section and highlight its key points. Then go to the problem section and solve problems pertaining to the section just studied. If there are problems with and without answers, do those with answers first to gain confidence. Once the section is well understood, proceed in a similar manner with the next section.

To use an answer to work backwards to find the solution cannot teach you what you would learn if doing the problem independently. It has been suggested that when you can't find the answer to a problem, you probably have not asked the right question. Asking detailed questions, you often find the answer. However, when you have tried a problem for ten to fifteen minutes without progress, it is time to seek help. Don't belabor a problem endlessly; usually you will waste the time. You may need just a little hint, some bit of information, or a correction to a mistake in the book.

Self-Quizzing–Pretend that you are to make the test for the class. What do you consider important? Write, say, ten good questions and lay them aside for a while. Then come back to take your own exam just as you would in the classroom setting. With a good study partner, questions may be exchanged.

The same procedure applies to old exams the professor might make available for study. Be sure you can do them one hundred percent. Incidentally, when taking multiple-choice exams, it is best, whenever possible, to work out the answer before looking at the alternatives given. It has also been shown that when students change an answer on such exams, sixty to seventy percent of the time they will change it from a right to a wrong answer.

Consultation–An often overlooked or unused study tool is the office hour provided by counseling centers, the professor, assistant, or fellow students. Whenever you confer with someone, remember to be well prepared. Know exactly what it is you are going to ask; in fact, write down the question in detail. Know exactly where the problem may be found in the book or in

your notes. Be prepared with writing material. Don't fear asking questions; it is one of your precious opportunities. After such a session, show your appreciation.

Study is not like a contest with a single winner. Study rewards everyone who attempts to succeed and excel.

> So, if you want to succeed,
> the word is *action*.

Expectations and Promises

Let's make a pact which binds both of us.

I expect you:

- to review what I said, using the active approach;
- to develop the best possible attitude;
- to live a clean, wholesome life;
- to set goals and schedules for yourself;
- to study in a peaceful environment;
- to devote two to three hours a week to studying for every one of your credit hours;
- to study by doing; and
- to respond to the professor's lectures: a nod, a puzzled look, a smile.

In turn I promise:

- to prepare myself as best I can;
- to teach by giving my very best;
- to be available to help;
- to maintain a positive, enthusiastic attitude;
- to inform you of any study aids known to me; and
- to be fair.

A quote from Emerson is the best motivation I can provide:

"There is nothing capricious in Nature, and the implanting of a desire indicates that its gratification is in the constitution of the creature that feels it. You would not have the desire unless you were capable of its achievement."

Further Reading

Froe, Otis D. and Lee, Maurice A., How to Become a Successful Student, Fawcett Publications, Inc., 1959

Chapter 7
Use of Gadgetry

In live presentations we still learn most visually, secondly from intonations, and last from the words spoken.

Our eyes seem to have a specially favored channel to the mind. We instantly recognize a person years, even decades after the last visual contact. The longest lasting impression on the mind appears to come by visual means. The change from concrete to abstract learning is quickest using visual aids. Audio tapes alone are of limited help, but audio learning is enhanced when accompanied by printed matter. The complexity of the visual presentation appears to make little difference, so that black and white photographs are found to be just as effective a teaching tool as a professional film.

If the visual media is special, then multi-media is even better. Learning takes place via associations; the use of multiple senses will increase the chances of learning. "Audiovisual" and "multimedia" learning have long been recognized as powerful combinations. We hear the sound-track, and we can virtually "see" the movie. The more associations the student can make, the better the chances of learning. A lasting impression is best achieved through the multiple input format.

Students throughout the world have grown up with a vast collection of multimedia input through television, films, arcades, etc. As teachers, we have no choice but to use modern technology. While it may be a discouraging thought to compete with television, it must be kept in mind that it is not so much the quality of the use of the technology, as it is simply the use of the media that enhances learning.

A study by Taylor clearly shows the effect of the use of lecture demonstrations on retention of material. Groups of students with indistinguishable class records were taken from five sections of a large course. The professor in group 1 used daily in-class demonstrations in addition to the standard lecture. Professors for groups 2, 3, and 4 did few demonstrations, while the professor for group 5 did none. After the course was completed, the students were dismissed for summer vacation and retested upon return after a three-month absence. The graph in Figure 7.1 shows the results: far more retention is possible with the use of demonstrations. So, for a lasting impression, use the multiple media.

Demonstrations are not always applicable in every course; however, role playing, skits, analogies, graphs, samples, diagrams, field trips, moot court, computer graphics, etc., all provide extra dimensions to learning. A history class becomes alive when artifacts of the civilization being studied are passed around; a poet's work is more tangible after visiting her birthplace; the needs of handicapped people become very clear after spending a day in a wheelchair.

An all-important teaching tool then is the use of media.

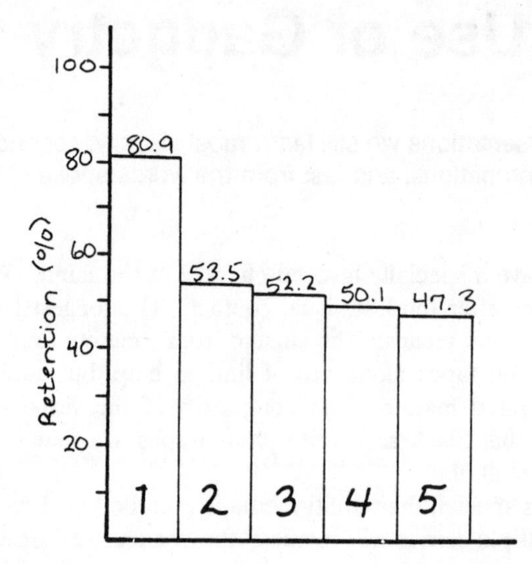

Figure 7.1 Student retention *vs* teaching method (see text).

Visual Media

Certainly the printed page is one of the most common visual aids to learning. Print styles, graphs, diagrams, photographs, colors, fold-outs, etc. all lend versatility to this medium. However, it is mostly a self-learning, not a teaching tool.

Blackboard

The blackboard, on the other hand, must qualify for one of the oldest visual aid teaching tools. It gives the teacher complete control of display: preparation before or during class, easy changes, use of colors, extra thick chalk for large classes, coordination of erasures with addition-al of new material, thereby providing a sense of flow. However, for all the advantages it offers, the blackboard has limitations. The speed of display changes is slow; the lecturer has to turn away from the audience; clarity is often wanting; it takes extra time to write in large, legible form; no actual motion can be displaced; and so on. Therefore, in many classrooms, the overhead projector has displaced, or at least complemented, the blackboard.

Overhead Projector

This device has all the advantages of the blackboard, overcomes its disadvantages, and offers some additional advantages. The writing need not be large, yet its display can be adjusted to virtually any size; the writing surface can be rolled horizontally or vertically; any transparent object can be displayed in color; dynamic processes in action can be shown (i.e., moving models or crawling bugs); material no longer needed does not have to be erased and can easily be retrieved for later reprojection; the teacher does not have to walk back and forth to use the available writing area; and the horizontal surface can be made vertical for specialty displays (i.e., liquids in test tubes).

Transparency preparation–Projectors are normally equipped with a continuous roll of clear plastic (acetate) which can be written upon, using any color of washable or permanent ink. These rolls may either advance up or down or sideways and allow for easy backtracking.

In addition, loose 8.5" x 11" *acetate sheets* are available in all colors and may be prepared prior to presentation, again using any color of washable or permanent ink. Normal sized lettering can be displayed for comfortable reading to groups of hundreds of persons. Prepared sheets can be used as background material by placing them underneath the projector acetate. This allows addition of new material by drawing on the projector acetate. These new drawings can easily be removed by erasing or advancing the projector acetate, thereby leaving the background material totally intact and ready for more secondary drawings. Acetates may also be prepared from computer generated material by allowing the computer printer to print directly on the acetate sheet.

Fairly intricate *overlays* may be prepared by having several sheets, each giving additional information on one base sheet. These sheets are taped to the various sides of the base sheet and flipped onto the original one as needed, either one at a time or one on top of the other (Figure 7.2). It is thereby possible to teach increasing complexity while still controlling it through the selective removal of any component and the use of colors.

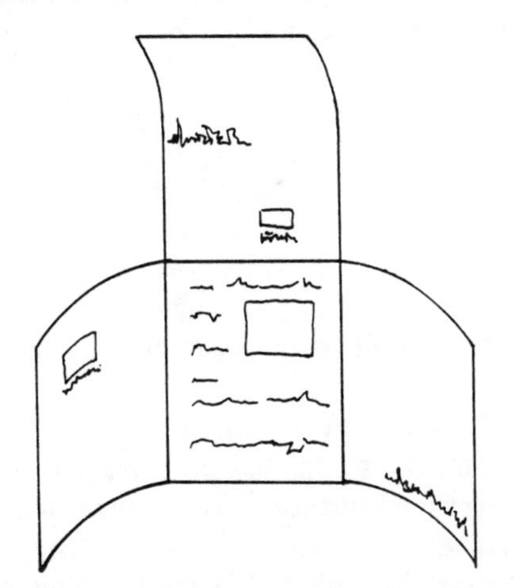

Figure 7.2 Transparency with three overlays.

The *Transparency Maker* allows the transfer of any xeroxed material onto a special acetate sheet. When accuracy or detail are important, such as in pictures, diagrams, print, etc., this method has no rival. The source must be transferred with good contrast to a xerox page, which is then covered with a light-sensitive acetate sheet and inserted into the Transparency Maker for a permanent image burn. Modern xerox machines permit the original to be reduced or enlarged to proper size. No colors are possible by this method, but since the image is permanent, pen writing may be added and erased.

If *dittos* are prepared for handout to students, it is quite possible to insert a sheet of acetate along with the paper to be run off. With a careful, slow run, the master will transfer the image onto the acetate just as it does onto the paper. This may then be used for class projection. It is particularly nice with multicolor dittos.

The *lift-off* technique allows the preparation of transparencies from original colored pictures. The process destroys the original picture, so it is most suitable for replaceable material, such as pictures from magazines. A plastic sheet, such as MAC-TAC, is stretched over the picture, rubbed with a blunt object, and then treated with hot water and soap. After a few minutes the plastic is carefully peeled off, and the picture has been transferred from the paper to the plastic. Specially made plastic, VIS-X Pic-Lift Plastic, is also available from Griggs Educational Service.

Commercial supply houses provide many materials for overhead use. First and foremost are suppliers of ready-made transparencies for any field and subject. These may be in color or black and white; they may be single issues or sold in sets; or they may even just be a printed master from which transparencies can be made. In addition, commercial houses also make available transparencies containing certain backgrounds (colors, graphing, grids, borders), transparencies with headings and headlines, fill-ins, maps, quotes, graphics, photos, pictures, and overhead kits containing labeling devices, and so on.

There are many *other uses* for the overhead. Flat-bottom glassware makes a good container for liquids. Any action within the liquid, such as stirring, mixing, addition of colors, a chemical reaction, bubbling of gases–all will be displayed in dramatic detail.

Two-dimensional nontransparent objects where only the shape is important, such as outlines, leaves, coins, or moving models are perfect for this medium. Display material may be small, yet everyone has a chance to see it. In my collection I have some hundred models ranging from adjustable chemical formulas, to glass beads in a vibrating container showing molecular motion, to an actual clock showing the moving second hand for timed displays.

Even three dimensionality may be displayed. For instance, a kit may be prepared by having stacked layers of transparent plastic with each layer showing the outline of an atom. The layers are separated by about 0.5 cm and held together by flexible corner pins. The stack may then be projected, and as the various layers are moved in concert, a feeling of three dimensionality is displayed. (Some layers will be out of focus, but this just adds to the extra dimension.)

PC displays–Newer technology allows the use of the overhead projector to display material from the personal computer. Kodak has developed a large Liquid Crystal Display unit which, when placed onto the overhead surface, allows images transmitted from the computer to be clearly displayed by the overhead. Because the data is stored in the computer or its disk, it may be changed, updated, revised, and resized instantly. This electronic transparency allows graphics, spreadsheets, and wordprocessing to be computer generated and displayed for the large audiences, even in color.

Vertical stage projection–The overhead projector proves its true versatility through this technique. Some things cannot be displayed on a flat horizontal surface (i.e., liquids in test tubes, any vertical motion, gas production). Projections of these displays are easily done by simply laying the projector on its back and turning its projection mirror down a few degrees. Anything displayed in front of the now vertical stage will be projected. In this manner it is possible to, for instance, watch the rusting of iron in a test tube filled with liquid acid solution, and do so in big living color. In fact this may be the only time that a teacher can literally walk into the (projection of the) test tube and be part of the chemistry, by moving about, showing color changes, bubbles, etc. The construction of some projectors may only allow ceiling projection while laying down. For such instruments there are two simple solutions: place a ring stand with an adjustable mirror above the projection head (Figure 7.3), or build an adaptor which is

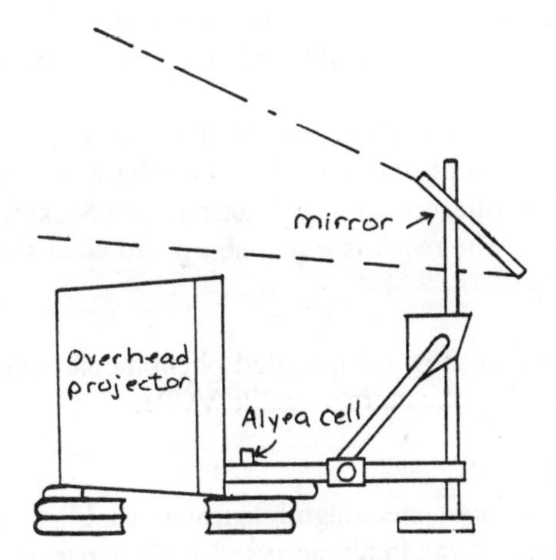

Figure 7.3 Vertical stage projection.

placed on top of the projector, thereby converting it to a vertical stage projector (for details contact Prof. Hubert Alyea, 337 Harrison St., Princeton, NJ 08540).

Finally, a word about the *variety of projectors* themselves. Features that are particularly helpful in teaching are, of course, a large writing surface, adjustable feet for easy leveling, focus and brightness controls. But such options as a mirror with 90 degree tilt, a flip-up side table to keep notes on, and a mirror projection arm that is either removable or easily swung out of place–all are desirable. If weight and transportability are important, the thin stage projectors are nice. Here the light source is not housed below the writing area but instead is mounted into the mirror projection device above the writing area. Light shines down from the top onto the mirrored writing area, thereby reflecting the image into the top. This allows the bottom portion of the projector to be extremely thin and therefore lightweight. The units are very powerful and suitable for projections for large groups.

Slides

This medium predates the overhead projector. It has the advantage of depicting extremely sharp, colorful and detailed features, but it suffers from a lack of versatility; it really does not permit superimposed writing during the lecture, and so serves best for finished and permanent material.

Slides are useful for the presentation of short segments of material or for lectures at professional meetings. Most dramatic is the use of the *lap dissolve* technique, which uses two projectors to fade one picture out as the new one fades in. Timed properly, it almost gives the feeling of motion and lends itself very nicely for depicting dynamic processes, such as a chemical reaction in progress. My students have also benefited from slide series which were prepared as review of the visual material presented in class. The set is made available to the students through the audiovisual center, where they may view it at their convenience. It is, of course, possible to couple the series with a synchronized sound track.

Slides may be prepared by professional or amateur photography and allow the capture of large or small objects. It is a particularly useful means of showing material taken from the printed media. I have a constantly active folder of collected magazine pictures labeled "Slides to be taken."

Black and white slides of any drawings, printed items, or even pictures may be conveniently prepared, first by successively reducing the original on the Xerox machine until the slide size is attained. The object is then run through the Transparency Maker, and the picture is cut out and mounted on a slide frame. The result is a very sharp and clear slide.

Homemade Films

Motion may be exploited to show complicated phenomena. Older filming technology was soundless and is being replaced by the more versatile VCRs.

Computer Aided Instruction

We have found CAI a most meaningful learning tool. It consists of professionally prepared materials, which may be randomly accessed to fit a particular course sequence. The nice feather is that the student is in control of the speed at which the lesson is given. The lesson in turn will not allow the student to go on unless the material is mastered. This is accomplished through text material, graphics, questions, hints, help, and referral to earlier material. The screen is touch-sensitive, thereby giving a quick means of response. At regular intervals the student may take a quiz which monitors progress.

For over a decade we have used *PLATO* (Programmed Logic for Automated Teaching Operations). Students may use the facilities at school, or, for a small fee, access it directly from their home computer. PLATO (also available on diskettes) is one of the best tutoring devices, being infinitely patient, yet challenging, and constantly demanding the student's input. Virtually every field is available: political science, Chinese, learning to play the piano, science, or even taking your own physical.

Other programs for the *micro computer* also abound; they seem to be a regular feature of most publishing houses and have created a host of independent software companies. Advertisements in virtually every professional journal attest to the widespread popularity of this new tool.

Audio Media

For the average student, sound is secondary to sight in the learning hierarchy. Yet without proper audio medium, the visual is quite helpless. Unless the classes and the room are small, I prefer a sound amplification system for several reasons. First, it ensures that sound is carried to all parts of the room, but it also allows me to speak at normal voice volumes and yet be clearly heard. I am free to use voice intonations, to lower the pitch and volume of my voice for emphasis, all of which is done more easily if I am able to speak at normal speaking levels. It also saves the vocal chords from exhaustion. Finally, the use of a public address system allows easy recording of the presentation, both by the students using their own devices, and the audiovisual center for an official transcript. We routinely make recordings available to the students within less than twenty-four hours of the presentation. Students may either listen to a tape in a studio or may purchase a tape at production cost.

Being tied to a microphone has definite disadvantages; it restricts the movement of the presenter, and, if longer cords are made available, embarrassing entanglements may take place.

The portable microphone is a marvelous solution. The microphone is connected to a small, lightweight FM transmitter clipped to the belt. The transmitter, in turn, provides clear and static-free transmission to a receiver placed in the public address system's amplifier box. This gives me all the advantages of the microphone, and at the same time gives me the freedom to walk into the class as I lecture.

Audiovisual Media

While the media discussed so far often combine live narration with the visual, a synchronized recording of the two calls for more professional technology.

Slide-tape series are perhaps the best known tools of combined media. While it is time consuming to prepare a series, it is still within the realm of the nonprofessional to do so.

Films on any subject are available from many sources. Schools, public libraries, and private institutions have their own film libraries. Professional organizations and commercial vendors also make films available, both for rent and purchase. It has been my experience, however, that films are rarely as well received by students as are personal presentations. This may be due to the fact that a film is flawless, not providing the chance of error always looming in the background of a live presentation, or the fact that a film dates itself easily through clothing styles, equipment models, etc.

Visual camera recording is a technology with fabulous possibilities. Like homemade films, it records motion and provides a sense of personal involvement; but unlike the homemade films, VCRs usually allow simultaneous sound/visual recording, are cheaper to operate, since the tape can be erased and no developing is involved, and the viewing does not call for the heavy film projectors or screens. It is possible to take a field trip by simply viewing a VCR; it is possible to peer into small and otherwise unaccessible areas, such as a nuclear reactor; and it is possible to do animation.

VCRs also allow an extension of the lecture recording service by providing both the visual and audio media for the student's later use. Oftentimes a lecture discussing formulations and proofs really needs the visual along with the audio. VCRs can be mounted in the classroom, thus avoiding the need for an operator. Mounting can be done so that the complete stage area is in view, or if all the important work is done on the overhead, the VCR may be mounted onto the overhead arm and focused onto the writing area. In fact, two VCRs may be used: one for wide shots and one for closeups with the instructor controlling the switch between cameras for recording onto one tape.

Video discs are fast making inroads into the educational market and so will other developing technology. It is, therefore, important to keep abreast of new opportunities and adapt and use them for the benefit of the student.

WHAT YOU CAN DO . . .

1. Remember, we have little choice but to compete with technology that the students are accustomed to.
2. Go ahead, try that new technology. You and your students will know if it works or not. Change if need be.
3. Become acquainted with your school's audiovisual center, its personnel and gadgets. Ask for ideas.
4. Go visit gadget stores.
5. Attend conferences and workshops.
6. Always check and compare how others use technology. (The thin stage projector first came to my attention at a conference in Tokyo.)
7. Explore all emerging technology for possible classroom use.

Further Reading

Talesnick, Irwin, Idea Bank Collation, 517 Science Supplies and Services Co., Ltd. Box 1591, Kingston, Ontario, Canada K75C8.

Taylor, T. E. Unlimited Learning, Information Unlimited, Box 361, Bryan, TX 77802, 1983.

Chapter 8
Effective Administration

Time is but the stream I go a-fishing in.
–Thoreau

Like streams, some lives are deep, while others are shallow; some are strong, others weak; some long, others short. Some have purpose and cut a well-defined path; others curl about aimlessly, consuming a great deal of energy in the process. Yet all have the same number of hours per day, per week, and per year.

As teachers we are particularly vulnerable to the disease of time mismanagement, because so often the unexpected happens: phone calls, salesmen, colleagues' visits, students needing help, urgent meetings, etc. Then there are always those projects on the back burner, which never seem to be getting their due: that letter I meant to write, the cooperative project I wanted to try, the grant I wanted to apply for, the book I wanted to write. On the short time scale these projects are secondary in urgency; however, they likely are the very ones which ultimately develop me into a better professional. So often these projects do not get done, because ultimately the lack of time encroaches on our efforts. There just are too many projects still left undone at the end of the day.

It is very revealing to do an analysis of how much (little) time is spent on those secondary, but yet so important, projects. A helpful exercise for me has been to log my time under two simple headings: maintenance and improvement. Maintenance items are the routine and expected items such as preparing, teaching, grading, counseling; whereas improvement includes items which allow me to learn, make me a better professional, and stimulate creativity such as reading, research, and writing.

There appears to be a paradox. On the one hand, we need to schedule time very carefully to get those extra projects in, which often might mean limiting persons' access to our time. But on the other hand, it is this very discipline that is necessary to be a better teacher in the class, a better counselor to the students, a better professional in the community.

The cure for the disease of time mismanagement is well-planned efficiency. Goethe said, "method will teach you to win time." It is motivating to know that, according to at least one source, well-arranged time is the mark of a well-arranged mind. Arranging and organizing is a time-consuming, never ending effort. As with physical objects which naturally tend to scatter randomly, so the law of entropy also applies to time; if left to itself it will randomly meander about.

While this eighth tool of teaching, effective administration, includes the supervision of time use by others, ultimate success is achieved only if a good example is set. So, what I myself do comes first.

Self-Supervision

Someone has calculated that if a person lives to be seventy years of age, on the average twenty-three years are spent sleeping, nineteen years walking, nine years playing, six years eating, four years being sick, and two years getting dressed. While most of us must spend time in each area, we do have control over the time allotted to some of these areas.

Once again it is instructive to run a self-analysis of time management. Over a period of a month I kept very careful and detailed records on how I spent my time. My eight chosen areas showed the following percentage of total time available: profession 30.4%, family 8.6%, rest 39.7%, hobby 2.6%, self-improvement 1.6%, home maintenance 6.3%, church 6.6%, entertainment 4.2%. A careful analysis of the findings led me to the conclusion that rest ought to be reduced, and that hobby, and self-improvement should be increased.

Some persons prefer that their time be scheduled for them. Teachers have the unique responsibility of determining the use of large blocks of their work time. Meeting classes is prescribed; however, the care taken in grading papers, preparing lectures and writing exams, and the time set aside for self-improvement and professional advancement are all self-determined.

Table 8.1 Take charge of your time by A. B. Harris and T. A. Harris.

1. Don't be a compulsive buyer. Things take time.
2. Learn to say NO.
3. Make decisions.
4. Interrupt the time taker. Politeness can eat up your day.
5. Avoid TV.
6. Plan.
7. Don't clutter.
8. Don't ignore maintenance.
9. Avoid idle waiting.
10. Don't agonize about the future.

The drive for **self-discipline** comes from within, and what comes from within can be directed. Reading and listening to motivational material, planning the day's work the night before, and setting goals, all aid self-discipline. The following list details ways in which one may determine the use of time.

- *Get to work on time*. Better yet, get to work well before it is time. Not only does this reflect on attitude, but arriving early also permits the body and mind to settle from the trip in preparation for the work ahead. In two decades of teaching, I have (fortunately) never been late to a class. To be able to do this means rising early in the morning, being neat and organized in personal affairs, and having contingency plans for the times when things do not go as planned.
- *Do it Now*. More time is wasted through procrastination than almost anything else. For years a sign above my desk has reminded me to "Do It NOW." I prefer doing hard and unpleasant tasks first thing in the morning. This may mean outlining a speech, making a phone call, or confronting someone. Once these chores are done, they are no longer plaguing the mind, allowing it instead to work without care.

• *Handle papers only once.* A constant stream of documents cross my desk on any day. It is extremely easy to say "I'll do this later." You have seen desks that are loaded with stacks of magazines, papers, books, and files. I try to dispose of each paper as soon as I receive it–put it in the file for a given lecture, outline the response to a letter, page through a magazine and clip any items of interest, etc.

• *File properly.* Much time can be wasted looking for missing items. And the problem usually is that there are too many papers per folder or too many folders without a system. Whether it is paperwork or items in a hardware store a good filing and retrieval system is mandatory. Its development takes time and constant updating.

• *Make lists.* They provide a sense of accomplishment when checked off. More than that, they work! Whether it is a list of plans for the day or a list of things to do on the way to town, lists organize thoughts and plan efficient routing of work. Thus, when a trip to a store is contemplated, accumulate related chores onto that list that can be done on that same trip. Prior to departure, establish a sequence according to geography and assign estimated times in units of 15 minutes for each item. The total time then sets the departure time and permits the journey to be most efficient. Someone said that the real secret of how to use time is to pack it as you would a suitcase, filling up the small spaces with small things.

• *Plan.* Put most succinctly, one should plan the work, then work the plan. No pilot departs without a flight plan. While he might depart and continue to fly, without a plan he would have nowhere to go. If we have plans to nowhere, we will certainly get there. Plans should be made for both small and large projects, whether this be a research project or an evening of leisure. Unexpected delays in waiting rooms can be productive if filled with planned activity. Specific planning tools are discussed in the next chapter.

• *Delegate.* Though we may be able to do a better job, there is no way that we can do all the work that should be done. When chairing committees I assign tasks to committee members; in staff supervision I expect student teachers and assistants to prepare quizzes; when teaching I ask students to look up the answer to a question I could not answer. Delegation motivates others, instills a sense of participation, and gives me more free time; but it only works if I carefully supervise the delegated work. Thus, task assignments to committee members may be tied to specific target dates for reports which I monitor. I review quizzes written by the staff, and I ask the students at the agreed upon time about the answer to the question. I provide the accountability for the task to be done.

• *Schedule time in blocks.* It is grossly inefficient to be constantly interrupted or to alternate between tasks. When not reaching a person by phone, rather than allowing that office to arrange for a return call, I prefer to return the call. In this way I stay in control of my time. The mind needs a certain amount of time to gear up for a task and to find a comfortable groove to flow in. This takes time, and frequent starts mean frequent start-up times. My students know that I set aside certain large blocks of time for writing which I protect jealously, but they also know that I do provide large blocks of time for them. When committee meetings are set, I seek to set them first or last thing in the day or cluster them with other like activities.

• *Maintain a clean desk.* Use of the above suggestions almost naturally will result in a clean desk. A clean desk is a mirror of the inner workings of the person behind the desk. It likely reflects on the looks of the bulletin board, on the person's use of time, etc.

• *Occasionally take the broad view.* It becomes necessary to occasionally take stock of the overall process. Does the filing system do what it is intended to do? Are there areas of work that pile up? Is there seasonal work? Is there a bottleneck? I like to come to the office on occasional weekends, in peace and quiet get above the forest of activity, and with a bird's eye analyze the flow of operations.

Student Supervision

The question is how to give students efficient quality time. The more I plan my time with students, the better the time is that I can give them. Planning is an absolute necessity when the number of students ranges into the hundreds. But planning does not mean that students have to make appointments. My students never have to–all others do.

The first strategy in planning is to know the needs of the students. Are there certain times of the term when the needs for help will be higher than at other times–registration, mid-term, finals? What days are students most likely to be free to come for help? Are there students with special needs and handicaps? A deaf student came with the request that I speak slowly, using plenty of facial expressions. Having recently lost his hearing, he was now learning to lip-read. I must also know about students with special conditions, such as epilepsy, allergies, pregnancies, and unusual drug requirements. Such knowledge has been necessary on numerous occasions when a student fainted or developed an uncontrollable reaction.

While I must know the needs of the students, they in turn must know my needs. They must know that there is a huge amount of work involved in writing six major exams, twelve quizzes, grade twelve laboratory write-ups and fifteen homeworks during the course of a term. While the many chances are to the students' advantage, the students must understand that in order to save time we will, for instance, make all exams multiple-choice and have them computer graded, and that we will not really grade the entire homework assignment, but instead will spot check it and assign grades on that basis. They must understand that, while I have many hours set aside for help, their office hour time must be prepared for. Thus, students will quickly learn that I get impatient when they come in and open the book, then the notes, and vaguely recall that they had a question "somewhere around here," but cannot locate the spot, let alone remember the question. My advice is to prepare for office hours by writing down every question in detail, with page reference. This has the additional advantage that often a properly phrased question tends to answer itself.

Students must further understand that I have set aside certain times for my work. This time I need with complete devotion to the task, just as I devote myself completely to help the students during office hour time. Most students respect and admire a clear policy, and only occasionally must I ask a student if the question can wait until the next office hour period.

Most routine office help takes no longer than about ten minutes per student. The efficiency can be improved when several students come in at the same time. I will encourage this by asking the waiting students if their concerns are personal or have to do with subject matter. Even if two students do not have exactly the same technical questions, it is still much more efficient to have several of them present at the same time, because likely there is overlap in the questioning. However, there are several reasons why the efficiency of office hours can be depleted very quickly.

One is the unprepared student, who is soon encouraged to come back when well prepared. Another reason is the student who would just like to visit; this happens daily, and for me turns out to be the most difficult situation to handle, especially if it is a former student. The student and I obviously have developed a rapport with each other, and it is the student's wish to nourish it. I do take the time to visit, but after some time I try to find ways to mention all the things that need to be done.

A third reason why unexpected time is taken from me is with students who have personal problems. In such cases, I stop all else and devote even a whole hour to a student. These are the times when listening does wonders. At times I feel that my role is that of a friend whom the student cannot find elsewhere, a parent the student perhaps does not have, or a counselor to offer a different perspective. These are the times when teachers have the opportunity to really touch a life through compassionate listening.

Staff Supervision

These are the vital helpers for whom I am at least partially responsible, and who can improve my efficiency many, manyfold. Aside from secretaries, these may include teaching assistants, part-time faculty, office help, laboratory personnel, summer help, etc. As true as always, good use of their time depends on good planning. The key to success is delegation with built-in accountability. My assignments must be sensitive to other schedules but should always be accompanied by an agreed upon deadline and a specific reporting mechanism. It is my job to keep track of the deadline. For part-time help, I have found it most helpful to spend some time to very specifically detail the work for an entire day. After this the helper is expected to work and not consult with me except at specified times.

Success in teamwork, such as teaching different sections of the same class, is directly related to the amount of communication among the team members. Our teaching staff meets weekly to work out details for the week's operations, anticipate difficulties, and suggest solutions. It was the staff's suggestion to increase communication even more by occasionally visiting each other's class sessions.

But perhaps the most satisfying aspect of staff help has been my increased productivity as a result of win-win arrangements between myself and staff members. A staff member, who particularly likes computer work, does all the record keeping for the class in exchange for services I render. Other special staff projects include writing of examination questions, search for appropriate clippings, and development of experiments and demonstrations. Some staff members become quite involved in their tasks by spending much time on what may become a hobby, or even taking extra courses to explore the area in detail. Monetary rewards are not the driving force behind such extra-mile efforts, but rather it is the satisfaction of accomplishment. Later my letters of recommendation can, of course, be much more specific and likely much more enthusiastic. I make sure that proper public acknowledgment is given, and whenever possible I provide joint authorship on a publication. Thus, a standing refereeing assignment for the Journal of Chemical Education routinely carries two of our names, and three of my recent books are joint authorships with staff members.

Interaction with Colleagues

Control of one's time with colleagues is perhaps easiest, since directness among peers is not threatening. Thus, social chatting, while not frequent, does occur and can either be steered to a professional topic, or the contact can be broken by a simple "I'm busy."

Committee meetings are notorious time consumers. It is enlightening to ask the question, What is the purpose of the meeting? What, specifically must be accomplished today? Based on the committee members' salaries, how much money (and time) is this costing the institution? Is the topic worth it?

To combat time fraud I often come to the meeting with the announcement that "I have one hour set aside for this meeting, then I must leave," or the suggestion that a time limit be set. Proper preparation by committee members saves time. Thus, if the topic is textbook selection, for instance, the texts under consideration should be reviewed before the meeting and a comparison chart prepared, listing authors and/or publishers versus desirable features, with a final rating assigned to each text. These may then be compared, substantive differences discussed, and a vote taken, rather than paging through the text during the meeting.

To me it is a conscientious move to skip meetings, or even ask to be relieved of that committee assignment, in cases where, beyond my control, repeated intrusion into my time takes place. It is a further responsibility to propose the abolishment of committees whose primary function appears to be solely the perpetuation of a tradition.

WHAT YOU CAN DO . . .

1. Analyze your time.
2. Set priorities.
3. Insist on lists, schedules, and plans.
4. Freely say "no" to unimportant requests on your time.
5. Visit with and learn from those who control their time well.
6. Go the extra mile, especially for those who help you.

Further Reading

Harris, Amy Bjork, and Harris, Thomas A. Staying OK. New York: Harper and Row, 1985.

Chapter 9
Office Time Savers

There can be no economy where there is no efficiency.
–Beaconsfield

The previous chapter dealt with efficiency in our relationship with those around us in the workplace. Here we discuss the proper management of things and obligations that surround us. As always, the driving force is to be more efficient, save time, and thus be able to help the student more and generally become a more productive person.

Things take time and the more things and obligations we have, the more time is demanded. Everyone manages things in some way; some do so by building a mountain of the incoming papers and working at it as time permits. In this manner many of the items at the bottom of the pile, when finally reached, are past their deadline and thus no longer significant. Others rarely, if ever, miss a deadline, are able to control a vast array of details, and are free to take on ever larger projects.

In this chapter then we explore the absolutely vital teaching tool of the efficient management of things and obligations about us. It is no great fun to spend time organizing and filing and planning; but unless time is taken to do this, we will have no time at all doing those things that are fun. Whenever possible, I do the unpleasant chores first and reward myself the rest of the day with those things I relish in. When called upon, I can quickly refer to a needed item.

Thus, by using good filing methods, I am able to easily access the complete data for any one of my approximately 15,000 students (about forty-four entries per student) who have gone through my classes in the past two decades. That is well over half a million pieces of information on students, in addition to many notes, comments, and course evaluations. Never is the advantage of the good file more evident than when a student enrolled years ago requests a letter of performance.

Calendars

Certainly among the oldest and most common office timesavers and organizers must be the calendars. These tools fulfill at least two functions: they are simple planners of activities, and they allow goal setting to take on written commitment.

- *Datebook.* Since my days in college, I have carried with me a little yearly pocket datebook in which I record reminders, meeting times, and places. It frees my mind from having to remember such details and, in addition, allows list making and goal setting.

When the contract for this book you are now reading was signed, together with the editors a deadline of February 15 was set for submission of the manuscript. This was in late September, leaving a little over five months to write the remaining five chapters. The outline and gathered materials for each of these remaining chapters had been in place for some time and was now studied in detail and an estimated writing time for each chapter established with the following target dates: October 18, finish chapter 5; November 8, finish chapter 7; November

29 and December 13 were the deadlines for chapters 8 and 9, respectively; and January 10 for chapter 10, leaving the rest of the time for taking care of loose ends. Having entered these dates into the datebook, the actual writing days and times (four hours on Tuesdays and Thursdays) were then determined for each week and followed. Except for some interruptions and delays, these were adhered to.

Plans cannot always be followed, nor can goals always be completed. However, it is an amazing fact that infinitely more can be accomplished with written-down goals than without them.

- *Three-Month Timeline*. During particularly hectic periods or for the execution of a project with unusually large numbers of details and deadlines, I have found it very helpful to establish a three-month timeline. Posted along the bottom of the office bulletin board, it is divided into months, weeks, and days, and each division is carefully labeled. Strips of paper of perhaps a quarter or half-inch width by two inches length are now used to note each little task, deadline, and reminder and are pinned below the corresponding day. As tasks are accomplished the strips are removed, or if need be, moved to other days. If many tasks fall on one day, the strips are pinned below each other. The beauty of this method is that it provides such good overview of the work ahead and allows easy planning in anticipation of heavy work demands.

- *Long-Range Planning*. We all have goals, and we all know the frustration of not being able to accomplish many of them. Some persons vent this frustration by constantly talking about what should or could be done. Popular wisdom expresses this in various ways: "Talk is cheap," "Actions speak louder than words," "Ideas come a dime-a-dozen."

There are many reasons why things don't get done as we like. Laziness, time restrictions (thoughts come fast, whereas implementation takes time), fear of failure, or–amazingly–fear of success, and so on. It is probably a fact of life that most of us will never get done all the things we plan. However, it is also true that we could get done much, much more if we took the time to set proper goals and had plans to implement these goals.

The steps to the successful accomplishment of a goal are astonishingly simple. First, we must set priorities among all the possibilities open to us, because likely we will have many more ideas than we will have time for. Second, we must write the goal down in as clear and precise a manner as possible, giving the exact things to be accomplished AND an exact deadline for its accomplishment. Telling others about it adds a sense of accountability for its attainment. Third, we need to break down the road toward its accomplishments into a step-by-step plan. This calls for an estimate of the overall work involved, a look at other obligations, and an assignment of daily tasks to advance our cause. Fourth, we must review the goal every day–in fact, read the goal aloud perhaps in the morning or in the evening before going to bed. This little exercise feeds the subconscious mind something to work on while the conscious mind is busy doing other things or is asleep.

Figure 6.2 showed a simple tool which aids in planning. We should always have short-range and long-range goals. The specifics for the accomplishment of a ten-year goal may be quite fuzzy at first; however, if constantly kept in mind, there will some day be an opportunity to reach it.

Project Organizer

Consider a given project such as chairing a search committee. There are dozens of tasks associated with the project which often have specific deadlines: minutes must be sent out; the date for the next meeting set; a phone call made; a week prior to the meeting a contact must be made; interviews must be set up; a final selection date must be met. When this project is one of a dozen going on at the same time, the timetables are indeed complex.

While calendars and datebooks are handy devices to put order to the task, they do not allow easy overview of the work ahead. I have found a Project Organizer to be a wonderful tool, since it provides the overview for a dozen projects over a period of a month; it is small and fits the coat pocket; but most of all, it is flexible where dates, projects, and tasks can be adjusted. Figure 9.1 shows the design.

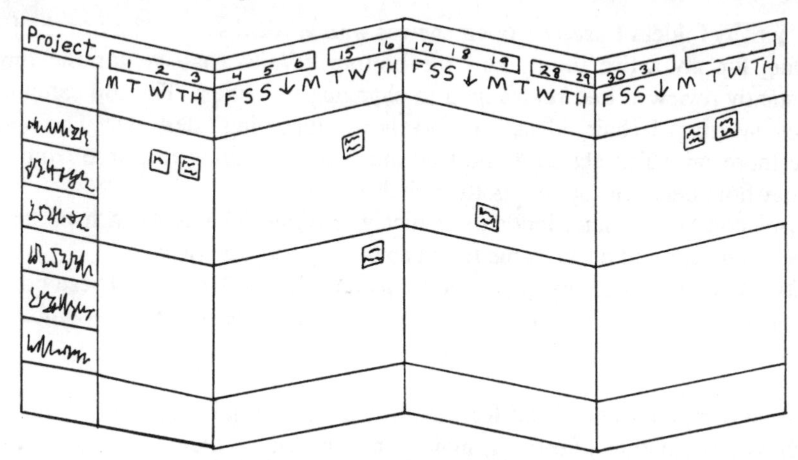

Figure 9.1 Project organizer.

The body is made from stiff cardboard. Across the top a movable continuous strip is numbered from 1 to 31 for the days of the month. The strip is held in place by weaving it through slits in the cardboard. The area below the strip is divided into four weeks and each week into seven days marked M T W T F S S. The strip is adjusted so as to match the date with the weeks. Small Post-It stickers are used to label the current month, the project titles on the far left vertical column, and each task matching date and project. The Post-It is removed when a task is done or moved to a new date, if need be. The projects can be arranged in any order. The entire Organizer folds four times to pocket size for easy transport.

Filing

How can one save time in the storage and retrieval of documents? A good filing system must be somewhere between the extremes of one folder for every paper and all papers in one folder. Assume that proper filing guidelines are followed: one filing cabinet for a given type of files; each drawer for a particular topic; within a drawer, dividers that separate subtopics; within these, colored folders for different entries, each folder labeled properly; and finally, no more than ten papers per folder, unless they are grouped with staples, paper clips, or dividers. Does this assure a properly working system? Of course not. Some persons whose system is a total disarray seem to always find the needed papers (eventually!), whereas those with good systems sometimes have difficulty. The answer is that periodically time must be devoted to the system. It is certain, though, that less time will need to be devoted to the orderly system than to the random one.

My system is a loose version of the proper guidelines: one cabinet for archive records, one for currently used materials, one for filing project ideas, one for lecture materials, one for books in the making with folders for each chapter, etc. While I attempt to file properly, retrieval may break down unless I use each section periodically. For this reason it is advisable to go through the files and rearrange, delete, and recode routinely. Rather than using new folders, I may choose to use that same tattered folder, since its appearance immediately announces the familiar content.

For high activity folders I use two open shelves with vertical slots. The top shelf is labeled "Action" (calling for my active input) and the bottom "Wait" (passive for the time being). These are constantly reviewed and rearranged to changing priorities. The top category may include folders on meetings I chair, ideas for workshops, upcoming talks, etc. The bottom shelf folders include those on which action was taken and is now awaiting response from other parties. Folders may float between top and bottom shelves.

My thirty-pigeon-hole cabinet lends itself nicely to filing documents with perhaps vertical or horizontal relationships and at the same time provide a good overview.

Boxed kits are set up for repeating experiments and demonstrations. These boxes contain all the necessary equipment and materials so that no time need be wasted reassembling prior to each use.

The personal computer lends itself for excellent filing and quick retrieval of huge numbers of details, such as examination questions, mailing addresses, problem sets, etc. Each can be tagged with any given characteristic and retrieved accordingly.

Examination Writing

Students like to be given a goodly number of examinations to provide many chances. For teachers, the work put into examination writing and grading must rank high in importance; therefore, considerable care (and thus time) is needed. When the above is coupled with large enrollment classes, teachers could conceivably be entrapped by their own work. Size can indeed be a handicap, unless efficiency goes with it.

Two solutions to this dilemma have already been discussed elsewhere: the use of multiple-choice questions and computer grading. Here, then, we discuss a time-saving technique of the examination assembly.

It is important to establish a large pool of good multiple-choice questions. Again, techniques of testing the usefulness of multiple-choice questions were discussed elsewhere. I have a collection of approximately a thousand multiple-choice questions usable on examinations. With such a large number, repeat use of a question is possible if a) new questions are constantly written and used, and b) repeat questions are not used for several years. My questions are typed vertically on 3x5 cards, using a good carbon ribbon for clear reproduction. As shown on the sample in Figure 9.2, the front of the card carries two codes: the correct answer to the question in the lower left bottom corner; and a filing code in the lower right bottom corner, written horizontally. The space between these codes and the text of the question may be used for editorial comments. The reverse of the card is stamped with the date each time the card is used. Let us first consider the *filing system*.

The cards are filed horizontally so that the filing code is at the upper right of the card. Tabs are used to separate topics. These divisions do not pertain to any particular text, but rather evolved as guided by convenience. Each chapter is divided into major sections, these into subsections, and these again into smaller topics. The index tabs for each of these divisions line up: chapters are all in the center, major sections all on the far left, subsections somewhat to the right, and so on. All the index cards for a given chapter then are coded with both name and sequential numbers. Each card belonging to a given section is given that section's number (8-31 in Figure 9.2a), which then allow for quick refiling after use. New sections can be added anywhere through the use of additional codes (i.e., 8-31-1).

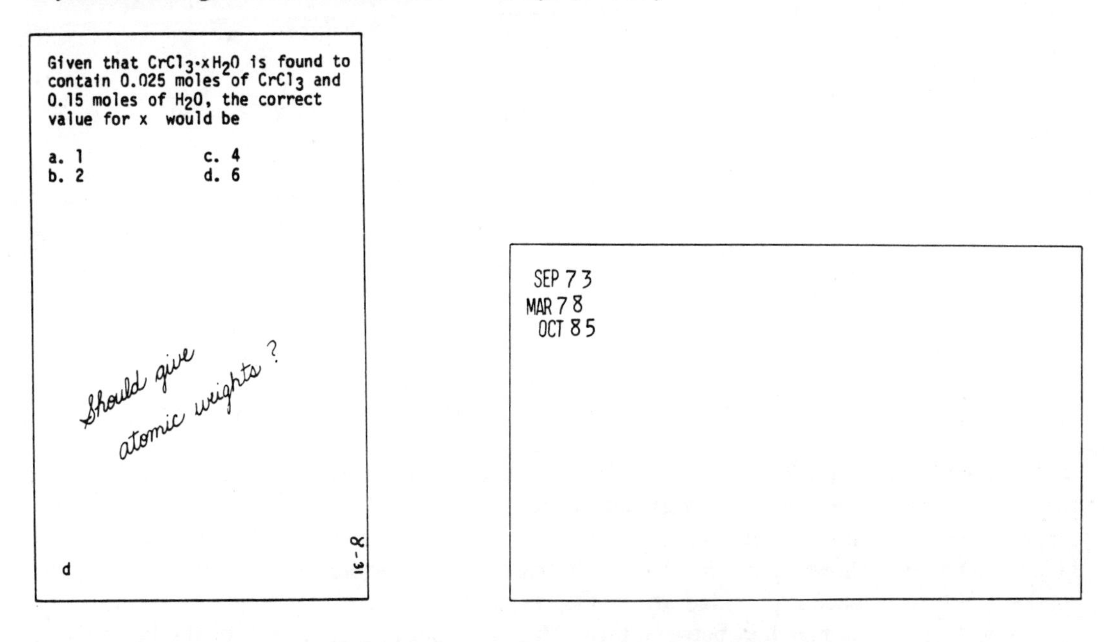

Figure 9.2 Using 3 × 5 cards for questions: (a) front, (b) back.

The question arises, why not use a computer for this? While I have access to many computers and own several, I have found my filing system comfortably tangible; that is, I have a good overview of all of it at once, I can lay any cards side-by-side, and I am not limited by growth demands.

Let us now consider the actual *assembly* of an examination. The chapters to be covered are divided into sections using the lecture notes and the text as a guide. Each section is then judged in terms of its importance, lecture time devoted to it, and the reasonable number of questions for it. These questions in turn are divided into recall, calculation, judgment, etc. Some questions are written and typed on 3x5 cards; others are selected from the large file, making sure no recently used ones are included. Once the proper number and sequence of questions has been determined, they are then assembled as shown in Figure 9.3.

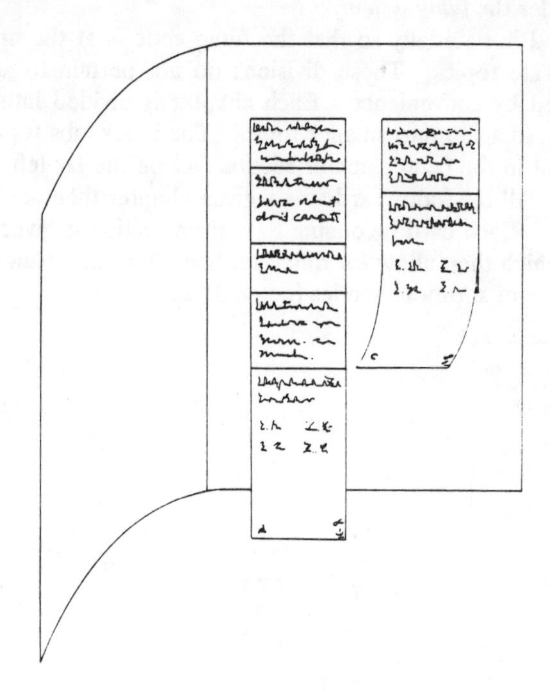

Figure 9.3 Assembling exam questions on photo album pages.

Large photo album pages with cellophane-covered adhesive make excellent backings for the arrangement. The pages are prepared by cutting them to 8.5" width but allowing a length longer than 11". With the cellophane laid back, the sticky surface is marked with two sets of blue parallel lines showing the line-up for the cards. The top and bottom margins are also marked, and some space is provided for the title and instructions.

The first card is now laid between these blue lines, starting at the top of the left column. The second card is laid over the first so as to cover the codes and any editorial comments of the first card and provide a comfortable reading space between the texts of the questions. This is continued to the bottom margin, after which the second column is filled similarly and the cellophane is once again stretched over the page.

After all questions have been arranged, the heading and instructions are added, page and question numbers are inserted, and the assembly may then be used as the master for any type of reproduction. Alternatively, the assembly of questions may be xeroxed, additional information added (question numbers, headings, etc.), and the finished work given to the duplicating shop.

The advantages of this system are indeed great. First, it saves repeated typing. Once the question is typed on a card and is found to be a good question, it will not have to be typed again. Second, the arrangement of the questions is totally versatile, allowing the addition of other materials such as charts, pictures, cartoons, etc. Third, if kept reasonably clean, the photo album pages can be used for a long time. I have used the same set for many years.

For short quizzes, where the number of students is manageable and computer analysis is not important, an adapted version of the above method may be used. Questions are assembled from files in much the same manner as for major examinations. Generally, I attempt to place ten questions on one sheet of paper, with a scoring box in the lower right-hand corner as shown in Figure 9.4. Grading is made very efficient by simply taking one of the quiz forms and punching out the correct answers, lining up this key to each of the student papers and counting correct marks. This will become the score out of ten, or it may be converted to percentage. The score box is located in the lower right-hand corner, since this area has a greater chance of being

Chemistry C 101 - QUIZ #1

January 30

Name ____________________

Answer all questions by filling in the appropriate circles below.

1. Which of the following is a chemical change or process?
   a. combustion; b. evaporation; c. freezing; d. melting; e. none of these.

2. A laboratory method used to separate one liquid from another is
   a. evaporation; b. distillation; c. solution; d. conservation;
   e. crystallization.

3. The list of the 15 most abundant elements in the earth, both core and crust, includes
   a. H; b. C; c. N; d. O; e. Pb.

4. The weight of an object is
   a. the same as its mass; b. a measure of the amount of gravitational attraction;
   c. the same no matter where it is measured; d. all of the above; e. none of the above.

5. The density of Al is 2.70 g/ml and the density of lead is 11.3 g/ml. How many grams of lead will occupy the same volume as 54.0 g of aluminum?
   a. 22.6 g; b. 12.9 g; c. 226 g; d. 56.5 g; e. 1,647.5 g.

6. The highest mountain in the world is Mount Everest - at least when measured from sea level. But if measured from the center of the Earth, the highest point turns out to be Mount Chimborazo, an Andean peak in Ecuador at eleven km. What is this height in feet? (1 m = 3.281 ft)
   a. 91,671; b. 36,091; c. 3,609; d. 3,353; e. 2,794.

7. Which of the following statements is true?
   a. the # of protons and neutrons in the nucleus of an isotope gives its mass #;
   b. the # of protons in any atom of an element determines its atomic number;
   c. the mass # minus the atomic # equals the # of neutrons in an isotope;
   d. isotopes have different # of neutrons within the nuclei of atoms of the same element;
   e. all of the above.

8. The notation $^{11}_{5}B$ indicates that
   a. the atomic weight of naturally occurring boron is about 11.5;
   b. boron has more than one isotope; c. this boron atom has 6 neutrons;
   d. this boron atom has 6 electrons; e. both b. and c. are correct.

9. The behavior of selenium is most like that of
   a. oxygen; b. arsenic; c. bromine; d. phosphorus; e. both b. and c.

10. Considering the position in the periodic table, which has the smallest radius?
    a. P; b. S; c. Se; d. Te; e. Cl.

____

EXTRA CREDIT Write the electronic configuration for S^{--}.

____

	a	b	c	d	e
1	0	0	0	0	0
2	0	0	0	0	0
3	0	0	0	0	0
4	0	0	0	0	0
5	0	0	0	0	0
6	0	0	0	0	0
7	0	0	0	0	0
8	0	0	0	0	0
9	0	0	0	0	0
10	0	0	0	0	0

Figure 9.4 Quick scoring quiz.

covered during the quiz by the working arm (at least for right-handed students), thereby enhancing security.

Assigning Letter Grades

Throughout the term we keep only numerical scores for all student work, which are used as a basis of assigning letter grades at the end of the term (or at any time during the term). The first step is to plot a histogram, showing the distribution of all student scores on an absolute or percentage scale. As a guide in letter grade assignments, we use several formulas as comparisons.

1. The *standard theoretical curve* is an idealized distribution of student performance and works best for very large classes where random distribution is most likely. Figure 9.5 shows the theoretical percentage of students falling in each category. This approach suffers from the disadvantages of absolute scales: there must be as many A's as there are F's, and B's as there are D's. It does not allow for the very unusual class, for the fact that some of the poorer students may have dropped the class, and of course insists on a large number of average students. However, it is a good comparison to judge against.

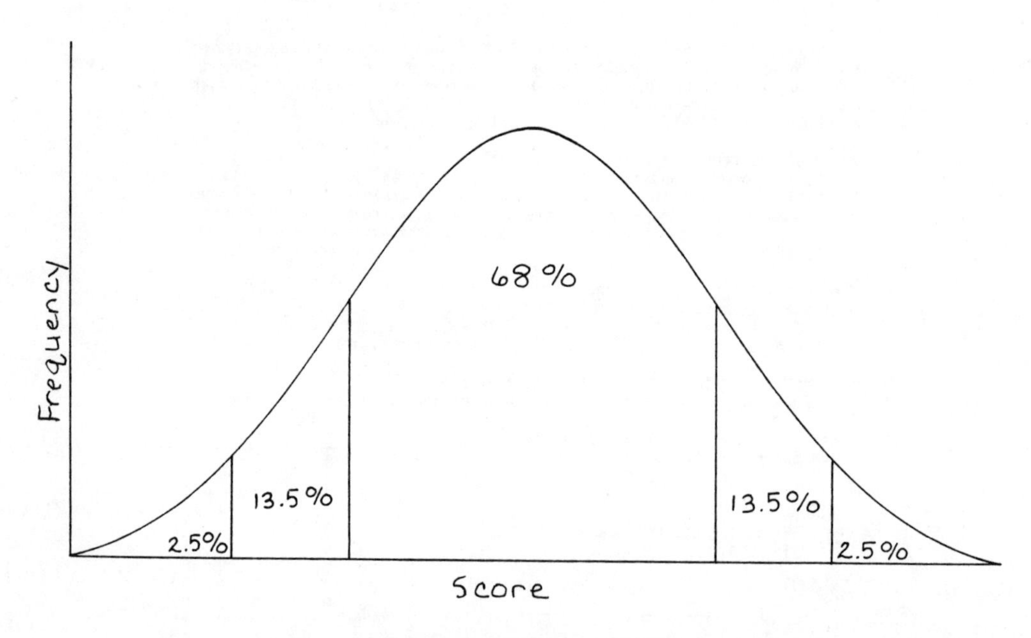

Figure 9.5 Theoretical histogram of scores.

2. The use of the *adjusted average* is a variation of the T-score. The latter shows what the student's score would have been if the mean (average) score had been 50 and the standard deviation had been ten units. In our simplified version of the adjusted average we simply slide the distribution curve so as to obtain an average of 75%, which is then used to assign letter grades according to one of the following scales:

90% = A	90% = A
80% = B	80% = B
70% = C	60% = C
60% = D	50% = D
50% = F	40% = F

3. Still another approach is to use the *formula*

   N = 1/2 (Total Possible Points + Highest Score)

   For example, on a total possible of 1000 points, the top student may have earned 948 points. *N* therefore is half of 1,948 = 974. Again, use one of two scales:

90% of N = A	90% of N = A
80% of N = B	80% of N = B
70% of N = C	60% of N = C
60% of N = D	50% of N = D
50% of N = F	40% of N = F

4. The *natural curve* is perhaps the best approach, since it uses the observed distribution and checks for natural breaks in that distribution.

During the final grading session a table is prepared showing the letter grade cuts for each of the four methods. Randomly chosen students are then looked at to see if they fall into expected grade regions. All of this is coupled with personal knowledge of the student, and the grade cuts are set. Each student close to a cut is considered individually for possible movement, either to a higher or lower grade.

Grading done with the use of the tools mentioned, and in the presence of several persons whose judgment is important, has always led to fair assignments and the resulting peace of mind.

WHAT YOU CAN DO . . .

1. Acknowledge the fact that for most of us there is always a more efficient way to do our tasks.
2. Keep a computer (or at least a typewriter) in your office.
3. Use and perfect at least one good calendar system.
4. Randomly pull three to five folders from your files. Is their content familiar, properly located?
5. Once a year clean out files and bookshelves.
6. Evaluate both the care and time devoted to examinations. Aim to improve both.
7. Study some published materials on the subject of grade assignments.

Chapter 10
Evaluate and Improve

Those who do not learn from the past, are condemned to repeat it.

–George Santayana

Those words ring harsh but true. Unless we are willing to expose ourselves to an examination of our past performance, we cannot hope to improve. No risk, no gain. Only through the pain of criticism does the joy of victory truly become amazing.

How well I remember the grueling sessions in graduate school where we took turns describing our research to fellow students who took pains to probe and question every possible angle of our work. Through these sessions our work became better, because our minds were sharpened and our data was double checked. The payoff was the joy of accomplishment when faced with the real examination before a committee of professors.

If we expose ourselves to the rigors of evaluation, we signal willingness to change for the better. We may find ourselves changing the content of our teaching material, our teaching style, our emphasis, even our personality. If we resist evaluation, we admit that we are set in our ways, that we are "gone to seed," that we are not capable of risking change.

Evaluation is the careful gathering of facts for the purpose of redirecting a course of events. Teaching evaluations check many facets, among which are instructor knowledge, course decisions, classroom behavior, student learning, organization, enthusiasm, rapport with the students, and motivation.

Research on evaluation as a tool has been conducted since the turn of the century and has generally found the above listed criteria as indeed being key characteristics of effective teaching. Research in this area continues by many: Centra, Doyle, Seldin, Cohen, McKeachie, Hilderbrand, Sorcinelli.

There are at least three reasons why evaluations are conducted. First and foremost must be the value for self-improvement. Second, scientifically run evaluations can be the basis for sound research; and third, evaluations are often conducted for the purpose of administrative decisions such as salary adjustments, promotions, and tenure. Evaluation for administrative purposes are usually subject to vigorous debate. Can one make such decisions by evaluating for just a short period of time? Is it fair to evaluate one professional on the basis of service, another on the basis of teaching and still another on the basis of research? After all, evaluation of research productivity is easier to measure, is more standardized across the disciplines, and is more universal with a peer refereeing system in existence.

It is therefore often suggested that favorable administrative decisions are easier to attain in the research arena than in teaching. My experience is otherwise. While one promotion was based on research activity, promotion to the rank of professor came on the basis of teaching activities. And I have found teaching to lavish rewards in many other ways as well: sabbatical, study leave of absence, grants, teaching awards, teaching fellowship, salary increases, much recognition from colleagues, speaking engagements, media interviews, publications, special committee assignments, consultantships, and most of all student response and gratefulness expressed in so many different ways.

Self-Evaluation

If the purpose of evaluation is to serve the student better, then self-evaluation by the teacher should be most helpful. While inherently true, the idea is fraught with controversy. Self-assessment of one's own abilities tend to be high, are usually conducted without a valid standard against which to measure, and the results, especially if negative, tend not to be divulged for scrutiny by any scientific method.

For these reasons, self-evaluation is usually reserved for personal use, where the safety of privacy may result in self-improvement. If self-evaluation is sought, several instruments can be of help.

1. **Written Self-Analysis**–To subject to the discipline of writing down what we think our abilities and shortcomings are can be very helpful. It organizes thoughts and has the potential of finding some solutions. Self-analysis can take the form of an essay on one's philosophy of teaching, a simple historical trajectory of growth, a listing of past weaknesses and victories; it can be the periodic use of a check-off list to monitor progress, or it can be the yearly submission to paper of goals and steps for the accomplishments of those goals.

Self-analyses are most useful if several steps are followed. First, they must be utterly honest. Second, self-analyses should be prepared routinely. Third, they should be reviewed periodically with the view of seeking improvement; and fourth, it is best to make oneself accountable by sharing them with someone trusted.

2. **Self-Observation**–As teachers we are constantly in the public eye. It is helpful to put ourselves in the public's place, thereby giving us a view of ourselves as the public sees us. How can this be done? One of the simplest ways is to look at student notes of our lectures. What did they hear and see? What the students perceived to be important will be in the notes. Is that what we meant to be important?

More powerful–and at first more intimidating–is the replay of our recorded lecture. How do we sound? Do we have annoying vocal mannerisms? Do we emphasize vocally or are we monotone? Do we speak at the proper rate?

Quite punishing can be the review of a video recording of our performance. To sit in the privacy of the office and watch what the students see is often humbling, sometimes enlightening.

3. **Self-Comparing**–It is a good thing to learn from those we admire and respect by comparing our styles to theirs. We can also compare to the ideal which may be gleaned from our reading, thinking, and observing of changing trends in education. We can compare by tracking our progress. A weekly chart of the average number of "ahs" uttered in a lecture will show progress over a term.

4. **Self-Testing**–There are many professional instruments which permit us a glimpse into our inner selves. These may be strict analyses of our gifts and traits or the matching of teaching with learning styles.

Isabel Briggs Myers has developed many materials which have helped thousands of persons. One test determines four major personal traits. The first of these is preference toward extroversion versus introversion; the second determines the mode of perceiving by sensing or intuition; the third describes the judging preference by thinking or feeling; and the last describes the overall preference as judging or perceiving. Assigned percentages to each give a fairly good picture of our preferences.

Another self-assessment instrument is Gregorc's Style Delineator. Less academic in nature, it is geared to the masses, resulting in a personality diamond whose corners may touch briefly or stretch far into the practical, probable, potential, or possible.

A third instrument of great help to me has been Palmer Becker's "You and Your Options." Through some very carefully thoughtout questions and exercises, it seeks to give a personal profile using eight areas: interests, abilities, attitudes, personality, values, world, decisions, and goals. This is followed by a ninth lesson on options and a final summary of a plan.

Student Evaluation

It is generally recognized that student evaluations are the most common instrument used for teaching evaluations (see Centra, Seldin). This is as it should be, since students are likely most interested in and affected by the teaching; normally they are the only ones who observe the instructor every day throughout the term, and, of course, they are the target of the teaching process. It is also true that student evaluations are perhaps easier to obtain on a continuing basis. They provide a relatively large data base and have been subject to much study over the years.

On the other hand, critics of student evaluations contend that students have little knowledge of the subject matter and should therefore not be placed in the position of judging teaching performance. Critics further argue that students will be tempted to evaluate based on their own performance in the course, or on the teacher's level of entertainment.

Most important in any kind of evaluation is the question of student learning. Exit interviews, alumni evaluations, and requests for letters all have been used to assure an assessment based on student learning. The findings are that, for the most part, student evaluations correlate well with other evaluations.

Well-designed student evaluations allow response to several areas: the instructor (preparation, enthusiasm, personality, flexibility); the instruction (explanations, balance of theory and practical examples, speaking ability, hand-outs); the course (organization, level of expectation, number of exams, homework); and student self-evaluation (does he work hard, expected grade).

Evaluation instruments must, of course, strive to be reliable (internally consistent), and valid (true to the facts). This can be attained only after much thought in preparation and testing of models. Unless this is an area of research interest, it is really best to use an existing professional instrument, rather than taking the time to develop one.

Student evaluations generally fall into one of the following four types.

1. **Universal**–Questions, usually with multiple-choice answers, are provided and may include the areas of instructor, instruction, the course, and the student. Table 10.1 gives an example.

2. **Cafeteria**–From a master pool of 200 to 400 questions, each discipline may choose questions applicable to its area. Often a core set of questions is required in each evaluation form. Table 10.2 shows an example.
3. **Essay**–The student is requested to write his assessment of the instructor, the instruction, the course, and himself. This method has the definite benefit of allowing the student to express himself freely without the influence of guided questions. It has the disadvantage that it does not lend itself for quick quantitative analyses.
4. **Diagnostic**–These are forms usually prepared for the purpose of addressing a specific area or problem. They are often initiated by the teacher for the sake of self-improvement.

Typical results from a questionnaire such as given in Table 10.2 might report the total number of students responding, the mean for each item, the standard deviation, and perhaps a report which is the difference between the score obtained for any given item minus the mean for that item obtained by a group of colleagues divided by the standard deviation of that group. The results allow for quick selection of one's very best and worst scores.

Average scores may also be obtained by selecting any group of questions. Thus, to check the adequacy of the instructor's grading process, items 11, 12, 23, and 24 may be averaged. The mean of items 13, 16, 18, and 19 would give an indication of the motivational quality of the student's experience. The mean of items 4, 6, 7, 8, and 12 is a yardstick of the rapport between the instructor and the students. The instructor's ability to communicate effectively is reflected in the mean of items, 1, 2, 3, 4, 5, 14, 15, 16, 17, 19, and 20. This eleven-item "global" score is perhaps the best index of how students rated the class.

Table 10.1 A universal teaching evaluation form.

Prof.______________
Department___________
Course Number________
Date______________

Student Evaluation of Instruction

I. EVALUATION OF INSTRUCTION

Please carefully evaluate the effectiveness of the teacher of this course. Place an "X" in ONE of the blanks under each of the major categories. Comments may be extended to the other side of the sheet.

KNOWLEDGE OF SUBJECT MATTER — Comment
__ Exceedingly well informed
__ Adequately informed
__ Not well informed
__ Very poorly informed

ATTITUDE TOWARD SUBJECT — Comment
__ Enthusiastic, enjoys teaching subject
__ Rather interested
__ Only routine interest displayed
__ Uninterested

Table 10.1 Continued

ABILITY TO EXPLAIN	Comment
___ Explanations clear and to the point	
___ Explanation usually adequate	
___ Explanation often inadequate	
___ Explanations absent or totally inadequate	
SPEAKING ABILITY	Comment
___ Voice and demeanor excellent	
___ Adequate or average	
___ Poor speaking distracting	
___ Poor speaking a serious handicap	
ATTITUDE TOWARD STUDENTS	Comment
___ Sympathetic, helpful, concerned	
___ Usually helpful and sympathetic	
___ Avoids individual contact, routine attitude	
___ Distant, cold, aloof	
PERSONALITY	Comment
___ Attractive personality; I would like to know him better	
___ Satisfactory personality	
___ Not an outgoing personality	
___ Personality conflict	
TOLERANCE OF DISAGREEMENT	Comment
___ Encourages and values reasonable disagreement	
___ Accepts disagreement fairly well	
___ Discourages disagreement	
___ Dogmatic, intolerant of disagreement	

COMPARED TO ALL COLLEGE INSTRUCTORS YOU HAVE HAD, HOW WOULD YOU RATE THIS INSTRUCTOR AS A TEACHER?

___ Outstanding
___ Better than average
___ Average
___ Below average
___ Poor

IF YOU COULD CHOOSE BETWEEN THIS INSTRUCTOR AND OTHERS IN A FURTHER COURSE, HOW WOULD YOU RATE YOUR PRESENT INSTRUCTOR?

___ Would prefer him/her to most teachers I have had.
___ Would be very pleased to have him/her again.
___ Would rather not have him/her again.
___ Would not have him/her again under any circumstances.

THE REVERSE SIDE OF THIS EVALUATION MAY BE USED FOR FURTHER GENERAL COMMENTS

Do not sign name. Please indicate class standing..

Major subject..

Approximate accumulative average..

Table 10.1 Continued

II. EVALUATION OF COURSE

Please evaluate this particular section of this course.

ORGANIZATION OF THE COURSE — Comment
___ Well organized
___ Inadequate, but could be better
___ Inadequate organization detracts
___ Confused and unsystematic

ORGANIZATION OF DAILY LECTURES (OR CLASS WORK) — Comment
___ Well organized in meaningful sequence
___ Usually organized
___ Organization not too apparent
___ Little or no organization

FREQUENCY OF TEST — Comment
___ Right number, well timed
___ Too infrequent
___ Too frequent
___ Timing should be improved

CONTENT OF TESTS — Comment
___ Satisfactory
___ Too detailed
___ Not comprehensive enough
___ Wrong type of test for this course

OPPORTUNITY FOR QUESTIONS AND DISCUSSION — Comment
___Ample opportunity
___ Occasional opportunity
___ Rare opportunity
___ Never

ASSIGNMENTS
___ Assignments clear and reasonable
___ Clear but too long
___ Unclear
___ Always unclear and unreasonable

TEXTBOOKS
___ Textbooks good
___ Textbooks satisfactory
___ Use of text should be modified
___ Urge a different text altogether

WORK RELATED TO CLASS LEVEL
___ Work suited to class level
___ Attempt made to suit class level
___ Work completely above class level
___ Work completely below class level

ON THE REVERSE SIDE OF THIS SHEET PLEASE MAKE SUGGESTIONS FOR IMPROVING THIS COURSE.

Do not sign name. Please indicate class standing..

Major subject..

Approximate accumulative average ....

Table 10.2 Sample cafeteria evaluation form.

Class		Grade You Expect		Major	
Freshman	0	A	0	Education	0
Sophomore	0	B	0	Humanities	0
Junior	0	C	0	Law	0
Senior	0	D	0	Medicine	0
Grad	0	F	0	Science	0
Other	0			Eng. & Tech.	0
				Other	0

Please read each statement carefully, then select one of these five alternatives: Strongly agree (SA), Agree (A), Undecided (U), Disagree (D), Strongly disagree (SD).

SA A U D SD

1. I understand easily what my instructor is saying.
2. My instructor has an effective style of presentation.
3. My instructor seems well-prepared for class.
4. My instructor displays enthusiasm when teaching.
5. My instructor has stimulated my thinking.
6. My instructor is actively helpful when students have problems.
7. My instructor deals fairly and impartially with me.
8. My instructor readily maintains rapport with this class.
9. I understand what is expected of me in this course.
10. Exams accurately assess what I have learned in this course.
11. Exams are fair.
12. Grades are assigned fairly and impartially.
13. Assignments are of definite instructional value.
14. I would enjoy taking another course from this instructor.
15. I like the way the instructor conducts this course.
16. My instructor motivates me to do my best work.
17. My instructor explains difficult material clearly.
18. Course assignments are interesting and stimulating.
19. Overall, this course is among the best I have ever taken.
20. Overall, this instructor is among the best teachers I have known.
21. Is this course in your major field of study? (Yes = SA; No = A)
22. Is this course required? (Yes = SA; No = A)
23. Grade you expected to earn at the start of class. (A = SA; B = A; C = U)
24. Grade you will actually receive. (A = SA; B = A; C = U; D = D; F = SD

– John F. Kremer

Peer Evaluation

Surprisingly, there has recently been a dramatic increase in the use of peer evaluation. It is surprising because the instrument has so many strikes against it. First and foremost, there is the threat of a colleague sitting in judgment of what could affect one's future. Nothing is of more sensitive nature. Most of us would prefer, if an evaluation is to be done, that it be done by someone unknown to us. A peer we see routinely and, therefore, negative evaluation results may affect collegiality, friendships, or, at best, be a continuing source of embarrassment. Furthermore, peer evaluation is very time-consuming. To provide a good sampling, a minimum of three classes need be attended per term, in addition to the training for the evaluation and the processing of results. Lastly, colleagues tend to overrate each other, thereby providing an untrue picture.

On the other hand, peers are the only ones who know the subject matter and have had experience in very similar settings. Therefore, they can provide another very valuable component in the total evaluation picture. Peers can give expert comments on the colleague's knowledge of the subject matter, course material, curriculum development, staff supervision, homework assignments, laboratory experiments, papers, exams, and grading. And, of course, they can also comment on classroom teaching itself: clarify, organization, enthusiasm, student rapport, student participation; however, it is the evaluation of classroom teaching that is most controversial, likely because it is touching a most personal part of the life of a teacher. It is for this reason that peer evaluation is often limited to course and curriculum advice and not classroom performance.

However, peer evaluation can be allowed to assess the entire teaching aspect, if it is done in a spirit of friendship, at the initiative of the faculty being evaluated, and where the express purpose of both parties involved is the improvement of teaching rather than a test for administrative decisions. I have benefited immensely from peer input.

HOW TO BE A SUCCESSFUL CLASSROOM PEER EVALUATOR

1. Be invited for the observation–know its purpose.
2. Discuss all evaluation details with your colleague *before* the visit.
3. Learn all you can about the class, the course, the instructor.
4. Arrive early and observe pre-class activities.
5. Take copious notes on student, faculty and teaching environment.
6. Analyze your findings.
7. Meet with colleague soon after the observation, inviting his self-assessment of the class.
8. Share your findings as another point of view.
9. Jointly make suggestions for changes.

–Adapted from G. W. Zimmerman

Peer evaluation can take several forms:

Vote. All peers rank each other, based on what they know about each other, have heard from students, or perhaps have observed. Alternatively, any teacher may ask his peers to rank him alone from among the group of peers. Evaluative comments by either method can be used for the purpose of improvement.

Video. The faculty member records his lectures and chooses his best sample for evaluation by the peer.

Visit. The faculty member invites a respected colleague of his choosing to attend his class in order to make constructive comments.

Microteaching. The faculty member gives a brief (seven-to-ten-minute) sample teaching in front of his peers for the purpose of generating evaluative comments.

In the last three methods, the evaluator's task is to observe carefully and in detail, checking teacher input (lectures, praises, gives instructions, uses student ideas, asks and answers questions, processes feelings); student input (asking, answering, commenting); or no input (thinking, silence, confusion). A notation should be made every three seconds, or whenever input changes. Prepared tables or grids help the recording process.

A faculty member's willingness to submit to an evaluation is a direct function of the institution's willingness to help and the teaching climate it creates. Here are some suggestions for schools.

- New faculty should be given orientations which go beyond the dos and don'ts and the physical aspects of the teaching process. Good orientations may include talks by senior faculty, brief sample teachings, study of cases, videos of teaching followed by evaluation, actual visits to classes in session, etc.
- Weekly teaching luncheons may be arranged where small groups of faculty, both new and experienced, get together and informally talk about their teaching. This can create an environment where young faculty soon will feel free to ask questions and bring out problems in their teaching.
- Teaching seminars are somewhat more formal, in that faculty take turns briefly presenting a particular aspect of teaching. It is important to allow enough time for discussion.
- A telephone hotline can be set up. A given number may be dialed at any time by faculty who just had a difficulty, an idea, for which they would like another opinion. Selected faculty are on call on a rotating basis.
- Mentor/mentee teams are set up between junior and respected senior faculty, to study a book together, go to conference, work on a joint project, and meet on a regular basis for discussion.

Expert Evaluation

Larger institutions of higher learning often have an office or a staff member qualified for professional teaching evaluation. The procedures used vary from institution to institution, and one must be willing to use their approach. I have benefited from such service and recommend it. It has the advantage of being less threatening than peer evaluation, is totally without bias, usually does not cost much since many institutions do it as a service, and its professionally compiled results are widely accepted.

Analysis and Documentation

Our style of teaching is the result of our personality, our training, and the influence all around us, past and present. However, our improvement of teaching is the result of evaluations by self, students, peers, and professionals. If improvement is truly sought, it is then important to carefully analyze and plot the trends in evaluation results. Professional help, such as that available from The Center for Research on Learning and Teaching at the University of Michigan, or the Center for Faculty Evaluation and Development at Kansas State University, is of great value.

In my own evaluations, I did notice that for "ability to explain" I consistently received my lowest score. After several semesters of conscious effort to improve my rating in this area, I did share my frustration with a colleague, who in turn shared his, and pointed out that his, too, were always lowest for that particular question. After some further investigation, it was found that this was a general experience among the faculty, and the data seemed to indicate that low ratings for that question come from low-achieving students. Nevertheless, I have ever since been challenged to greater efforts in explaining.

In addition to the standard evaluation at the end of the term, it is helpful to also run an evaluation at about midterm. This reveals any problems and allows these to be rectified early enough so students can benefit. I publicly share the problem areas of my evaluations with the students, and together we search for the best means to overcome the problem. This tells the students that I am willing to expose myself because I care.

Teaching Dossier

Documentation of teaching activities is important to allow quick overview and to provide an organized report usable for administrative decisions. If done well, there is no reason why positive decisions on tenure, promotion, and salary could not be made, based strictly on teaching accomplishments. What follows is a checklist to be used as a guide in preparing a teaching dossier.

The successful teaching dossier is based on a continuing effort of collecting all evidence. At least once a year this is organized in a meaningful manner, making the strongest possible honest case for you (if you don't do it, no one else will). The challenge is to be complete, yet avoid duplicating and stuffing with trivia. A well-prepared dossier pays off well.

Class Activities

1. Courses taught should be listed by code, title, date, and enrollment.
2. Outlines and syllabi are helpful additions.
3. Curricular developments document creative changes in courses and programs.
4. Creating of new courses represent major efforts.
5. Team teaching and guest lecturing give evidence of professional cooperation.
6. Individual teachings may include research students, seminars, or private students.
7. Teaching outside the school reports on activities such as continuing education.

Indirect Teaching

8. Thesis direction is time consuming and can be of major impact.
9. Involvement in honors programs is evidence of the extra mile.
10. Supervising of teaching assistants is a necessity in many courses.
11. Giving public lectures is a desirable community service.
12. Invited lectures usually refer to professional meetings.
13. Workshops prove the expertise of the presenter.

Teaching Impact

14. Carefully summarize self, student, peer and professional evaluations.
15. Use tables and graphs to show trends in evaluation results.
16. Compile any and all unsolicited notes and letters from students, colleagues, and administrators.
17. List gifts received.
18. Compile any and all solicited letters from students, colleagues, and administrators.
19. Prepare a record of students taking several courses from you.
20. Summarize any exit interviews done with former students.
21. List worthy student accomplishments (admission to graduate school, scholarship, promotion, highly placed job, public notoriety) where you can claim some contribution.

Creative Endeavors

22. List research in teaching topics.
23. List, and separately file, all publications.
24. Compile all published reviews of your work.
25. Grant support shows the opinion others have of your work.
26. Audiovisual course materials help students and show creative effort.
27. Organizing a conference is major work with potential for major payoff.
28. Educational enterprises could include the founding of a center, an institute, a company to create and market products, etc.

Icing on the Cake

29. Honors and awards are a tremendous boost.
30. Special committee assignments are the result of earned respect.
31. Teaching committees are an opportunity to help.
32. Offices held in professional organizations.
33. Appointments to national committees.
34. Consultantships to accrediting teams, national and international agencies, schools and associations, all are evidence of national stature.
35. Patents and licenses on created products are special.
36. Reviewer of planned textbooks for major publishers are noteworthy and often lucrative.
37. Referee for professional journal articles requires expertise.
38. Membership on school boards are for select people.

WHAT YOU CAN DO . . .

1. Resolve not to let a single term go by without evaluation.
2. Have someone administer two student evaluations
   a. an informal one at midterm, and
   b. an extensive one at the end.
3. Study the results, learn from them.
4. Tell your weak areas to the students, ask for help.
5. Visit classes taught by good teachers.
6. Discuss course content, objectives, exams, etc. with colleagues.
7. Share your problems with a trusted colleague.
8. Do a self-analysis at least once per year.
9. Have a professional analyze your teaching.
10. Watch your teaching on video.
11. Prepare a good teaching dossier.

Further Reading

Becker, Palmer. You and Your Options, Faith and Life Press, Newton, Kansas, 1979.

Braskamp, L., Brandenburf, D. C., and Ory, J. C. Evaluating Teaching Effectiveness, Sage Publications, Beverly Hills, 1984.

Centra, J. A. Determining Faculty Effectiveness, Jossey-Bass, San Francisco, 1980.

Cohen, P. A., and McKeachie, W. J. "The Role of Colleagues in the Evaluation of College Teaching," Improving College and University Teaching, 28, 147-154, 1981.

Doyle, K. O., Jr. Evaluating Teaching, D. C. Heath and Co., Lexington, 1983.

Flanders, N. A. Analyzing Teaching Behavior, Addison-Wesley, Reading, Mass., 1970.

Gregorc, Anthony F. An Adult's Guide to Style, Gabriel Systems, Inc., Maynard, Mass., 1982.

Gros Louis, K. "Preparing a Teaching Dossier for Promotion and Tenure," Teaching and Learning at Indiana University, September, 1985.

Hildebrand, M., Wilson, R. C., and Dienst, E. R. Evaluating University Teaching, University of California, Berkeley, 1971.

McKeachie, W. J. "Student Ratings of Faculty: A Reprise," Academe, 65, 384-397, 1979.

Myers, Isabel Briggs, Introduction to Type, Gainesville: Center for Applications of Psychological Type, Inc., 1979.

Myers, Isabel Briggs, Gifts Differing, Palo Alto: Consulting Psychologists Press, 1980.

Seldin, P. Changing Practices in Faculty Evaluation, Jossey-Bass, San Francisco, 1984.

Sorcinelli, M. D. "An Approach to Colleague Evaluation of Classroom Instruction," Journal of Instructional Development, 7, 11-17, 1984.

Travers, R. M. W. Handbook of Teacher Evaluation, edited by Millman, J., chapter 2, Sage Publications, Beverly Hills, 1981.

Epilogue

The highest compliment I as a teacher can receive came to me from Jim. Jim was my student last term, who, like other students, often came in to see me. As we spoke, as we worked through chemistry problems, as I watched him respond, I did notice something special about him. His eyes reflected a sincerity, his questions revealed a hunger for knowledge, his attitude mirrored concern. As time went on I got a glimpse of his life.

Brought up in an underprivileged home, learning was never cared for. His parents, school dropouts at age sixteen, never once asked about homework, books, or grades. When he reached the fifth grade he still could not read. A caring teacher saw his plight, encouraged him to stay after school every day for the rest of the year, and taught him to read.

Following the example of his parents, he dropped out of school at age sixteen, married, and at seventeen was a father and had joined the army. All four of his siblings were later to follow that very same routine.

Jim learned a trade and became a successful, independent business man. Driven by a rare sense of mission, he spends three hours every evening with his young children: one hour at play, one hour with homework, and one hour reading to them. However, by age twenty-six the example set by Mrs. Meacham, his fifth-grade teacher, still spoke loudly. Jim sold his business, reduced his living standard, obtained a high school diploma and entered college with one goal in mind: to become a middle school science teacher in a system populated with underprivileged children.

Today he is a very successful, mature student. His trailer home is a center of learning for many neighborhood children who come for help. Jim is helping one of his brothers to finish high school; and he tutors his mother as she attempts, at his suggestion, to obtain a high school diploma.

As Jim's awe-inspiring study unfolded before me, details of another student's life came to my attention. Kurt was fresh out of high school and failing my course. One day he came to me, confessing: "Dr. Boschmann, I am lazy, and I am ashamed of it." I was struck. Here was a young man, saying something that I, more than twice his age, would have a hard time saying. Kurt continued by describing his home. Father comes home from work, gets a beer, turns on the TV, and settles for the evening. He falls asleep, wakes up the next morning, goes to work, comes home, and repeats the cycle. Kurt followed the parental footsteps. I sensed in Kurt a maturity beyond his years and a real willingness to change. I inquired whether he would be willing to talk with someone, eight years his senior, who has a bold story to tell. Kurt was eager.

I checked with Jim. "Would you be willing to spend some more of your time helping a fellow student who is ready for a change?" Without hesitation Jim volunteered.

At the appointed hour they appeared in my office. I introduced Jim: "Kurt, this is Jim. He is older than you, has had a difficult beginning, but through sheer willpower has turned his life around and is in the process of helping many others. I think you can benefit from his counsel." I introduced Kurt: "Jim, this is Kurt. He has startled me with unusual self-insight and a deep wish for self-improvement. Will you help him?" They shook hands, and a preview of the care to come was evident in their voices and the setting of future meetings.

To no one's surprise, academically Jim and Kurt did very well in the class. But beyond that, my very small contribution allowed Jim to lay the seeds for major changes in Kurt's life. I must confess that I now understand the Teachings of Zen: "The highest compliment to a teacher is the realization that your students have surpassed you."

Appendix

Wonderful Thoughts about Teaching and Teachers

Learning is becoming, and teaching is being.

Teachers are forever.

Today's world of high tech needs teachers of high touch.
–Naisbett

Teaching rewards and rewarding teaches.

Teaching techniques don't teach–teachers do.

Attitudes are more important than facts.
–Menninger

Teachers are salesmen of intellectual curiosity.
–Alyea

Teaching is pedagogical intercourse.
–Buber

My pupils teach me the art of teaching.
–Tolstoy

Good teaching is seduction into the subject matter.
–Rassias

If you become a teacher, by your students you will be taught.
–Rodgers & Hammerstein

Education is for the individual, training is for the masses.
–Nietzsche

A teacher affects eternity; he can never tell where his influence stops.

–Adams

Teaching itself does not make much difference in student outcome – but teachers do.

–McGee

My task is not so much to share my gifts with others, but to enable others to discover theirs.

The teacher gives not of his wisdom, but rather of his faith and lovingness.

–Gibran

The secret of education lies in respecting the pupil.

–Emerson

In all things we learn only from those we love.

–Goethe

A good teacher is one who listens and elicits information.

–Kalash

Capture a teacher, and you capture a generation.

Teaching is the process of arranging learning experiences to facilitate student achievement.

–Wong

The key principles of the scholarly life are devotion, diligence, humility, organization, collaboration with students and renewal.

–Davies

The marks of a good teacher: To know the subject and to keep up with it; to care for the students, and to motivate them.

–East

The ideal college is Mark Hopkins on one end of a log and a student on the other.

–Garfield

Teaching is the business of life enhancement.

–Wong

The value of an education is not the learning of many facts, but the training of the mind to think something that cannot be learned from textbooks.

–Einstein

Whoever is a teacher through and through, takes all things seriously only in relation to his students–even himself.

–Nietzsche

What makes a great teacher? I believe it is the ability to inspire in students a dedication to the subject of instruction.

–Hook

When I am lecturing I experience a curious mixture of being immensely at east and stagefright.
–Whitehead

The whole art of teaching is only the art of awakening the natural curiosity of young minds.

–France

Instruction ends in the schoolroom, but education ends only with life.

–Robertson

The education of the human mind commences in the cradle.

–Cogan

To educate a man is the art of arts, for he is the most complex and mysterious of all creatures.

–Gregory

The important thing is not so much that every child should be taught, as that every child should be given the wish to learn.

–Lubbock

The aim of education should be to teach us rather how to think than what to think.

–Beattie

Teaching teaches the teacher.

–Fuller

We teach what students can do with what they have. That is real education.

–Gandhi

The best teacher is the one who suggests rather than dogmatizes, and inspires his listeners with the wish to teach himself.

–Bulwer

What nobler employment, or more valuable to the state, than that of instructing the younger generation?

–Cicero

More is to be got from one good teacher than from ten books.

–German proverb

Every man who rises from the common level has received two educations: the first from his teachers, and the second from himself.

–Gibbon

What is most needed for teaching is a humble mind.

–Chinese proverb

To be a good teacher one must first be a good human being.

–D israeli

Great discipline generates enormous strength.

–Schuller

Students who are consistently treated with dignity and respect, are not likely to cause problems in the classroom.

–Purkey

If teachers are to be effective in the classroom, they need to develop and maintain a positive view of all students.

–Purkey

A good education may not make you a good leader; but it will teach you which leaders to follow.

The best teacher is one who, though establishing a personal relation, frees the student to learn. Learning can only take place in the student, and the teacher can only create the conditions for learning. The atmosphere created by a good interpersonal relationship is the major condition for learning.

–Patterson

The great and good teachers of all times have exemplified humanistic education. They have respected their students, have treated them as individuals and persons.

–Patterson

Teachers might manage to bring students to a desired level of achievement, but fail to motivate them for further learning; indeed they may have dampened any further interest.

–Centra

The greater the ignorance, the greater the dogmatism.
–Osler

If your plans are for one year, plant rice.
If your plans are for five years, plant trees.
If your plans are for a thousand years, educate.
–Hall

A student is not free from evaluation to the extent that the instructor withholds it. He is free from it to the extent that he can accept himself as a person.

–Rogers

Make students feel that test results concern his work and not his absolute worth.

To know is nothing at all; to imagine is everything.
–France

For rigorous teachers seized my youth.
And purged its faith, and trimmed its fire.
Showed me the high, white star of Truth.
There bade me gaze, and there aspire.
–Matthew

The true teacher defends his pupils against his own personal influence. He inspires self trust. He guides their eyes from himself to the spirit that quickens him. He will have no disciple.

–Alcott

To teach is to learn twice.
–Joubert

A teacher who can arouse a feeling for one single good action, for one single good poem, accomplishes more than he who fills our memory with rows on rows of natural objects, classified with name and form.

–Goethe

But where's the man who counsel can bestow? Still pleased to teach, and yet not proud to know?

–Pope

Let such teach others who themselves excel, and censure freely who have written well.

–Pope

Truth persuades by teaching, but does not teach by persuading.

–Tertullian

Teaching is to be involved with something greater than oneself.

A teacher is the mediator between the audience and the images presented.

Education is the best provision for old age.

–Aristotle

Teaching is an act of love.

–Davies

A good teacher is a gadfly, stinging his students into a state of confusion, from which only hard thinking can rescue them.

–Socrates

A wise teacher makes learning a joy.

–Proverbs 15:2

Although teaching, writing and consulting are his principal professional activities, Dr. Boschmann also lectures and leads workshops in the areas of teaching, learning, and motivation. For details contact:

Dr. Erwin Boschmann
425 Agnes Street
Indianapolis, IN 46202
U.S.A.
(317) 274-3786

What others say about his presentations . . .

"Dr. Boschmann's gentle, satirical introduction will highlight all the errors you make as a teacher. He will get your attention in a delightfully unconventional way. Then as a caring, compassionate colleague, he will show you how to realize your best self as a teacher."

–Patricia A. Boaz
Dean of Student Affairs
Indiana-Purdue University

"I am pleased to thank you for the outstanding presentation which you made on Teaching Excellence at our opening Convocation."

–Marshall Yovits, Dean
School of Science
Indiana-Purdue University

"I was delighted both with the content and the response of your audience. [You are] a most distinguished teacher."

–Dorothy Webb, Director
Children's Theater
Indiana-Purdue University

"It is a mere statement of fact that [you] have been just about the most effective visitor to date. It was indeed heartening to be associated with one so dedicated who put his best efforts into teaching."

–Carl A. Baumann
Professor of Biochemistry
University of Wisconsin

"I learned a great deal from you that I can utilize in my own class room efforts. You demonstrate a very interesting combination of attributes in your teaching–the systematic approach of science with a high degree of imagination, wit and wisdom. That interesting mix affords delight and learning for your audience."

–Ray Koleski
School of Social Work
Indiana-Purdue University

"Thanks again for the very stimulating talk. I was so impressed with it that I listened to the tape several times, and each time got something new from it."

–Walter Buchanan, Engineer
Naval Avionics
Indianapolis

"Good teachers have always been favorite people of mine. It takes that extra something, however, to make the really ideal teacher, and I think you are one."

–James R. East, Assoc. Dean
School of Liberal Arts
Indiana-Purdue University

"I felt that your presentation was unique, interesting and displayed a caring concern for your students, their feelings and goals. I personally plan to evaluate my own situation and try to present this sincere, caring approach to all my students."

–Stephen Like
South Knox High School